# THE HOUSE OF DAVID

*endpaper* David and Bathsheba from a brussels tapestry entitled 'The Story of David' *frontispiece* Michelangelo's David

# THE HOUSE OF
# DAVID

Jerry M. Landay

Saturday Review Press/ E. P. Dutton & Co., Inc.
New York

Designed by Alex Berlyne
Photography and picture editing by Ronald Sheridan

ISBN: 8415–0290–0

Library of Congress Catalog Card Number: 73–87729

# Contents

To my beloved Jonathan, Woodrow, and Stephanie Lisa

'. . . That this may be a sign among you,
when your children ask in time to
come, "What mean these stones?"'

# Acknowledgements

In Chapters Five and Ten, the author has drawn in part and expanded upon material originally contained in his book *Dome of the Rock*, published by the Book Division of Newsweek Inc. in 1972. The author wishes to thank the editors of Newsweek for their courtesy. The Scripture quotations in this publication are from the *Revised Standard Version Bible*, copyrighted 1946, 1952 and © 1971 by the Division of Christian Education, National Council of the Churches of Christ in the U. S. A., and used by permission.

# Photography Credits

All the photographs in this book are by Ronald Sheridan, with the exception of those cited below, and the author and publishers express their gratitude to him for his permission to reproduce them. They also wish to thank, Mrs Irène Lewitt, Dr Bezalel Narkiss, Mr Uri Avida and the Archives of the Encyclopaedia Judaica for their kind assistance in the photo research and to the following individuals and institutions for their aid and permission to reproduce the photographs that appear on the following pages: Monastery of San Isidoro, Léon, Spain, 75, 101; The British Museum, London, 58, 146, 256, 265; Pierpoint Morgan Library, New York, 30, 32, 60, 68, 80, 96, 102, 110; Studio Allix, 184; Graf Harrachische Museum, Schloss Rohrau, Austria, 151; Ramsey and Muspratt, 166–7; Herzog Anton Ulrich-Museum, Braunschweig, 39, 67, 251; B. P. Kreiser, 67; Biblioteca Apostolica Vaticana, 165; Kölnisches Stadtmuseum, Cologne, 49, 148–9, 211; Metropolitan Museum of Art, New York, 54, 153; Verlag Karl Albor, 12; Uffizi Gallery, Florence, 47, 48; National Gallery, Washington D.C., 28–9; Universitätsbibliothek, Erlangen, 26; Bibliothèque Municipale, Amiens, 25, 45; Zev Radovan, 23, 87, 200; Israel Museum, Jerusalem, 87, 131 (bottom), 200, 201, 209, 230; Israel Department of Antiquities, 23, 87, 131 (bottom), 200, 201, 209, 230; Osterreichische Nationalbibliothek, 83; Statens Museum for Kunst, Copenhagen, 82; Reunion des Musées Nationaux, Paris, endpaper, 97, 134, 142; Oeffentliche Kunstsammlung Basel, 133, 253; Basel Kunstmuseum, 127; Cambridge University Library, 118; Staatsgalerie, Stuttgart, 139; Rijksmuseum, Amsterdam, 225; William Rockhill Nelson Gallery of Art, Kansas City, 113; Bibliothèque Nationale, Paris, 234; Musées de la Ville de Strasbourg, 103, 232; Photo Leroy, 194; Bibliothèque Municipale d'Arras, 194; Staatsbibliothek, Berlin, 160; Kunsthistorisches Museum, Vienna, 93; Erich Lessing/Magnum, 93, 155, 213, 224; Caisse Nationale des Monuments Historiques, Paris, 263; Scala, 34, 36, 51, 56, 98, 178, 180–1, 213, 222; Giraudon, 86, 171, 172, 175; David Harris, 264; Walters Art Gallery, Baltimore, 266; Department of Archaeology, Hebrew University of Jerusalem, 260; Cathedral of Sens, 218; Basilica of St Paul, Rome, 17, 236; Musée Kircher, 218; Stadelschen Kunstinstitut, Frankfurt-am-Main/Photo Blauel, front cover, 52, 154; Musée Royaux des Beaux-Arts, Brussels, 85; Stiftsmuseum, Klosterneuberg, 221.

# Chronological Table

| | Judah | | Israel |
|---|---|---|---|
| 928–911 | The reign of King Rehoboam | 928–907 | The reign of King Jeroboam I |
| 911–908 | Abijah | 907–906 | Nadab |
| 908–867 | Asa | 906–833 | Baasha |
| | | 883–882 | Elah |
| | | 882 | Zimri |
| | | 882–871 | Omri |
| | | 871–852 | Ahab |
| 867–846 | Jehoshaphat | 852–851 | Ahaziah |
| 846–843 | Jehoram | 851–842 | Jehoram |
| 843–842 | Ahaziah | 842–814 | Jehu |
| 842–836 | Athaliah | | |
| 836–798 | Joash | 814–800 | Jehoahaz |
| 798–769 | Amaziah | 800–784 | Joash |
| 769–733 | Uzziah | 784–748 | Jeroboam II |
| 758–743 | Jotham (regent) | 748–747 | Zechariah |
| | | 748–747 | Shallum |
| 758–743 | Ahaz (regent) | 747–737 | Menachem |
| | | 737–735 | Pekahiah |
| | | 735–733 | Pekah |
| 733–727 | Ahaz | 733–724 | Hoshea |
| 727–698 | Hezekiah | 722 | Samaria captured by Shalmaneser V |
| | | 720 | Samaria becomes an Assyrian province |
| 701 | Sennacherib's expedition against King Hezekiah | | |
| 698–642 | Manasseh | | |
| 641–640 | Amon | | |
| 639–609 | Josiah | | |
| 609 | Jehoahaz | | |
| 608–598 | Jehoiakim | | |
| 597 | Jehoiachin | | |
| 597 | Nebuchadnezzar's expedition against Judah; Jehoiachin exiled to Babylonia | | |
| 595–586 | Zedekiah | | |
| 586 | Destruction of the First Temple and Jerusalem and exile of Judah | | |

# Introduction

I am a journalist whose personal interest in his origins have led to the study of an archaeological, historical and religious record spanning thousands of years. Against that background, the pivotal developments of our own turbulent epoch have begun to acquire shape and meaning. Patterns are discernable within the seemingly senseless torrent of events. One pattern, it seems to me, is the universal nature of all human experience. We are essentially little different from our ancestors. The ruler of a great oriental state some four thousand years ago must have felt the same awe of responsibility, the same anguish of decision, the same sense of inadequacy in the face of history as does the leader of a modern technological-industrial state. The political leader was and is, first and foremost, an aspiring human being, struggling not only to deal with external forces, but to confront under pressure again and again his own essential nature, warts and all.

Somehow, in our unrestrained pursuit of 'progress' (while having little idea of *how* we should progress), we have been afflicted by what I call the conceit of contemporaneity. This conceit tends to delude us into believing that no age was ever better, wiser, more informed, more clever, more original, more productive, more unique than our own; that we somehow have achieved a monopoly upon technological ingenuity, courage, justice and wisdom which makes us superior to our forebears.

I profoundly disagree. In one degree or another, every problem we confront today has been faced again and again through endless generations. Solutions to these problems were repeatedly devised, then lost; and it is for us not to invent or create, but to rediscover them. We have basically experienced nothing new.

It is within this context that I have tried to approach David and Solomon. I have watched their counterparts in our own age. I have seen them struggle to achieve power, to survive, aspire to immortality, bid for the support of their peoples, manipulate their allies and adversaries, create consensus through sheer will, extract order from chaos, stage comebacks against unbelievable odds, risk all in the public arena. I have watched them succeed or fail, and, often, succeed and fail.  I have seen powerful men struggle to seek a rational balance between warring tendencies – to conceive of themselves as more than human and less than human. I have watched them victorious as politicians and vanquished as men. I have observed them stand forewarned of the proposition that power corrupts, and then, corrupted by power, deny that proposition.

All of this we read in today's newspapers. All of this, too, we may study and surmise in the histories of the greatest leaders of ancient Israel – David and Solomon. Yet we rarely view the two monarchs in this very real light. They are claimed as part of the heritage of three major faiths. The age in which they governed held profound consequences for the future. Yet somehow they have been seen unidimensionally within the restricted confines of institutionalized 'sacredness', which has tended to strip them of whatever mortality and humanity they surely possessed. David and Solomon were real men – not myths or legends, wizards or demigods. They were no less concerned with the problems of leadership – military balances, trade deficits, balances of power, strategic relationships, personal popularity and personal weakness – than are today's presidents and prime ministers. And it is in this context of living history that I have tried to present them.

This effort has presented challenging problems, and I can easily anticipate the reactions of some highly territorial biblical scholars who detest popularization as an invasion of their 'field' by untutored intruders, or who oppose humanization as a barbaric assault against the pristine purity of Academe.

Where large gaps occur in the historical-biblical record, I have taken the liberty of attempting to bridge them in a responsible manner, basing my judgement wherever possible on the interpretations or assumptions of respected scholars and the discoveries of archaeologists and historians. Where the Bible records a series of conflicting traditions dealing with the same event, largely in the chronicle of David, I have taken the liberty of serving the flow of the tale by selecting the one version of the event deemed most likely, reasonable or consistent.

The Old Testament itself presents other inherent problems. It supplies us with vivid accounts of the life of David, many evidently written by contemporary biographers, but resorts largely to an enumeration of the acts and achievements of Solomon – clearly lifted from court chronicles – rather than continue with a detailed biographical account. Thus a reader may detect differences in my stylistic approach to the Davidic and Solomonic sections. These were unavoidable and reflect the approach of the scriptural texts themselves.

My prime source, of course, is the Bible, one of the most brilliant historical, political, diplomatic and military texts ever composed.

Jerry M. Landay<br>
Laguna Beach, California<br>
August 1973

# 1 The House of Saul

On a day around the year 1050 BC (we are not given the exact date, but it matters little), a messenger of the tribe of Benjamin bore his burden of urgent news along a trail which meandered upward towards the hilly spine of Canaan. The messenger's way, less a trail than a rough track, began near Aphek on the Plain of Sharon, which guarded the pass to the Israelite hill country. The way ended at the gate of the walled city of the People of Israel called Shiloh, high in the central mountains. Shiloh was the seat of the holiest of sanctuaries, for it sheltered the Ark of the Covenant.

The messenger had made the laboured 18-mile climb in under four hours. He had run much of the way, pausing only to ease his pounding heart and, once, to rend his garments and pour handfuls of the reddish soil of the Sharon upon his head – a sign which told all who saw him that he bore mournful news.

Only on the outskirts of Shiloh did the messenger share with those he met the barest portions of his tidings – disaster had befallen the tribal militias on the field at Aphek. Some were stunned, and merely stared dumbly at him. Others vented their grief in anguished moans, and, like the messenger, rent their garments. Anxiety drove yet others into agitated flight – they clambered ahead to bring word of his coming to Shiloh.

The massive body of the blind and aged man seemed one with the carved seat of stone before the main gate at Shiloh. The tumult which reached his ears seemed to confirm his premonitions. And even before the exhausted messenger dropped to his knees before him, Eli, the High Priest of the holy tribal centre at Shiloh, knew precisely what he would be told. Before Eli's body had begun to fail him, such powers had elevated him not only to the position of High Priest, but to the titular leadership of the Twelve Tribes of Israel.

Samuel anointing Saul, as represented in a gothic relief on the Freiburg Cathedral

13

Eli masked his emotions and asked the messenger: 'What is the uproar? What news from Aphek?'

And he heard the worst. The Philistines had drawn the militias of the Israelites into a set-piece battle before Aphek, the very kind of fight her leaders of old had warned Israel never to wage. Three-man chariots had shattered the ranks of the charging Hebrews, and those who had not been killed or maimed had fled or been cut to pieces by the swords and javelins of the enemy infantry.

In the van of the fruitless Israelite charge had been the Ark of the Lord, dispatched by Eli himself to lead his people into this crucial battle. It had been borne by a cart and oxen led by Eli's sons, the priests Hophni and Phinehas. For them, retreat had been impossible. The Ark had been their sacred charge. Besides, the lumbering cart could never have outraced the Philistine horsemen. The knights had circled about the Ark like a wheel around a hub and when they had tired of the game, the circle closed. Phinehas and Hophni were cut down, and the Philistine knights, not a little awed at their unexpected prize, drew the Ark back to their lines.

Over two centuries earlier, at Mount Sinai in the Desert of Wandering, Israel had made her Covenant for all time with the sole,

the single, the only God – Yahweh, Jehovah – the universal deity
who embodied all creatures and whose spirit ruled all things. To
the wandering Israelites Yahweh had made the pledge of divine
patronage in exchange for everlasting fealty. This pact sealed
between Yahweh and Moses, their leader, had made the Israelites
unique among the many peoples of the polytheistic Orient. The
terms of the Covenant comprised a code of ethical conduct which
made men responsible to Yahweh and to each other. Its Ten
Commandments had been inscribed on two tablets of stone. These
sanctified tablets had been housed within the Ark of the Covenant,
Israel's only material testimony to its formative spiritual experience
at Sinai.

 The Ark had preceded the Israelites across the Desert of Wandering to Canaan, the land promised by Yahweh. The Ark had
advanced before them across the Jordan to the walls of Jericho,
where the armies of Joshua had begun to redeem the pledge of
Yahweh. Rarely had it led the Israelites into defeat. Never before
had it been abandoned on the field of battle.

 Even when the Hebrews had been slowly transformed into a settled people on the flanks and ridges of Canaan's mountains and the

uplands east of the Jordan, the portable Ark, a permanent reminder of their semi-nomadic past, remained the receptacle for the tablets of the Law – the common link that bound the tribes to one another and to their traditional sources. To a people that spurned idols and other material relics of faith, the Ark was the one tangible symbol of the ever-present sovereign – Yahweh. And now it had been lost.

The wave of shock and grief killed old Eli. He heaved a sigh of inexpressible anguish, his sightless eyes gaped, his heavy body toppled backward, and when his head struck the ground Eli's neck snapped. He was ninety-eight and had been the priest and Judge of Israel for forty years. Eli's last conscious thought, overriding the loss of two sons, was that he had failed his people and his invisible sovereign.

As he directed the preparation of the family burial cave of the Eliads for the interment, the young acolyte Samuel, Eli's adopted son, was numbly aware of two things: the dimensions of Israel's crisis and the knowledge of imminent danger. Samuel knew that the Philistines would now be advancing in force up the pass towards the gates of Shiloh itself. They would certainly level the sanctuary to the ground and kill all its inhabitants. He ordered the people to begin hasty preparations to abandon the city and the sanctuary.

Samuel retired to his family seat at Ramah in the territory of Benjamin, 12 miles south of Shiloh. There he began calmly to assess the situation and his own role in it. It was not the Ark alone that was gone – though the impact of its loss upon the spirit of the tribes was incalculable. And few mourned the passing of Phinehas, and Hophni. As he had grown older, Eli had transferred the burden of his priestly duties to his sons, and they had perverted responsibility into licence. They had misappropriated meat from the sacrifices of the pilgrims to satisfy their own hunger, in defiance of the holy statutes. They had wantonly sated their sexual appetites, too, at the shrine of Shiloh, in the manner of the heathen Canaanite priesthood. And Eli had lacked the will and the strength to control them. But he knew neither son could succeed to the high priesthood upon his death, for the Eliad House had squandered its right to lead.

The burden of leadership, both spiritual and political, had now devolved upon Samuel, as indeed Eli had carefully planned, but at the darkest hour of Israel's history, when the Philistines had chosen to extend their hegemony to the uplands and challenge the right of young Israel to survive. In planning the invasion, the Philistine commanders had hardly been unaware of the strategic importance of the shrine and its Ark. Now they possessed one and would soon claim the other. They would impose their will on the fragile union of the Israelites by dismantling it.

The story of Saul's life (from upper left) told in a fresco from the Basilica of St Paul, Rome. Beginning with the messenger informing Eli that the Ark has been lost, it portrays Eli's death, the anointing of Saul, the exploits of David during Saul's reign and Saul's death by falling on his sword in his final battle with the Philistines

The loose structure envisioned by Moses and established by Joshua was a confederation of Israelite tribal units which stretched from Asher and Naphtali in the Galilee to Judah and Simeon in the Negev Desert of southern Canaan. For the most part, the land-hungry Israelite invaders had been unable to subdue the great walled fortress towns of the Canaanites in the fertile coastal lands and broad plains they controlled. So the bulk of early Israelite settlers staked their claims on the less hospitable, and therefore underpopulated, heights of Canaan, where they could more easily defend their slender foothold in the Promised Land.

Here the tents of the Wandering were laid away. The Hebrews built crude stone huts and founded hamlets and towns on the slopes and along the mountain crest. They cleared the forests, dug cisterns, learned to plant wheat, flax and barley, to press olives for their oil and grapes for their wine in the manner of the Canaanites.

Those few Canaanite cities on the heights, such as Gibeon, were isolated by the Israelites. Attracted to the theological concepts of the newcomers, the Gibeonites peaceably became a part of the fabric of Israel. Still other enclaves in the rugged hill country had been peopled centuries earlier by the Semitic kin of those who had gone down to Egypt; and their descendants readily joined the Israelite tribal union and adopted the Sinaitic tradition as their own.

Tribalism suited the needs and circumstances of Israel. It followed naturally from the social and military organization which arose in the desert. The relative autonomy of the tribal structure appealed to the many diverse Semitic elements in the Hebrew ranks, in view of the varied local problems with which each tribe had to cope. Self-rule by councils of tribal elders also served that streak of individualism which is inherent in the Jewish character.

'In those days,' the Bible tells us, 'there was no king in Israel; every man did what was right in his own eyes.' Anarchy? Far from it – a radical experiment in theocracy conceived by Moses. A king there was, but it was Yahweh. A law there was – a remarkable social ethic based on the Decalogue, born not of legislative act but the mystical Covenant to which all subscribed willingly and by which all were equally judged. The classless society for which so many have agitated existed then in rudimentary form, three thousand years ago – a society whose statutes provided neither for legislature, nor nation, nor monarch. And it is unlikely that the diverse tribes would ever have submitted to a single central government had the defeat at Aphek not confronted them with a general crisis so grave that the tribal essence as a whole was mortally threatened.

In the days before Aphek, there had been a need for some form of central authority which the tribes could accept – an instrument

The excavations at Aphek, where the Ark was lost to the Philistines

of Yahweh which would interpret and apply the Mosaic code in complicated legal questions, arbitrate feuds between clans and tribes, mobilize the militias in time of military threat, oversee the maintenance of the great cultic centers – at Gilgal near Jericho; in the central hill country at Shiloh; and at Bethel – and serve as the vessel through which Yahweh might communicate His will from time to time.

That instrumentality was the Judge (*shofet* in Hebrew). The Judge was an actor in search of a role, a charismatic summoned by need, a mystic into whom Yahweh's spirit might rush in time of danger, a galvanizer of the body politic. It was the unique personal qualities of the Judge which placed him or her momentarily in command – not the right of succession, not formal election, not ambition, coercion, or the lust for power. And there were no formal constraints upon the tribes to heed him. When the need had passed, the danger had been averted, the crisis ended, his role fulfilled, the Judge's power was surrendered, and he vanished from the slate of history.

The Judge might be an emissary like Ehud, a farmer like Gideon, a disinherited freebooter like Jephthah, a prophetess like Deborah, a priest like Eli, or Samuel. His enemies were the Canaanite cities, which for a time tried to deny Israel access to the fertile plain of Jezreel, and the raiding nomads from the desert called Amalekites and Midianites, who burst forth on their camels from the forested fringes of the hills, ravaged Israelite fields like locusts, emptied grain silos and drove off Israelite flocks.

Serious as these incursions were to the newly settled tribes, they were largely local struggles, limited in character and extent. The tribal militia system provided a ready reserve force. Warriors of one tribe could be called upon for help by another. The men of Benjamin or Manasseh might be reinforced by the men of Ephraim. Benjamin, Ephraim, Zebulun and Issachar could support an operation commanded by Barak of Naphtali.

As long as the Israelites of the confederation felt secure – as long as the system could be seen to work – the idea of monarchy was anathema. Understandably, some were tempted to imitate the royal institutions of their neighbours – the Canaanite city-states, the nations of Ammon or Moab, or the states beyond the Euphrates. The Judge Gideon had been offered the crown of Israel after his decisive defeat of Midian, but he refused, saying: 'I will not rule over you, and my son will not rule over you. The Lord will rule over you.'

A gold and wood box decorated with scenes of lions hunting deer testifies to the advanced artistic culture of the Mycenaeans, one of the Sea Peoples that concentrated on Cyprus and later settled other parts of the Mediterranean Basin

But all that was before the tyrants, the *serenos* of the Philistine Pentapolis, adopted their policy of expansion against the Israelites. The setting for this epic struggle takes us back to the late thirteenth and early twelfth centuries BC, a period of great instability and change comprising one of those cyclical time pulses that determine the shape of human affairs for centuries to come. It was a time when the old empires – Egypt and the empire of the Hittites – were dying; a great new power – Assyria – was being born. Egypt's grip on feudal Canaan weakened, and Israel was one of the peoples who arrived to exploit the vacuum. But there was a second exodus to Canaan shortly after Joshua's arrival. The only vestige of that ancient migration is the name Palestine, a name derived from the Sea People who dominated the affairs of Canaan for so long.

The exodus of the Philistines stemmed from the same convulsions in the Mediterranean Basin which sired ancient Greece. The first impulse occurred in the Aegean, when the brilliant civilization of Minoan Crete was shattered by earthquakes and monumental volcanic eruptions. Many of the surviving remnants found refuge in Cyprus, which also gathered in a host of peoples uprooted by the Trojan War. Later they were joined by wandering bands of Mycenaeans from the Greek mainland displaced by the barbaric Dorians. Cyprus was overcrowded. The homeless sought land and sailed east in tribal groups to the Syrian coast. Here the Philistines were effectively resisted, so they probed south, mounting a land

A drawing taken from the reliefs at Medinet Habu, Egypt, showing Philistines (in feathered head-dress) in battle with Egyptians. The Philistines later became Egyptian mercenaries and settled the coast of Palestine

and sea invasion against the Palestine and Egyptian coasts. Again they were defeated – this time by the forces of Pharaoh Rameses III. But the long struggle sorely depleted Egyptian strength. The pharaoh promptly hired the vanquished Philistines as mercenaries, installing them in Canaan as guardians of Egyptian interests and trade routes and as watchdogs over Rameses' vassal Canaanite princes.

The Philistines were given land on the coast of southern Palestine, where they founded a confederation of five cities: Gath, Ekron, Gaza, Ashkelon, and Ashdod (the latter three exist today). As Egyptian power waned, Philistine influence grew. Their holdings stretched from Gaza to Tell Qasile, on the northern outskirts of modern Tel Aviv, and inland to the fortress-city of Beth-shean, which they had also garrisoned for the pharaoh. They built fleets of merchant and fighting ships which effectively controlled the entire Palestine coast. They grew rich on trade and on levies upon caravans which moved north and south through Philistine territory on the great international highway known as the Via Maris. They adopted Canaanite ways and Canaanite gods. Economically, they came to dominate Israelite settlements on the western fringes of the hill country.

Eventually, both for reasons of military security and population pressure, the *serenos* of the five city-states agreed that the heights must be taken from the rival newcomers, the Israelites. A carefully waged campaign was mounted eastwards from the port of Tell Qasile, the northern boundary of Philistia, towards the heights. Strategically, the Philistine thrust through Aphek to Shiloh all but divided the tribes of Israel, reducing the ability of the militias to offer coordinated resistance. Beyond that, possession of Shiloh gave the Philistines a foothold on the mountain ridge along which the most important pockets of Israelite settlement lay.

Philistine forts and garrisons soon dotted the hill country. The Aegean warriors impressed Israelite labour and forcibly drafted Israelite conscripts. Other Hebrews voluntarily went over to the conquerors and helped to maintain order over their own people. Israel was all but subdued. The *serenos* might well rest content that, in time, their new subjects would be peacefully absorbed into the Philistine ethos, as had the Canaanites on the coast.

With the cities of the Pentapolis as their base, the dominion of the Philistines now extended east across the Valley of Jezreel to the great fortress mound of Beth-shean and southwards to encompass a portion of the Jordan Valley. The hill country was effectively theirs as well.

The *serenos* had every reason to feel superior to the unsophisticated

A Mycenaean seal ring, further testimony to the advanced material culture of the Sea Peoples

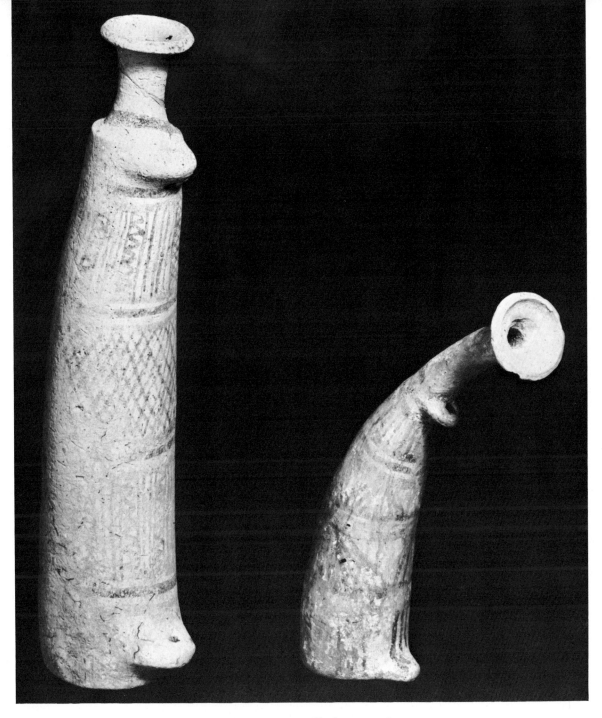

Hebrews, whose stern and austere desert ways still clung to them as wool to hide. Their primitive mountain villages bore sorry comparison to the walled cities of Ashkelon and Gaza, with their temples, markets and busy harbours.

The Philistines boasted a magnificent material culture whose roots lay in the long-vanished grandeur of the Minoan palaces of Crete. Their magnificent pottery, painted with glowing scenes and colours taken from nature, was coveted from the courts of the

Philistine pottery drinking horns unearthed in Palestine

pharaohs to the bazaars of Byblos. Artistically the Israelites had no material culture to compare. Clumsily shaped, hastily fired pots and urns, with not so much as a single decoration or image to grace their sides, testified to an appalling lack of taste. The Israelites cared so little for the appearance of things that they would not so much as trouble to shape a stone for their houses or walls; they were satisfied to slap it in place as hastily as they found it, without mortar, and to fill in the irregular chinks with pebbles. They had no plastic art at all – no statues, for instance. In fact their law forbade them.

To the Philistines, the Israelites worshipped a deity that was like air. If you could not shape him in stone or clay, how could you see him, bring sacrifices to feed him, pray to him or revere him? Little wonder that Yahweh could not cope with Dagon – the Philistine chief god – on the field at Aphek.

Like conquerors before and after them, the Philistines were possessed of a conceit that clouded their imaginations and blinded them to the nature of the conquered. What they could not understand they classified as inferior and slandered with pejoratives. The Philistines were a mighty people who had survived much, a people of tradition, of fine artistic sensibility, with a mastery of classic military strategy and tactics. Their instruments of war were unrivalled by any but the Egyptians. They were, as we will later see, the military technologists of their day. But they lacked the humanity to be great. They lacked the humility to survive.

The young priest Samuel knew this. He understood that the Philistines had demoralized Israel but had destroyed neither its heart nor its head. What they had captured or burned were merely symbols. The national essence of Israel could neither be captured nor burned. It was as intangible as the air, and as pervasive. Samuel understood, too, that the hilly terrain of the Israelite territory was unsuited in any protracted campaign to the fighting style and equipment of the Philistines.

Samuel had been dedicated to the priesthood as an infant by his mother, Hannah, at the sanctuary at Shiloh, to which the Israelites dutifully made a holy pilgrimage each year. At an early age, he had displayed dramatic signs that he possessed the powers of revelation. Old Eli had seized upon him as a likely substitute for the sons who had proven themselves unworthy of the succession. Samuel's oracles attested that Yahweh had accepted him as his herald. His knowledge of the sacred law was unrivalled; and he possessed the charismatic power to move men worthy of the Judges. They called him *navi*, prophet.

Samuel travelled quietly from village to village to preach sermons of faith and patience to his people. His message was a simple one:

Poro philistu quenes i raphes i istruxes acie qu isrt. into ar etam
ne vga uur isrt philisteis.

The Philistines were
equipped with superior
weaponry in their wars
against the Israelites. This
portrayal of the fighting
between the two peoples is
from the Picture Bible of
King Sancho (Léon, 1197).
The Ark, represented as a
small box, is carried by a
figure in the lower right

'Direct your heart to the Lord, and serve him only, and he will
deliver you out of the hands of the Philistines.'

'The Ark of Him we serve is with the enemy,' Samuel told his
dispirited brethren, 'but Yahweh himself is neither in Gaza nor Ekron
nor Gath. He is still with us. Have faith that He will honour His
pledge to deliver Canaan into our hands, if you but honour yours.'

As the years passed, the Philistines believed the hill country firmly

pacified, and they withdrew more and more of their main force to the coast, leaving routine occupation duties to small Philistine garrisons reinforced by Israelite mercenaries. In the event of civil disorders, the main force was less than a day's march away.

But meanwhile, in Philistia on the plain below, there had occurred an event which terrified the conquerors, fired the Israelites with new hope and seemed to confirm the message of Samuel. In those days, the polytheistic peoples of the Near East attributed omnipotence to their own gods, but nonetheless acknowledged the powers of neighbouring deities. The powers of these foreign gods were not to be taken lightly.

The Philistines thus treated the Ark of the Israelites with deference. They installed it in the temple of Dagon at Ashdod. Then bubonic plague struck Ashdod. The priests hastily transferred the Ark to Ekron, but the plague spread there as well – in fact, it soon afflicted all of Philistia. The fearful priests concluded that Yahweh was the vengeful agent of the mysterious contagion. Better to be rid of Him!

They yoked two milch cows to the cart, pointed them in the direction of Israelite territory and doubtless gave them a spirited prod or two. The news spread throughout the hill country that the Ark had miraculously returned. Samuel ordered the joyful Hebrews to lodge it in a makeshift shrine at Kiriath-jearim, once a site sacred to the Canaanites, now in the territory of Benjamin and only 9 miles from Samuel's seat at Ramah. What to the Philistines had been a curse was viewed by the Israelites as an omen of imminent salvation. But it also fired their impatience.

Nearly fifty years had passed since the disaster at Aphek. And now the elders of the tribes of Israel sought an audience with Samuel at Ramah. They declared openly what he already knew – their people were growing restive under Philistine domination and they sought freedom. Some mustered the courage to state what the others dared only admit to themselves: the system devised by their ancestors was clearly not able to cope with such a situation. The young clamoured for action, cried for a leader. And they spoke not altogether flatteringly of the ageing prophet.

Youths must of course be forgiven for their rashness, the elders said. Yet it had to be reported. It was being said that liberation would demand far more military skill than Samuel possessed. He was a priest, a prophet. And the times demanded a Joshua, a Gideon – more, a king who could arouse and unite the masses and then lead them into battle. The neighbouring nations were so governed, and they had not succumbed as had the Hebrews. Yahweh had ruled through Samuel. Now a monarch was required for Israel, to rule

The story of the capture and return of the Holy Ark, from the Erlangen Picture Bible. The central panel portrays the plague that afflicted the Philistines and prompted them to send the Ark back towards the hill country
*overleaf* Detail of 'The Return of the Ark' by the 17th-century artist Sebastian Bourdon

The election of Saul – the tallest of the Benjaminite warriors – to serve as the king of the Israelites, from the 13th-century St Louis Picture Bible

in Yahweh's name. But the Lord would remain the divine Sovereign, for He would choose through Samuel the temporal king. All the tribes would accept the king's will, and thus Yahweh's will, in the cause of liberation. But, the elders added, there would be a clear separation of powers. The king would rule their mortal affairs. But Yahweh would reign. And Samuel would remain their spiritual shepherd, serving as a check on royal excesses.

Samuel was reluctant to submit. On the one hand, he had been supremely charged with the maintenance of the Mosaic Law and the institutions created to administer it, and he could not preside over any radical changes in the system. The statutes contained no provision for a monarch, nor the means to define or circumscribe his duties. On the other hand, Samuel recognized the dangers of being overtaken by the masses in this feverish time. He must harness them, perhaps by seeming to bend to them.

He was, after all, being given the power to select the king. He could, therefore, hand pick a candidate who would remain subservient to him yet fulfil the role of king. The monarch could be dispensed with once the victory had been won. Samuel reasoned that leaders in war were unfit for peace, and people readily tired of their heroes in settled times. They would turn again to the High Priest of Yahweh when Aphek had been avenged.

Samuel withheld his decision from the elders and retired to ponder the matter. The monarch, he decided, must be drawn from the tribe of Benjamin. His reasoning was both brilliant and cunning. In size, Benjamin was the least of the Twelve Tribes, and thus inter-tribal jealousies would be minimal. Yet history and circumstance had bred into the warriors of Benjamin a ferocity and ruthlessness worthy of giants. In the early days of settlement, Benjamin had borne the brunt of Canaanite resistance in the hill country and had never lost its aggressiveness thereafter. The tribe seemed to have drawn vigour from the rugged territory it had won. By the very lips of Jacob, Benjamin had been portrayed as 'a ravenous wolf, in the morning devouring the prey, and in the evening dividing the spoil'. The Benjaminites excelled at ambushes. They were uniquely trained in the use of slings and the bow and arrow, which they could fire with the left hand as readily as the right. Finally, Benjamin was geographically located in the centre of the tribes.

Saul came quickly to Samuel's mind. He was a handsome young warrior who had gained some attention in guerrilla operations against the Philistines. Benjaminites spoke of his bravery and stature. Saul was the tallest of the Benjaminite warriors. He stood head and shoulders above his companions both figuratively and

The Territories of
the Tribes of Israel

SIDONIANS

DAN

ASHER

NAPHTALI

ZEBULUN

ISSACHAR

Mediterranean Sea

Megiddo●

Beth-shean●

MANASSEH

Jabesh-gilead●

Jordan River

Aphek●    Shiloh●

EPHRAIM

GAD

AMMONITES

Rabbah●

Mizpeh●    Gilgal●
      ●Michmash
Gibeon●  B E N J A M I N
    Gibeah●  Ramah  Jericho●
         ●Nob
Ekron●   Jebus●

Ashdod●  ●Bethlehem

Gath●

Ashkelon●

REUBEN

Dead Sea

PHILISTINES

JUDAH

Debir●

Carmel●

MOABITES

●Beersheba

SIMEON

0    10    20
                miles

The anointing of Saul by Samuel, from the St Louis Bible

literally. In him also resided more than an ample portion of the tribe's characteristic brashness and pride and a fiery temperament, which, taken together with his height and self-confidence, gave him the bearing of a king.

But Saul's strength also stemmed from another source. He was of the family of Kish, one of the most successful of Benjaminite farmers. The holdings of the House of Kish in land, herds and flocks had earned him a place of prominence in the tribe, and he had become an elder. There would be no question that the Benjaminite establishment would take up the cause of Saul, the son of Kish, and use its influence among the other tribes to win the necessary consensus for Samuel's choice. But Saul would rule only by the leave of Samuel.

Now the prophet shrewdly began a phased campaign to devise for his unwitting candidate an image worthy of a king. The campaign began, of course, with Benjamin. Samuel tendered a dinner for the most prominent members of the tribe at Ramah, and Saul was given the place of honour beside the prophet. The event was duly noted and widely broadcast. Privately, Samuel made his decision known to Saul, whose ambition, when kindled, proved equal to his size. Next Samuel ordered him to fall in with a band of priestly disciples at Gibeah, Saul's home, and during prayers to feign a state of prophetic ecstasy. He did as he was ordered, and this omen of Yahweh's favour was also telegraphed quickly throughout the land. Finally, Samuel summoned representatives of all the tribes to an assembly at Mizpeh, a few miles north of Ramah, where he proclaimed the monarchy and anointed Saul. The House of Saul became the royal house of Israel.

Most in that awed assembly shouted as one, 'Long live the king!' and rose before him to proclaim their fealty. But not all. Jealousy inflamed the large and favoured tribe of Judah in the south. Militants from Judah moved throughout the assembly muttering: 'How can this man save us?' and they withheld their homage. With the monarchy only hours old, Saul was confronted with a supreme test. Not only the fate of the throne, but the unity of Israel hung on the outcome.

Saul's struggle to win the critical support of Judah came within months. Nahash, king of Ammon, across the Jordan, laid siege to the city of Jabesh-gilead in the territory of Manasseh, and Saul won a crushing victory, giving Israel its most profound taste of success since the humiliation at Aphek a half century before. Samuel and Saul quickly exploited the victory. The king was escorted to an assembly of southern tribes at their cult centre, Gilgal, where Joshua had first set foot in Canaan some 250 years earlier. There

A Philistine funerary mask, one of the artefacts which testifies to the advanced art of the Philistines

Saul was again anointed by Samuel, as a tribute to his reluctant southern subjects. Samuel proclaimed the rights and duties of the kingship, both to rectify the omission in the statutes and to ratify his own pre-eminence in the ruling hierarchy. Judah was pleased by Saul's gesture and disarmed by his triumph at Jabesh-gilead, and it tendered him the pledge of support it had withheld at Mizpeh.

Israel, until now a people, had become a nation. But it had yet to win its freedom. It remained effectively subject to the *serenos* of Philistia.

Saul organized and trained Israel's first standing army. He assembled his soldiers in small units and deployed them against the Philistine garrisons on the heights as a guerrilla striking force. A detachment commanded by Saul's son, the prince Jonathan, fell without warning upon the Philistine outpost at Geba and wiped it out to a man. When they received word of Saul's coronation and the spreading insurrection on the heights, the *serenos* dispatched their main force to Michmash with instructions to restore order among the Hebrews. The Hebrew mercenaries rose against their Philistine commanders and went over to Saul. The king deployed his forces brilliantly and, again with Jonathan's help, won a decisive victory at Michmash. The Philistine power was by no means destroyed, but the *serenos* could no longer effectively pacify the hill country.

Saul went on to inflict a series of crushing defeats in local border actions against Edom, Moab, Ammon, Zobah and the nomadic raiders of the Amalekites, who had tried to capitalize on Israel's preoccupation with the Philistines. Beyond the fact of his matchless ability to command, Saul had also given his nation a prince truly worthy to be a successor – Jonathan. He had not only inherited his father's military prowess, including a brilliant grasp of tactics, but displayed a degree of humility which pleased citizen and soldier alike.

The royal house had demonstrated it had no intention of serving as a mere figurehead for Samuel. He was a sorely troubled old man; and the rigidity of age caused him to assess events in absolute terms. Samuel convinced himself that he had lost his gamble. In embracing Saul and Jonathan so passionately, his people were in effect rejecting him – and rejecting Yahweh. At least that is how Samuel viewed Saul's achievements. Israel would never again accept a return to the ancient ways. Frustration, envy and anger now commanded the prophet, and the pride of righteousness unique to the ambitious priest drove him to folly.

The Philistines, at least for the time being, had been humbled. So, now, would Samuel humble the king.

Saul leading his men in battle, a detail of Ghiberti's 'Gate of Paradise', the doors to the baptistry of the Florence Cathedral (1424)

# 2 For This Is He …

The priests of Israel, the servants of God, were the guardians of the Covenant of Sinai and the body of law which flowed from it. They preached that each man's primary duty was the attainment of moral perfection; that each man's primary allegiance and salvation lay in the Glory of Yahweh. On the sacred altars of Israel, men rich and poor consecrated tokens of their worldly wealth to the ultimate Sovereign and, secondarily, to the maintenance of the priesthood. Samuel reigned over a priestly class which conceived that the People of Israel had no greater obligations, no more fundamental priorities, than these. In the harsh and empty desert where the basic tenets and precepts of early Israel had been formulated, the demands of nationhood, the concepts of monarchy and fixed borders, the stresses of domestic power and foreign affairs were wholly irrelevant, if not wholly unknown.

Samuel saw history not as a record of the deeds of man, but the acts of Yahweh made manifest through man. And if Yahweh, through his people, had now ordained that a king, Saul, be set over Israel to shepherd her through crisis, then it was Yahweh, through his agents the priests, who could unseat him.

The demands of temporal power confronted Saul with a totally different set of realities which could allow for no such theological preemption. He ruled in Yahweh's name. He aspired to the salvation of the new nation he had begun to forge from a host of petty tribes. The first duty of his citizens was national survival; their first allegiance was to the glory of Israel and the maintenance of the throne. Saul's priorities of sacrifice were of a different order than Samuel's. What good if an Israelite offered a cow, a bull, a measure of grain to Yahweh upon a flaming altar and his nation were lost? The primary sacrifice of the citizen, as Saul saw it, was that which led to the defeat of Israel's mortal enemies. And that

David holding the head of the slain Goliath, by Caravaggio (1565–1609)

meant the primacy of the throne, the subordination of all else to the dictates of the king. Thus would the glory of Yahweh be achieved.

The priesthood was intent on maintaining the *status quo* in the visionary yet demanding Israelite conception of the relation between man and God; whereas Saul conceived of his mandate as the securing of a stable anchor on earth for the Kingdom of God. Saul's misty notion of the new national order was that of a triangular hierarchy – the spiritual and temporal authorities coequal at either end of the power base, and, at the apex, Yahweh. But Samuel refused to accept any order which implied permanent alliance, even coexistence, with Saul.

Israel's enemies were not yet tamed. Saul hardly had the time, let alone the temperament or inclination, to engage in a power struggle with the priesthood. He was a warrior-leader, taxed with unending battle, with the unrelieved burden of fashioning a single victorious fighting force from the militias of the fiercely independent tribes.

Yet Saul was politician enough to wish to avert a head-on clash between the rudimentary apparatus of government and the far older and more stable priestly establishment. Such a potentially divisive struggle was unthinkable, particularly while war still raged. But he was also aware that Samuel viewed each military success as a defeat for the old order. Saul attempted to defer to Samuel where possible, consult with him on major decisions when practical and to passively endure Samuel's provocations, challenges and insults each time the old priest tried to force an open breach. For Saul's downfall was the old man's sole object; and Saul was keenly reminded that Samuel's authority with the people was still great – often, he feared, greater than his own.

Israel's foes had not granted Saul the respite to perfect the new central administrative authority. Samuel, on the other hand, controlled a complex apparatus of priests and levitical auxiliaries who served local and regional cultic shrines throughout the land. Through them, Samuel had ready access to virtually every member of his flock, and the priestly apparatus in turn provided him with instant intelligence of all that transpired from the humblest farming village to the very palace of Saul at Gibeah.

Samuel did not hesitate to exploit this advantage in his campaign to subvert the king; and his underlings willingly joined in the cabal. Samuel preached to the people, invoking the angry image of a wrathful Yahweh: 'You shall know and see that your wickedness is great in the sight of the Lord, in asking for yourselves a king.' He repeatedly intoned the warnings he had uttered when

A portrayal of the High Priest of Israel, detail from 'David Playing the Harp' by the 17th-century painter Jan de Bray

the elders first gathered at Ramah to petition for the monarchy:

> [The king] will take your sons and appoint them to his chariots and to be his horsemen, and to run before his chariots; and he will appoint for himself commanders of thousands and commanders of fifties, and some to plough his ground and reap his harvest, and to make his implements of war and the equipment of his chariots. He will take your daughters to be perfumers and cooks and bakers. He will take the best of your fields and vineyards and olive orchards and give them to his servants. He will take the tenth of your grain and of your vineyards and give it to his officers and to his servants. He will take your manservants and maidservants, and the best of your cattle and your asses, and put them to work. He will take the tenth of your flocks, and you shall be his slaves. And in that day you will cry out because of your king, whom you have chosen for yourselves; but the Lord will not answer you in that day (I Samuel 8: 11–18).

Recklessly Samuel had invoked phantoms in his campaign to undermine Saul, and it was for that very reason that Samuel's sedition had little effect. For Saul had neither the time, the luxury nor the vanity to enjoy the excesses and indulgences of high office. He had superimposed no royal bureaucracy upon the old tribal structure, save Jonathan, his son, and Abner, his cousin, who commanded the tribal militias. He had constructed no splendid court in the manner of the kings of Egypt, Hitti, or Akkad. Saul dwelled in primitive simplicity in a spartan palace-fort with four towers, atop the summit of a hill in his home village, Gibeah. In battle he commanded not from the safety of a royal tent behind the lines, but at the head of his troops, risking no less sacrifice as commander-in-chief than what he demanded of his humblest foot-soldier.

His only innovation, and this is readily understandable in the light of military necessity, was to found the nucleus of Israel's first standing army, a far more efficient fighting force than the relatively unwieldy system of tribal militias. Saul required warriors whose first duty would be to king and country rather than to the tribe or clan. Like most new states, Israel's first bid for survival was waged on the battlefield. Thus, as history repeatedly shows, it is a military aristocracy which is paramount in the turbulent

life of an emerging nation. Saul enlisted from the various tribes young warriors who had distinguished themselves in action against the Philistines and bound them to the service of the throne.

This iron sword, believed to be Philistine, was recently brought to light by Bedouin in the Gaza area

The People of Israel had given Saul a single mandate – liberation. All else was subordinate to the struggle, like Castro in the rugged Sierra Maestra, or Mao Tse-tung in the caves of Yenan in our own day. Saul was confronted by an enemy far more experienced in combat, superior in numbers and far better equipped both in quantity and technical quality of weaponry than his own.

The Israelites had nothing to compare with the Philistine chariotry, the enemy's mobile striking force, whose three-man crews, armed with maces and spears, tore through the ranks of the opposing infantry like a scythe through wheat. Behind them, paired into four-man units, ranged the infantry, seemingly invincible in their coats of mail, bronze helmets, greaves and shields. The Philistine warriors were armed with a formidable arsenal of weapons: straight swords for hand-to-hand fighting; deadly javelins with loop and cord about the shaft, which they hurled with precision in combat at greater range; and leather slings which laid down a deadly shower of fire over long distances.

Nor could the Israelites match the skill and technology of the Philistine weapon makers. For the Aegean wanderers had acquired a great secret in the lands of the Hittites before they ventured south against Syria and Palestine. They had learned how to smelt and forge weapons and implements from iron. They fashioned swords far more durable than those of the Israelites and finely honed javelins and daggers whose points and cutting edges retained their keenness far longer than brittle weapons of bronze. So closely did the Philistines guard their technological advantage that Israelite farmers in far more peaceful times had been forced to go down to Philistia for their ploughshares, mattocks, axes and sickles and seek out the services of Philistine smithies each time their tools needed sharpening.

If the coveted advantage of iron-making tilted the military and economic power in the *serenos*' favour, a rigid feudal structure and a superb grasp of conventional military tactics maintained it. Saul's select standing army numbered no more than three thousand men. He was forced to depend largely upon the call-up of tribal militias for additional levies. But he could not arbitrarily conscript them; he could only petition. And the welfare of each tribal warrior was less dependent upon the grace and favour of the king than upon his own kin, for it was the family of each fighting man which delivered his main rations to the field of battle.

The king nonetheless gave the young Israelite nation the gift of life in its decisive struggle with Philistia. Saul developed the strategy which turned the military balance in Israel's favour – a martial philosophy as old as the history of human conflict, as young as the irregulars of Ethan Allen or the Viet Cong in the modern era. In Israel's seeming weakness lay her strength. Saul found his inspiration in the sagas of the Judges – of Gideon, who used surprise attack to overcome the superior forces of the Amalekites; of Abimelech, who resorted to ruse and ambush to overcome the redoubtable defences of the fortress city Shechem; of Deborah and Barak, who exploited the advantages of terrain to immobilize the chariotry of Hazor's king.

If the Philistines were pre-eminent in set-piece battle, Israel would turn the rules of war to her advantage by avoiding such engagements. She would resort to unconventional warfare – overcoming mass with speed and strategic retreat; superiority in weaponry with sudden attack. She would strike in the hills and mountain passes, where Philistine chariots were useless. She would fall upon the enemy when he least expected it and melt away into the hills, caves and hamlets before the foe could recover and mass. She would stand and fight only at times and places of her own choosing. If the *serenos* warred by day and slept at night, Saul would strike by night and vanish at dawn. Using small, highly mobile fighting units, Saul would employ the stratagems of the fleet tiger to humble the plodding elephant. And if Israel could not manufacture weapons of iron, she could steal them from the enemy dead.

For maximum manoeuvrability, Saul deployed his forces into three groups. Each could attack on a fixed front, or against the Philistine flank, or be held in reserve. He could use one force as the hammer, flushing and pursuing the enemy as he scattered in wild retreat; while the other two units became the anvil, a deadly human wall picketed with spears planted across the escape path, against which the fleeing foe dashed itself, like a wave smashing to foam against a jagged cliff. In this manner had Aphek been redressed at Michmash, had Saul raised budding Israel toward nationhood.

God does not decree victory or defeat, but plants within each of us the capacity to strive. Saul the warrior knew this. His was the

ability to confront reality with naked power and tame it. But he could never accept that not all men cheer good works. For Samuel had raised Saul to give Israel victory and then had come to fear and hate the change that Saul's victories wrought. The exclusivity of the prophet-priest in Israel was at an end; nationhood now demanded that priest and king share their mandate to guide the Elect of Yahweh. But Samuel, old and brittle, blinded by the envy that condemns bitter men to absolutism, would never accept a symbiotic alliance with a lesser creature of his own creation.

And so, on the eve of the climactic battle with the Philistines at Michmash, the old man laid snares to discredit the king in the eyes of the people and the army. Saul's army was encamped at Gilgal in the Jordan rift to the east. Before the battle was joined, it had been arranged that Samuel would come to minister to the troops and

Philistine charioteers in their three-horse chariots, shown in a drawing taken from the reliefs at Medinet Habu, Egypt officiate at a ceremony of sacrificial intercession for victory and peace. But Samuel failed to appear. For a week, Saul stayed the critical assault out of respect to Samuel, his forebearance tinged with fear that the advantage might pass to the enemy. His men grew restless, tense and anxious with the agony of waiting. Samuel's prolonged absence was seen by the restive multitudes as a sign of Yahweh's disapprobation. Some spoke of mutiny. Others began to desert. Saul's discomfiture grew until, in desperation, he led the sacrificial service himself, usurping the function reserved by the law expressly for the priesthood.

Only when this had been done did Samuel deign to appear. Saul personally lead an escort of honour across the desert plain to meet him. But Samuel, dissembling, was a tower of wrath, and would not be placated by the king's gesture.

The prophet thundered: 'What have you done?'

Saul tried to explain the fearful predicament in which Samuel's tardiness had placed him; but reason is often impotent before guile. Barely acknowledging the king's words, Samuel said, so that all might hear: 'You have done foolishy; you have not kept the commandment of the Lord your God, which he commanded you; for now the Lord would have established your kingdom over Israel forever. But now your kingdom shall not continue!'

Before the king could respond, Samuel turned and was gone. There is hardly a threat to a monarch more grave than that which calls into question the continuity of his house and his seed. Yet Saul heard Samuel reject his royal designation, and within the hearing of others. Nonetheless, Saul reasoned, the prophet had spoken out of rage, and with some cause. Saul had, not wantonly, usurped the priest's role, and in this Samuel had grounds for anger. But when it cooled, Saul thought, and the battle over, there would be time for a reconciliation.

When the victory at Michmash was won, Samuel was temporarily thwarted, but more determined than ever to prevent the triumph of the new order over the old. The final break was not long in coming. The predatory Amalekites again tried to exploit Israel's preoccupation with the Philistine threat by staging raids from the south against Israelite territory. Samuel approved of Saul's decision to launch a punitive strike against the Amalekites, but again saw the opportunity of ensnaring the king by commanding in the Lord's name that he take actions which would be repugnant to him – so distasteful that he could not obey. Invoking the holy tradition of the Exodus, in which the Lord had cursed Amalek for opposing the Israelites, Samuel commanded the king: 'Now go and smite Amalek, and destroy all that they have; do not spare them, but

Saul's disobedience to
Samuel (left to right),
which ended in the angry
prophet anointing the
young David, from the
Picture Bible of King
Sancho (Léon, 1197)

kill both man and woman, infant and suckling, ox and sheep, camel and ass.'

Saul's columns fell upon the unsuspecting Amalekites, put them to rout and captured their king, Agag. Saul ordered the captive warriors slain, but chivalry demanded that he spare Agag's life; and the rules of spoil prompted him to share out the enemy's sheep, oxen and cattle to the victorious troops as booty.

The news of Saul's disobedience was brought to Samuel, who travelled swiftly down to Gilgal, where Saul's army was again encamped. Once more he angrily reproached the king, who sought to mollify him by offering to sacrifice the spoil to Yahweh. In vain, Saul begged for a reconciliation. 'I have sinned,' he said, 'because I feared the people and obeyed their voice . . . Pardon my sin, and return with me, so that I may worship the Lord.'

But the vengeful Samuel remained firm: 'I will not return with you; for you have rejected the word of the Lord, and the Lord has rejected you from being king over Israel.' Then Samuel called for a sword, and ordered that Agag be brought before him. Pitifully, Agag pleaded: 'Surely the bitterness of death is past.' But Samuel, the apotheosis of vengeance, ran Agag through; then, without a word, turned and departed.

Saul desperately reached out and grabbed Samuel's arm, to stay him. But the prophet's robe tore, and with it the fabric of any hope that king and priest might be reconciled. They were never to see each other again: Saul would brood over his rejection by the spiritual head of Israel until the shadows of his mind overwhelmed his reason; Samuel, in bitterness and anger, would plot Saul's final overthrow. Samuel, too, was a haunted man. For though he had in prophetic tones declared the stewardship of Saul null and void, he lacked the absolute power to carry out his prophecy and remove him from the throne. Saul continued to rule, and the aged priest had no recourse but to seek an alliance with one who could help him realize that which he could no longer accomplish himself.

For Samuel was old and knew he would soon die. He knew, too, that the dissolution of the monarchy and a theocratic restoration were by now quite out of the question. Though Saul's stature had been considerably diminished among the elders and the priestly establishment, the people throughout Israel held the king and his heroic son Jonathan in the highest regard. They had brought victory, avenged Aphek, freed Israel from Philistine domination and prepared the way for her evolution from tribal confederacy to nationhood. The Philistines remained a serious threat, but Saul

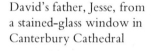

David's father, Jesse, from a stained-glass window in Canterbury Cathedral

had given Israel the means of defending herself and redressing the military balance. Most important, he had done all this without imposing upon the people the excesses of which Samuel had so often warned.

Against all this, Samuel could no longer hope to demolish the monarchy. And so, to his discredit, Samuel settled for the limited objective of destroying Saul. A holy cause had deteriorated into a mere personal grudge, a prideful exercise in prophetic self-fulfilment.

There was in Saul's small court an exemplary young warrior from Judah named David – average in stature, but with finely chiselled Semitic features, dark hair, a ruddy complexion, and almond-shaped eyes of exceptional beauty. He was of humble origins – the youngest of eight sons of a farmer of Bethlehem named Jesse. His brothers had monopolized their father's favour and attention. They were warriors in Saul's army, veterans of the Philistine wars. As the junior member of the family, David had inherited the menial chores of guarding Jesse's flocks of sheep on the stony and sun-bleached hills above Bethlehem and carrying battle rations to his brothers in the field.

But nature has a mysterious way of compensating a handful of her chosen creatures for the deprivations of their youth. Paternal neglect bred into the young shepherd a self-reliance and resourcefulness rare among those of his age. With only bleating sheep on the hilly pastures of Bethlehem as his companions, David made time and stillness his allies. He gave himself fully to them, and they offered him in return the imagination of an artist, the reflective inner eye of a poet and a mystical oneness with the land which drives the inspired warrior to heights greater than himself.

The young David, by Verrocchio (1435–1488)

David's solitary life gave him an elementary choice – stultifying boredom or the grand adventure of self-discovery; the honing of his inner resources; the ripening of the talents which in most of us lie fallow, condemning us to a living death. David chose to grow. Not consciously, of course. He was not consciously grooming himself for greatness. At least, in the formative years before Gibeah, he would not have been aware of the drive we call ambition. What some ascribe to genetic inheritance and the fortunes of circumstance, what others vaguely call a lust for life, what the mystics refer to as the capacity for knowledge compelled him to reject the humdrum, the ordinary.

David had come from a deeply religious household. At least once a year, Jesse would take his sons on a holy pilgrimage to Judah's cultic center at Gilgal in the steamy, steep-sided bowels of the southern Jordan rift, where the Ark had first been installed in the days of Joshua; and to Nob, 5 miles north of Bethlehem, between Jerusalem and Anathoth, where many of the priests had fled after the destruction of Shiloh and where, some think, the Ark rested in David's youth. As each flaming oriental dawn summoned the family of Jesse to the olive orchards, the vineyards, the pastures, they would first gather at a primitive stone altar on a rise dominating Jesse's fields, seeking Yahweh's blessings upon their labours and the day's yield.

But it was in the solitude of tending the sheep, as the sun moved across the ark of azure sky, tinting and shading the pale honey stone, the alarm cry of the hoopoe bird and the flushing of a startled gazelle punctuated the mountain silence, the stifling eastern wind, the *sharav*, of the desert warred with the sea-laden clouds from the west, and the very foundations of the hills reeled and rocked with the thunder of the angry firmament, that David found exaltation and comfort in the faith of the wilderness, the essential deism of his fathers. Through these, the Lord spoke to David with a voice that town dwellers have never heard.

David's antidote for loneliness, fear and boredom were his lyre, on which he composed psalms of praise and penitence to the all-present Yahweh, and his sling, which he came to use with exceptional skill in warding off the lions and bears which threatened his flock and ghostly Philistines, the demons of his youthful imagination, whom he conjured in the shadows of the trees and recesses of the boulders which littered the hillsides.

He would also occasionally take his rest upon, and silently study, the amputated stumps of old Canaanite walls and temples; or dig absent-mindedly into the ground, distinterring the fragments of what had once been a fine Canaanite pottery jug, a Hyksos urn, or an Egyptian amulet. He wondered upon the people who had once shaped and used these objects in the land on which the Israelites now lived. As his fingertips lightly, gingerly, established communion with these artefacts, David came to grasp intuitively a sense of the flow of history, of men with other gods and other pasts, of a much older and more experienced world that lay beyond the physical and spiritual ken of his own young country and his own times.

Others came to know of David's compositions on the lyre and the sweet, lamenting voice with which he sang them – paeans to Yahweh, laced with rapture, hope, redemption and the vivid imagery of the Israelite countryside. On errands to the field of war, bearing rations of bread, parched grain, cheese and wine to his brothers, David also brought his lyre. And he would often stay through the long still nights, comforting the soldiers with his

David as a youth, by
Donatello (1386–1466)

DAVID·DE·ORE·LEONIS·ARIETE·MERVIT

DAVID

music. In time, it was natural that David join the ranks of Saul's fighters – a youthful poet-warrior whose sling began to earn him as much renown as his lyre. The qualities of artist and fighter are far from strangers in the bundle of paradoxes known as man. Both merged in a single passion in David's breast – fervency for Yahweh and His land. And these were combined in turn with a

A 9th-century mosaic from the Church of St Gereon, Cologne, showing David killing a lion

growing sense of his uniqueness—the budding seed of ambition.

On ambush and patrol, David combined the stealth of the shepherd, and the endurance of the peasant with the self-nurtured confidence and independence of a youth who before his time had come to terms with himself, his fears and loneliness and the unfathomable mysteries of the unknown. It was inevitable that David rise to command and that, in time, word of him should reach Saul in the fortress-palace at Gibeah.

There agitated courtiers, and tribal elders, who came regularly to consult and pay their homage to the king, spoke of little else but the grievous spiritual affliction that had begun to rend Saul's soul, like feet treading upon the bursting grape. The king, they whispered, was surely being consumed by an evil spirit. Could it be that Samuel had brought the very wrath of Yahweh himself down upon the king?

Saul had reigned now for over two decades. He had mobilized his people; pressed, urged, cajoled them into efforts of unstinting sacrifice and greatness as only Moses and Joshua had done before him. Saul had savoured moments of unsurpassed triumph against overwhelming odds, had been borne upon the shoulders of his joyous people, had stood alone atop the rounded summit at Gibeah, offering hymns of thanksgiving to the God who had given him the leadership of Israel.

Yet what had he really earned? Few moments of peace, for the Philistines had been humbled but not defeated. They continued to harry Israel at every turn, hoping again to restore their hegemony over the hill country and the alien people who lived there. There had been little time to consolidate the throne's authority over the quarrelsome Israelite tribes. And, for all of his achievements, Saul had earned only undying hostility and envy from Samuel, who plotted unceasingly against him and invoked the holy forces of heaven to bring him down.

Saul's fiery Benjaminite spirit grew weary of its fetters. Forces of psychic darkness seized him. They taxed his spirit, drained him of energy, paralyzed his will. Alternatively, moods of impenetrable blackness and frenzies of aimless excitement overwhelmed the king. For hours or days, he would not speak; then suddenly he would lash out violently against those closest to him. Paranoiac mistrust undermined Saul's relationships with his courtiers. In his most profound depressive or manic seizure, not even Jonathan could restore him to lucidity. Saul had become a figure of tragic proportions. And word was spreading throughout the land, in part encouraged by Samuel, that the king was sorely afflicted by evil spirits, and the Spirit of Yahweh had departed from him.

David beheading the fallen Goliath, one of Michelangelo's frescos in the Sistine Chapel

Saul's wife Ahinoam was distraught and urged his servants to seek remedies which might relieve the king's torment. Saul's fondness for music was well known. One of his stewards, braver than the rest, approached the king one day when the melancholia had abated and said: 'Behold now, an evil spirit from God is tormenting you. Let our lord now command your servants, who are before you, to seek out a man who is skilful in playing the lyre; and when the evil spirit from God is upon you, he will play it, and you will be well.'

One of Saul's young military aides overheard the suggestion and quickly approached the throne. 'Behold, I have seen a son of Jesse the Bethlehemite, who is skilful in playing, and he is also a man of valour, a man of war, prudent in speech, and a man of good presence; and the Lord is with him.'

A royal messenger found David in his father's house in Bethlehem, where he had long ago superseded his brothers in Jesse's eyes. David seemed relatively unsurprised by the summons to Gibeah, but Jesse, moved deeply by the unexpected honour, quickly prepared a humble tribute to Saul – loaves of bread, a skin of the wine of Judah and a young goat – and David loaded them upon a donkey and bore them to the king. Thus, David entered the service of the royal household at Gibeah.

Saul at once took to this youth who reminded him so much of himself. The roots of both lay in the very soil of Israel. Both had sprung from farming families. Both had learned to covet every rock and tree of the land while working in the grain fields or vineyards or tending livestock for their fathers. And Saul saw in David the very incarnation of himself as the youthful warrior – courageous, almost reckless, and with the natural grace and charisma of a leader.

They spoke of their fathers and their farms, their exploits against the Philistines, and entered into religious disputations which once again taxed and whetted the intellectual capabilities of the ageing king. And David soothed the fevered soul of the king with songs upon his lyre of the majesty of Yahweh, of his justice and compassion for the lonely and the oppressed, of his redemptive mercy for those in spiritual and material need. Saul wept, found comfort in David and forgiveness for himself. Saul was reborn in the blaze of the young warrior-poet's grace and spirit.

If Saul found a kindred spirit in David, Jonathan found a cherished and trusted companion and friend. One was a reflection of the other. Both shared the adventures of battle, but the trials of combat attenuated their deeply human, deeply sensitive natures and their youthful passion for life itself.

The chemistry of David, easing the torment of the weary king,

'The Anger of Saul', by Rembrandt

David at Saul's court
depicted on a 7th-century
Byzantine silver plate

kindling the spirit of the prince, magically transformed the house
of Saul. Both came to love David greatly, and Saul and David became inseparable, so much so that when Saul once again returned to
battle at the head of his troops, David accompanied him as the royal
armour-bearer.

And to herald the advent of David to the royal household, Saul
paid Jesse the unusual honour of a royal visit to the farm in Bethlehem, where he told the deeply moved father, 'Let David remain
in my service, for he has found favour in my sight.'

In time the people came to hear of David, companion to Jonathan, confidant of Saul, who fought in battle by the side of their

rejuvenated king, whose inspired psalms marked him truly as a warrior moved by the spirit of Yahweh. And they came to learn his psalms, and sing them as they worked in the fields, or offered sacrifice at their high places. And Samuel observed all of this and wondered.

The people also began to speak of David's skill and valour in combat, his marksmanship with the leather sling. David carried the smoothly rounded slingstones in a shepherd's bag at his side. He could unerringly plant a slingstone in a Philistine's forehead and lope out of range before the enemy could avenge their loss. Unlike the Philistines and many of the Israelites, and over Saul's vehement protests, David scorned the wearing of heavy armour in favour of speed and mobility. His ability to outrun the enemy more than compensated for the questionable protection of a burdensome coat of mail and bronze helmet. Besides, the inferior armour and weaponry of the Israelites had served David poorly in hand-to-hand combat at close range with the Philistines.

In time, the people came to devise a legend about David's prowess; in part based in truth, as myths are, but also encompassing mythical exaggerations which are a measure of the impact of greatness on the popular imagination.

In the legend, David takes on in single combat a giant of a Philistine from Gath named Goliath, who is over 9 feet tall. And he fells the well-armoured, heretofore invincible, warrior, armed only with a slingstone, sending the enemy into pell-mell retreat.

David may well have come to serve as Israel's champion in contests of single combat, for it is known that this was a custom both of the Canaanites and the Philistines in David's day. Of his prowess as a warrior, there is no doubt. For his accomplishments were such that they eventually came to eclipse those of Saul and Jonathan. So much so, that the women of Israel chanted a popular ballad as they worked or danced in the festivals:

> Saul has slain his thousands
> and David his ten thousands.
> (1 Samuel 18:7)

Saul, too, heard the ditty, and the demons of his spirit, which David had caged, now broke loose and began to gnaw at the king with triple fury. There is no greater evil than that which erodes the bonds of deep love and trust between men.

Samuel sensed what had occurred. It was too late to reverse history. But at long last, he had found the agency through which his prophecy of wrath against Saul and his house might now be fulfilled.

# 3 A Partridge in the Mountains

King Saul submitted to the phantoms of madness. He thought the thoughts that feed upon themselves and cannibalize reason. Saul's monumental efforts at nation-building had earned him the hatred of Samuel. God had placed in his hands the fiery sword of Joshua and then abandoned him. Like Moses on Mount Nebo, Saul had led Israel to the promise; but he had been, in the end, denied its savour. And now, the lamb he had brought into the midst of his own house had proved a serpent.

'They have ascribed to David ten thousands,' Saul brooded, 'and to me they have ascribed thousands. What more can he have but the kingdom?'

Now Saul recalled with horror the prophecy of Samuel which he had so lightly banished from his mind in the days before Michmash: 'The Lord has rejected you from being king over Israel!'

A proud man wronged by others may find shelter in righteousness or moral rectitude. But he may not so easily ignore the scorn of others. Saul imagined his persecutions into being and nurtured them so obsessively that in time they became real. He fastened his wrath upon David, who now came to personify in the king's tortured mind the vengeance of Samuel. Thus does the paranoid seek to externalize his anguish. Saul conjured David as a mortal threat to his person and to the throne, to the rightful succession of Jonathan, to the permanence of the Saulide House itself. Saul could not comprehend Jonathan's blindness to danger.

In those days, men of kindred natures took vows of loyalty and comradeship that went far beyond the shallow, self-seeking affinities of our age. The fellowship of Jonathan and David was the embodiment of the sheer love of man for man, an intimacy based on shared experiences and dangers, the mutual admiration of noble and sensitive spirits – a kind of intuitive trust that transcends the taint

David playing the harp to comfort Saul's anguish, a painting by Lucas van Leyden (1494–1533)

57

A woodcut by Julius Schnorr von Carolsfeld of the friendship of David and Jonathan

of ambition, jealousy or the claims of sex. Such bonds are foreign to our own comprehension because we live in an epoch without honour.

In ancient Israel a particular word was used to describe the bond between David and Jonathan: *hesed* (loyal love). The word denoted that unique quality of the bond between Yahweh and his people and its extension into the relations between men. *Hesed* was formalized by a unique personal covenant made binding between men in the presence of the Lord. In other oriental societies such private pacts had been sealed ritually in blood. In Israel the parties to a compact of loyal love exchanged garments or weapons, which symbolized the admired qualities of each friend.

In this way David and Jonathan made their covenant of friendship – an unbreakable pledge between two honoured sons of

Israel which transcended self-serving considerations of ego, ambition or power. But in Saul's distorted view, Jonathan's action was a capitulation to artifice – to a calculated plot by the son of Jesse to usurp the throne.

Saul was once again seized by his affliction. As before, the courtiers summoned David, with his stringed lyre and sweet shepherd's voice, to still the demons that possessed the spirit of the king.

> How long, O Lord? Wilt thou forget me forever?
> How long wilt thou hide thy face from me?
> How long shall I take in my soul,
>     and have sorrow in my heart all the day?
> How long shall my enemy be exalted over me?
>                                         (Psalm 13:1–2)

It was different this time. In the past David's songs had stilled the manic rages of the king or eased the paralyzing grip of depression. Now Saul seemed indifferent to the music, at times distracted and inattentive, as though attuned to other quite arcane voices, other strains. Haggard, unkempt, slumped upon his throne or reclining upon his couch, Saul watched David in sullen silence and with an intensity that was often disconcerting. David could sense that the king was no longer master of himself. He seemed a prisoner of fantasies which were somehow alien, almost hostile. David's music was now quite incapable of penetrating Saul's private world. Yet, each day, David was summoned to play before the king. And each day, he left the king's chamber depressed by the suffocating silence and with an intuitive sensation of danger.

'The inward mind and heart of a man are deep,' David later is said to have written. Was he thinking of himself; or, perhaps, of Saul? Or, of both: the watcher and the watched; the man of power who cringed at power's waning, the youth of steel to whom power coursed without summons? David was hardly unaware of the consequences, the potential dangers, of his triumphs and achievements – the growing adulation of the people, the fame of his songs, the popular refrains which eulogized his conquests and enraged his sovereign. He noted, too, the almost fawning deference of the priests toward him, and knew of their hope that he might soon succeed the ailing king.

David thus came to perceive the growing danger of his position, to understand that the venom which coursed through the king's veins had much to do with him. David was able to appreciate how Saul in his madness must have seen him – a hungry vulture feasting upon the rotting body of the royal house.

To David, the irony of his position was agonizing. Fidelity to his royal patron had been instinctive. He was the son of a humble farmer, admitted by fortune to the innermost counsels of the king and to an honoured role in the historic events which had shaped his nation. The wonder he had first sensed in the pastures of Judah had, if anything, ripened with time. Ambition had never diminished or corroded it; nor had it been tarnished by the lust of ambition or material desire. He had known petty wants, but he was readily satisfied, and he had sought little.

Now David took further pains to avoid anything which might tend to reinforce the king's suspicions of him. He kept to himself, avoided the subtle probes of gossiping courtiers or their petty intrigues, the blandishments of priests who might report to Samuel of David's ambitions or intentions. He even tried to pay no heed to the growing attentions of Saul's comely daughters Merab and Michal. Such dalliances could bring him down.

Yet, each time Saul commanded his presence in the king's chamber, an inescapable feeling of dread coursed through David. He chanted to ears incapable of hearing, to a mind beyond reach. Saul raged or brooded, in agitation or silence, ravaged by a hurt beyond hurt. On one occasion, while David played, Saul paced the chamber, mumbling as though in heated contention with himself. Suddenly he lunged clumsily for a spear which leaned against the wall. David, whose eyes had never left the king, rose quickly from his stool and sprang aside as the ill-cast spear struck the stone floor nearby and clattered into a corner. Saul moaned, as though in pain, and slumped weakly to a couch, slack-jawed and distant.

David slipped from the chamber without a word. He was surprisingly aware that he had not at all been shaken by what had just occurred. David had come quite naturally to accept the possibility of physical danger and had been wary when the spirits of evil had possessed the king. Now that the attack had come, there seemed no alternative but to leave the king's service – and quickly.

Yet, when David related the event to a stunned and sorrowful Jonathan, as well as his intention of retiring permanently from Gibeah, Jonathan passionately urged that he reconsider. It was out of the question for David to consider leaving forever, as such a move might be taken as confirmation of something amiss between him and the king. Jonathan also appealed to David's personal loyalty, claiming that he needed his strength and love more than ever, since his father was clearly unable to conduct the affairs of state, and within the court there was discontent and plotting, not to speak of the fact that beyond the Israelites' borders the Philistines

In a fit of rage, Saul attacked his young servant, an act which ultimately drove David from the court. Saul casting his spear at David, from the 13th-century St Louis Bible

were waiting to take advantage of any weakness within. They would surely exploit David's absence, and the mutual alliance between the young prince and his warrior comrade appeared to be the only hope for Israel until the king recovered his health.

Beyond that, Jonathan claimed that he had plans to place Israel's administration upon a firm foundation against future reverses of health or fortune such as the king's present malady. In the meantime, however, it was critical that David remain bound to Israel's fortunes – although, Jonathan granted, it would probably be best for him to leave Gibeah until the king recovered his senses. He would recommend to Abner that war be resumed with the Philistines and that David be placed in command. That would remove him from the court for a while but at the same time would dissuade the *serenos* from attempting to capitalize on the king's indisposition, should they learn of it.

Abner, who had come to depend greatly upon David's skill as a commander, readily assented to Jonathan's plan. Surprisingly, even Saul raised no objection when he heard of it. His rage had abated, the psychic storm had run its course. The king seemingly had no memory of his attempt upon David's life on the preceding day. But David wondered whether Saul did not secretly harbour the perverse hope that a Philistine sword might succeed where his own spear had failed.

All Israel cheered the news that David was embarking on a new campaign against the Philistines. He marched down the Way of Beth-horon at the head of a legion of a thousand men. And it

The Way of Beth-horon (above) was the route taken by David and his soldiers in their attack against the Philistines. This expedition was a convenient excuse for David's absence from the royal court, where his life was in danger

was not long before messengers to Gibeah from the border country of the Shephelah were reporting stunning successes in operations against the Philistine outposts on the frontier. David even began staging daring strikes deep into Philistine territory. The balance of power appeared to be shifting decisively.

Popular acclaim for David mounted. New tales of his courage spread from mouth to mouth. And, since man is a myth maker, they were exaggerated greatly as they spread. Young women spoke with passion and yearning of his physical beauty. And his songs were sung from Asher and Naphtali in the north to Judah and Simeon in the south.

In Gibeah, Jonathan worked desperately to stave off the tragedy he knew could destroy the young country if Saul's conflict with David were not resolved. First, he ordered all reports of the popular acclaim for David scrupulously withheld from his ailing father. Only the most routine dispatches from David were permitted to reach the king. And, at Jonathan's suggestion, David liberally embellished them with florid expressions of praise, fealty and blatant flattery. Ailing egos may be intoxicated by the most cloying of wines.

Jonathan's second goal was of a far more difficult and profound order. It was to establish a permanent bond between the son of Jesse and the House of Saul. David must be married to a daughter of the king, and Saul must somehow be convinced to permit it. To many, Jonathan would have seemed a fool. Power, they would argue, is not divisible. Yet the heir to the throne of Israel was prepared to legitimatize a rival, perhaps even to abandon the succession in his favour.

There are a perennial handful of men who are not shackled by what passes as conventional wisdom. They are not enslaved by the obvious or handicapped by the tunnel-vision of self-seeking. Their genius is the ability to penetrate to the essence of things. Jonathan understood that the young monarchy could well perish in a confrontation between David and Saul. Yet Samuel's rigidity and Saul's deterioration were making the confrontation inevitable. With David's tribe, Judah – the largest of the tribes – supporting him, David could well triumph – but at the cost of civil strife so devastating that Israel's external enemies could sweep across the land. Jonathan was prepared to sacrifice his personal ambitions if this might spare his country such a fatal schism. So, too, might the union of David with a daughter of the royal house avert a power struggle which could tear the country apart.

A match with Merab was clearly out of the question. She was already betrothed to Adriel, the prince of Abel-Meholah, on

Israel's north-western border. Besides, Jonathan thought, Merab's spirit was composed not only of a generous portion of Benjaminite wilfulness, but the petulance and haughtiness of a first-born daughter. Merab was a shrew, used to getting her way. David deserved far better. Michal was Jonathan's favourite: beautiful, olive-skinned, passionate and endowed with the warmth and generosity of her mother – which tended to overcome the Benjaminite bluffness in her. Yet she was regal and elegant – a princess of Israel no less noble in presence than a daughter of Pharaoh. It was abundantly clear to Jonathan that Michal was drawn to David, wanted him.

In David's presence, Jonathan had noted, Michal measured him with her eyes too intently, almost greedily. She blushed too readily; giggled too generously at his self-conscious jokes. Alone with her brother, Michal would often question him about David with an insistence born, it seemed, less of curiosity than of ardour.

Jonathan had often teased Michal about her interest in David, but he had rarely discussed the matter with David himself. He was aware of how scrupulous, how compulsively meticulous, David was in dealing with the daughters of the king. Whether his reserve sprang from the young commoner's consciousness of his lowly origins, his resolve not to offend Saul, or rejection of his own sexuality, Jonathan was not certain. Yet he was certain that Michal's desire would find its response in David and that such a union would find favour in the eyes of the elders and citizens of Israel.

So right did the match seem to Jonathan that the difficulty of ever obtaining Saul's consent never appeared to intimidate him. First, Jonathan shrewdly obtained the support of his younger brothers, Abinadab, Melchishua and Ishbosheth, and of Merab, by playing to their self-interest. He spoke of how the marriage would cement the shaky union between the southern tribe of Judah and the House of Saul; of how it would insure the long-term loyalty of a royal protégé whose popularity now rivalled their own; and, thus, how the marriage could strengthen the prospects of the royal house.

Michal readily agreed to Jonathan's plan, as he had anticipated. She did not doubt that the match would receive her father's blessing. He had denied his daughters nothing, in atonement for the long periods he had been forced to spend away from them. Jonathan now waited for favourable reports of his father's condition, which would occasionally abate for long periods at a time, and on a day when Saul's affliction had greatly improved and his servants reported him in good spirits, Jonathan proposed the marriage.

Michal passionately declared her love for David. The monarch listened to their petition in silence, then asked his children to withdraw. Michal was certain the answer would be no. But the next day, Saul, surprisingly, gave his consent.

When David returned from the Philistine frontier, Jonathan eagerly drew him aside and told him the news. As Jonathan had hoped, David spoke of his deep feelings for Michal, ill concealing both the tenderness and desire he felt for her. But he was understandably suspicious of the king's sudden show of altruism towards him. He told Jonathan: 'I am a poor man, and of no repute. Does it seem a little thing to you to become the king's son-in-law?'

Jonathan replied: 'David, my friend, your humility becomes you. Of no repute, indeed! Would you insult me by so belittling the judgement of those who love you? You are deemed worthy by your friend, your wife-to-be, your people, and your king.'

Saul seemed uncharacteristically communicative, solicitous and affectionate when David was summoned before him to discuss details of the wedding. He felt it necessary to remind Saul that it was quite impossible for him to provide a dowry worthy of a princess. Saul had clearly been expecting the subject to arise. 'The king desires no marriage present,' Saul said, 'except a hundred slain Philistines, that he may be avenged of the king's enemies.' David and Jonathan were both shaken. Was Saul asking for a dowry of a hundred lives, or one life, his own? David was amazed at the extent of Saul's wilfulness and perversity. He would sacrifice even the feelings of his beloved daughter in a grotesque gamble that a Philistine spear might rid the king of a feared enemy.

Never before, David thought, had he been so conscious of man's capacity for perfidy and deception. Jonathan looked at him fearfully. But David only smiled and said: 'The king shall have his marriage present.' He bowed and left the throne room, considering with some surprise the intensity of the rage which Saul had aroused in him, rage he had somehow barely managed to suppress. David thought, for the first time, that he, too, was capable of evil. His religion was in large part an attempt to help men discriminate between good and evil. But it was easy to make moral evaluations in the abstract. In the real world, such value judgements came less easily. Take his own case. Yahweh had commanded: 'Thou shalt not kill.' But David might be capable of murdering Saul, as he had in fact slain Philistines. Both had challenged his right to survive – and the fight for survival always seemed to justify a very special set of rules which clashed with sacred law. Moses himself had invoked them in his wars against the Amalekites, as had Joshua in his struggle to redeem the Promised

Saul betroths his daughter Michal to David, from the St Louis Bible

Land from the Canaanites. Good and evil could not be discussed in limbo, for without a specific context good and evil did not exist. David's moral context was defined simply: anything was good which helped him survive. Sheer survival was now the issue in his bizarre relationship with King Saul.

David spoke secretly to a priest of the court whom he knew to be an agent of Samuel. He advised the priest of what had happened, and asked that Samuel be informed that David would shortly visit him at Ramah. Through intermediaries, Samuel had often let it be known that he would look with favour upon any attempt by David to seize the throne; that Yahweh now favoured David as His elect, His annointed. David had feigned indifference to these overtures. Now, however, he knew that survival might soon come to depend upon the goodwill and support of the priestly establishment. The time had come to cement an alliance with Samuel.

On the march to the coastal plain of Philistia, David slipped away from camp one night and doubled back to Ramah, where the aged Samuel sat in splendid isolation, awaiting reports of the physical and mental decline of Saul. David enlarged on the priest's report, telling Samuel all that had transpired at Gibeah, of the impending marriage, the blood dowry, of his perilous relationship with the jealous king. Ironically, it was the old man who seemed intense and impetuous, the younger man who counselled patience and restraint; for Samuel's days were numbered, the time left for the realization of his prophecy slipping swiftly away.

The prophet urged the anointing of David before an immediate convocation of the elders and the launching of a rebellion if Saul refused to abdicate in David's favour. David resisted. Surely he, above all, had reason to see the king removed. But it was folly to think the king might passively retire before such a challenge. Furthermore, the king was still popular, for few outside the court knew the full extent of his malady. An uprising would mean civil war. Beyond that, David would not mount the throne as an assassin or despot. He told Samuel of his confidence that events would surely dictate the way out of Israel's dilemma. In the meantime, David asked the old man for aid should Saul ever move against him. Samuel pledged the help of the priestly establishment. He suggested that David could count on sanctuary and sustenance at Nob, the holy city of the priests where the Ark now resided, should his life be in danger.

Then David returned to his mission in Philistia. He and his soldiers went on to slay two hundred of the enemy, twice the number the king had demanded as Michal's dowry. Returning safely to Gibeah, David presented the foreskins of his victims as proof of his success. The king was distraught. He must now submit to the unspeakable indignity of losing Michal, of seeing her taken to the bed of the young rival who had eclipsed him, of welcoming that rival to his own table as son-in-law and of watching the marriage prosper. But Saul had given his word to his eldest son, and his daughter, and could not withdraw it.

So Michal and David were wed, and the marriage was enthusiastically acclaimed throughout the land. As Jonathan had anticipated, it proved an agreeable match. To Saul's profound displeasure, Michal and David were well suited to each other and found satisfaction and happiness in their relationship.

But the king could not suffer it to continue. He called in several of his most trusted servants and told them that his son-in-law was now plotting to seize the throne. The crime of treason, Saul continued, justified the most drastic counter-measures. They must arrest David; and if they encountered resistance, he would not be greatly upset if it were deemed necessary to take David's life on the spot.

The king's men interpreted their instructions as Saul had intended. David was a hardened soldier, a cunning adversary. It was clear he would resist arrest. They must move against him when he least expected it and slay him – before he could react – in his bed as he slept.

One member of the band, however, had helped rear the king's children and was deeply fond of both Jonathan and Michal. The thought of slaying the heroic son of Jesse, the friend of one and husband of the other, horrified him. He revealed the plan to the prince and princess. They were overcome with disbelief and told David at once. The three agreed that the servant's tale was of such gravity that it was essential to be certain of its accuracy.

David proposed that on the appointed night he would slip out of the window of his bedchamber unseen. Michal would prepare a decoy under the bed-clothes, using a waterskin and a pillow of goat's hair. When the night arrived, Michal heard the intruders steal through a window. She rose from her bed to confront them.

Although Samuel anointed David king, the youth refused to rebel against Saul and usurp the throne of Israel. 'David Anointed by Samuel' by Jan Victors (1653)

Michal saved David's life by placing an effigy in his bed, but after the murder attempt David avoided further dangers at court by fleeing to sanctuary at the city of the prophets. This episode is among the illuminations in the St Louis Bible

'We have come to arrest David,' shouted the leader, shaken at finding the princess awake. And he nervously eyed the outline of the inert figure beside her. Surprisingly, it had not moved.

'He is ill,' Michal hastily explained. The assassins pulled down the coverlet to reveal the waterskin and rushed to advise the king. For the moment, at least, David's escape concerned him less than Michal's apparent perfidy. Michal's paramount loyalty had been to David, not to him. He had been abandoned by Yahweh, the prophet Samuel and now by his own children.

He summoned Michal before him, and Jonathan accompanied his distraught sister. Saul stormed at her: 'Why have you deceived me thus, and let my enemy go, so that he has escaped?'

It was Jonathan who replied in a calm, steady voice: 'Let not the king sin against his servant David; because he has not sinned against you, and because his deeds have been of good service to you; for he took his life in his hand and he slew the Philistine, and the Lord wrought a great victory for all Israel. You saw it and rejoiced; why then will you sin against innocent blood by killing David without cause?'

Jonathan's firmness caused Saul to tremble. He sent Michal from the room, then turned to his son and shouted: 'You son of a perverse, rebellious woman, do I not know that you have chosen the son of Jesse to your own shame, and to the shame of your mother's nakedness? For as long as the son of Jesse lives, neither you nor your kingdom shall be established. You know where he hides. Send him to me. He shall surely die.'

Jonathan now resolutely approached the throne and asked his father: 'Why should he be put to death? What has he done?' Jonathan's certitude drove Saul beyond the edge of reason. He lunged for the spear held by a nearby bodyguard. Jonathan defiantly turned his back on his father. Now Saul was forced to make a choice and, staring at the broad back of his eldest son, he hesitated, then dropped the spear. Defiantly Jonathan walked slowly and sadly from the chamber.

He rushed to David and related all that had happened.

Saul my father seeks to kill you. Therefore, take heed in the morning, stay in a secret place and hide yourself. I will go out and stand beside my father in the field were you are [hidden], and I will speak to my father about you; and if I learn anything I will tell you.

May the Lord be with you. If I am still alive, show me the loyal love of the Lord, that I may not die; and do not cut off your loyalty from my house forever. When the Lord cuts off every one of your enemies from the face of the earth, let not the name of Jonathan be cut off from the house of David. And may the Lord take vengeance on David's enemies. You shall be king over Israel, and I shall be next to you; Saul, my father, also knows this.

They wept and embraced. David asked Jonathan to advise Michal of his flight. A meeting with her would only compromise her further in the eyes of a father who had come close to murdering a son. The two friends looked at each other in silence. They knew they had committed themselves to an act from which all else would now flow – to which all would be traced.

'Go in peace, quickly,' Jonathan said. And David turned and departed.

He rode in darkness along the road that clung to the rocky spine of the hills of Benjamin. There had not been time to collect either food or weapons, or to inform his army comrades of his intentions. But then David was not yet certain of his intentions. He needed time to think in safety and seclusion. David rode towards the sanctuary of Nob, 4 miles south-east of Gibeah. Samuel had proposed Nob as a convenient place of refuge. There David might send word to Samuel of his final breach with Saul. He might also formalize an alliance with the priesthood. At Nob, David might find food, rest and a chance to consider his next moves. It had suddenly occurred to David that he was the quarry in a desperate pursuit. Saul could not afford to let him remain at large. He was now an outlaw; technically, an enemy of the crown and state. The idea would take some getting used to.

David received an uncordial welcome at Nob. He had covered the distance to the shrine before daybreak and stood before Ahimelech, a great-grandson of the prophet Eli. As Eli had presided at Shiloh, Ahimelech now served as chief priest at Nob. When the priest recognized David, he became nervous and agitated, wrung his hands and plucked nervously at the fringes of his linen cloak.

'Why are you alone?' Ahimelech whispered, his voice tinged with suspicion. Ahimelech was plainly not anxious to see him. For some reason the priest was not anxious to disclose, David was not welcome at Nob. And he determined that he must tell Ahimelech nothing, seek no counsel from him, depart as quickly as he had come. He did not respond to Ahimelech's question. He asked only for food and sword, promising that once he received them he would be gone. He had not eaten since the afternoon of the preceding day.

Ahimelech grudgingly agreed to provide David with the weapon and several loaves of unleavened bread, which had been consecrated as a sacrifice to Yahweh. The holy bread could, by statute, be eaten by the priests at the end of each week, when it had been replaced with fresh loaves.

Ahimelech's cautious attitude towards David's request was undoubtedly brought on by the presence at the sanctuary of one of Saul's trusted servants, Doeg, and the priest's fear of reprisal should he be tagged a collaborator. For Saul had reacted far more swiftly than David had expected, foreclosing most of his options. His choice was a simple one: to linger, facing imminent capture and execution; or, to follow the way ordained in those times for the fugitive – the road to the south, the barren hill country of his tribe, Judah. And, he wondered, if the foundations are destroyed, what can the righteous do?

David opened his eyes and stared at the rock above him, coated thickly with the soot of ancient fires. Caves, too, must carry the mark of Cain, he thought. He had not been the first hunted man to find shelter here. These caves, which honeycombed the heights of Judah, had been shared before by desperate men and squalid clusters of bats.

David knew the area well. During the early phases of the liberation struggle against the Philistines, Saul's guerrilla bands had used the Judean caves both as hide-outs and bases from which to launch raids and ambushes. The region was a twilight land, far too rugged

The barren hill country of Judah, to which David fled from Saul's anger and jealousy after his cool reception at Nob

and sparsely populated to pacify; so the wilderness belonged to no man, neither to Israel nor the *serenos*. It was ideal for the purposes of a fugitive.

Those purposes had begun to crystallize in this cavern David had chosen. It was sited near the summit of the fortress-like hill called Adullam. From its mouth David could look west across the undulating foot-hills of the Shephelah to the fertile plains of Philistia and the curving arc of sea that stretched beyond sight to the land of the pharoahs. Far to the south the verdure of the coastal plain melted into the tawny tinted sands of the Negev and Sinai deserts.

The sun flooded the mountains and plains beyond with a golden light. As it warmed David's skin, it seemed to burn away the paralysis which had threatened to numb his body and brain. The clarity of even the farthest object in the still, dry air seemed to stimulate a clarity of thought of which he had not been capable in days.

Food, water and shelter would be no problem here. A nearby spring provided the latter. Wandering nomads bartered enough olives, figs, rye and unleavened bread for his sword to suffice until contact could be made with his family in Bethlehem. The basic challenge would come from Saul, to whom the thought of a rival on the loose would be insufferable. The king would surely mount well-manned and well-armed expeditions to capture him. David needed comrades to help counter them. His own fighting force must not be too large at first, for it must be capable of speed and mobility and possess the stamina and craftiness to live off the land – and be loyal enough to follow him anywhere. It must be composed of first-class fighters whose exploits would attract others to his ranks. To fight, they must be promised booty, and, ultimately, glory. The force David intended to raise would be the nucleus of an army that would eventually remove Saul from the throne of Israel.

First, David dispatched a trusted nomad to Bethlehem, 12 miles to the north-east, to inform his family of his hiding place, and he bade them come secretly and quickly. David had to remove his parents from the reach of a vengeful king. He also needed the unquestioned loyalty of his brothers. They came, bringing food and supplies. Word was also sent to David's comrades-in-arms to join him at Adullam. Some were fearful and remained in the service of the king. But others deserted to David. And with them, singly and in pairs, drifted young adventurers motivated only by the prospect of seeing battle under David, rebels disaffected with the king and brigands without a cause, in search of booty and a fight. The force amounted to some four hundred men.

News of David's defection had reached the Philistine *serenos*. They moved quickly to exploit the situation and launched a series of lightning assaults against Israelite border settlements. The desertions to David had whipped Saul to a fury, and in his paranoiac blindness he made his first fatal error. Saul chose to oppose David rather than the Philistines. He sent units in force into the Judean highlands in search of David, stretching his forces too thinly to provide adequate support for the Israelite settlements.

David responded brilliantly in two ways. He withdrew his own force further south into the wilderness, where the advantage clearly lay with the quarry, not the hunter. Then he began to generate popular support in Judah, his tribal base, by launching operations against the marauding Philistines whenever the opportunity presented itself.

David's raiders were able to dart quickly from their cave bases in the wilderness, lifting the Philistine siege of each Israelite settlement, and, in return, earning both the goodwill of the townsfolk and generous contributions of supplies. These, together with enemy booty, permitted David's men to survive in the wilderness with tolerable ease. In time, David was able to carve out a sort of personal fiefdom within Judah.

But his operations against the Philistines were precarious, for they served to advertise David's whereabouts to Saul. From time to time, intelligence was delivered to Gibeah by citizens satisfied to accept both David's military protection and the king's gold.

On one occasion, Saul mounted an expedition into the wilderness of Ziph. David and his men were encamped on the heights. Saul had grown careless. He ordered Abner to bivouac the army on low ground. David observed the king's approach and the disposition of the camp itself from a distant ridge. Night would soon fall. The terrain and the darkness provided the optimum condition for a surprise attack.

But David's judgement counselled against such an attack. The essential elements of political greatness, of statesmanship, are a sense of timing and an exquisite perception of cause and effect. In David, these were innate. The vision of others is fogged by the prospects of immediate reward. The vision of the great is of a different order. The essence of Yahwistic law was that blood begets blood. David knew that he could not hope to found a dynasty or command the mandate of a united nation with the blood of the king on his hands. Assassination is the road to despotism, not glory. Besides, the assassination of Saul could well undermine the vital relationship between David and Jonathan, for Jonathan still loved his father. For David, the key to the throne was Jonathan's willingness to surrender the right of succession. David's sword, however, could destroy all this with the murder of the king, and foreclose the hope of any reconciliation with the other of Saul's heirs.

Nonetheless, the present situation was not entirely to be wasted. As an accomplice, David chose Abishai, his cousin and brother to his trusted lieutenant Joab. Early in the dark morning, when sleep is deepest, the two crawled noiselessly past drowsing pickets, sentries and bodyguards. They made their way to the royal tent in the very centre of Saul's camp. Excitedly, Abishai whispered: 'God has given your enemy into your hand. Now let me pin him to the earth with one stroke of my spear, and it will not be necessary

to strike him twice.' David restrained Abishai, saying: 'Do not destroy the king. Who can put forth his hand against the Lord's anointed and be guiltless?'

Instead, David motioned to his mystified follower to take the spear which was stuck in the ground at the head of the sleeping form of Saul. David quietly picked up a water jar, which lay beside the king. Then they crept away and climbed a hill adjacent to the camp, well out of spear shot, though within easy voice range.

Below, Abner, Saul's commander, was hastily awakened by an excited sentry and emerged from his tent to listen incredulously to the voice of David calling from the darkness: 'Will you not answer, Abner? Why have you not kept watch over your lord the king? Someone came into camp and could well have destroyed him. Instead, they took the king's spear and the jar of water by his side. You deserve to die for your carelessness.'

Saul emerged from the tent, his fury greatly muted by the shock of a narrow escape. And he shouted: 'Is this your voice, David?'

'It is, my king. Why does my lord pursue me? What have I done? What am I guilty of? Why has the king of Israel come out to seek my life like one who hunts a partridge in the mountains? Here is your spear, O king. Let one of your young men come up and fetch it. The Lord delivered you into my hand tonight, and I would not put forth my hand against the Lord's anointed.'

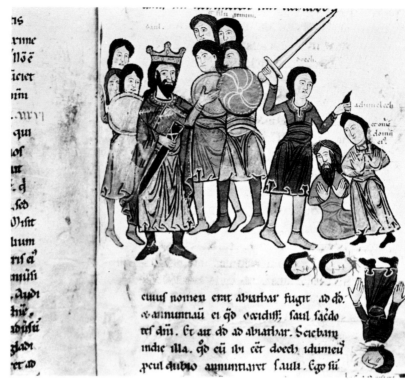

When Saul mounted an expedition into the Wilderness of Ziph (above, left), David used the opportunity to warn the king of his vulnerability, but he spared Saul's life
The massacre of the priests of Nob (above, right), Saul's reply to David's challenge in the Wilderness of Ziph, as portrayed in the Léon Bible (Spain, 1162)

In his fright, Saul was convinced the camp was surrounded and that David might order a full-scale attack upon the camp if he were angered. The king swallowed his pride and tried to mollify David: 'I have done wrong, my son. I have played the fool and erred exceedingly. I will no more do you harm, because my life was precious in your eyes. Please, return to Gibeah.'

David signalled to Abishai to follow him away and back to the heights. The only reply to reach Saul was the faint soughing of the wind, a sound as barren of life as the wilderness itself. For the remainder of the night he lay in his tent, unable to sleep. With the first light, he ordered the expedition to return to Gibeah.

Some days later, spies brought David news of Saul's response. He had ordered Michal's marriage annulled, against her will, and offered her to another man. He had commanded Doeg to massacre Ahimelech, who had given David food and a sword, together with the other priests of Nob. When word of the massacre reached the aged Samuel at Ramah, the shock killed him. The priestly establishment, upon which David had so heavily counted for support, was now leaderless, demoralized and in disarray.

David's escapade in the wilderness of Ziph – what had it earned? David spent long days and nights in anguish pondering the thought. It troubled him deeply.

# 4 The Anointed of Judah

David assessed the cost of his bravado in the Wilderness of Ziph – for that, he sadly conceded, was what his single-handed foray against Saul had amounted to, sheer bravado. He had driven the king to commit an act of brutality, in violation of the most sacred statutes, unparalleled in Israelite history – the massacre of the priests of Nob. He had lost his prime supporter, the prophet Samuel; and now, Saul had robbed him of Michal, forcing her to wed Paltiel, the son of a minor courtier named Laish, a man for whom she had no feeling, whom she barely knew.

Jonathan was horror-stricken at his father's remorselessness. But his eldest son's feelings were of small concern to Saul. The king denied Jonathan, as he had denied reason. Jonathan was banished from the king's presence. Furthermore, he was placed under constant surveillance to prevent any contact or communication with David.

In the Negev, the position of the fugitives was becoming increasingly untenable and threatened to become desperate. Saul had redoubled his efforts to close in on the insurgents. More often now, royal scouts and military patrols were sighted combing the wadis and heights of the wilderness in search of David's camps. The fugitives were constantly on the move trying to evade detection or costly battles, engaging in limited harassing actions only when conditions were favourable. David divided his force into small units, both to increase their mobility and make them more difficult to locate. This greatly complicated David's communications and logistics problems. But the greatest danger lay in the relentless erosion of support in the villages and settlements upon which David had counted for supplies, shelter and intelligence. Saul's massacre of the priests of Nob had alarmed the elders of Judah. They feared that in his wrath the king might unleash a similar

The desert landscape where David and his men kept on the move to avoid Saul's patrols

reign of terror upon their settlements should they be caught collaborating with David. Their concern proved justified. Messengers of the king were dispatched to each settlement bearing a royal edict which they read before the gates. Those found aiding or abetting the insurgents would be considered enemies of the throne and punished by banishment or death.

The manoeuvre produced the expected results. David and his men became pariahs. They were unwelcome in the towns and settlements, and the gates were barred against them. One after another, vital sources of supply dried up, and provisions became scarce. David was trapped between the hammer of Saul and the anvil of the Philistines.

His force had now swelled to six hundred men. Many were motivated by loyalty to David, or to their nation, or by grievances – real or imagined – against the throne. These men could be expected to endure great suffering and hardship in David's service. But many others were, at best, soldiers of fortune, some from foreign lands; at worst – and David freely acknowledged it – ruffians and outlaws. The depth of their loyalty was in direct proportion to the fullness of their stomachs or purses. Their likely reaction to the prospect of starvation would be either desertion or revolt. And, indeed, their stirrings and grumbles over the unfavourable turn of events had already reached David's ears.

It was vital that his force be kept intact and its strength husbanded. David coldly examined the problem. There were only two options left to him: he could extort or steal his supplies from Israelites; or he might try to obtain what he needed from Philistines. But the latter required delicate negotiation. He would have to resort to the first for a time, while attempting to arrange the second. To stop and consider whether or not his actions were just was a luxury in which David could not indulge at present. The interpreters of Yahweh's statutes envisioned a perfect world. He must survive in an imperfect one, as nobly as circumstances allowed. And, in the circumstances, his supplies would have to be 'donated' – willingly or otherwise – by well-to-do farmers who could afford to part with a portion of their figs and grapes, olives and rye.

But brigandage could only serve as an interim step at best, lest David permanently incur the enmity of the entire Israelite establishment and undermine his loyal following among the peasantry. He would have to find a new base of operations, one in which he would be beyond Saul's reach, militarily secure and assured of dependable sources of provisions until it was safe to return. Only one place satisfied the conditions – Philistia. David would have to persuade the enemy to enter into an alliance of convenience with him. The idea was as brilliant as it was outrageous.

David explained his scheme to the trusted emissaries he was sending to Achish, the *sereno* of the great Philistine city of Gath in the fertile lowlands. Their shock slowly gave way to grudging admiration. David's plan was audaciously simple. He had long esteemed Achish as the most chivalrous, as well as the shrewdest, of Philistine leaders. Achish had been first to understand the import of the rupture in David's relations with Saul and had accordingly been first to begin tentatively exploiting the situation. It had been Achish's troops whom David's men had faced in their relief of the settlements of Judah.

This was the essence of David's proposal to the *sereno* of Gath: he and his men would cease opposing Philistine forays into Judah, provided that Achish annex to David a small portion of the territory of Gath at the fringe of the Philistine frontier with Israel. In exchange, David and his men would serve as mercenaries under Achish. However, they would not fight fellow Israelites. They would restrict their military service solely to the defence of

The view of the lowlands from Tell Gath, which includes the remains of the biblical city of Gath ruled by Achish

Philistine territory against the incursions of Amalekite raiders who emerged from the southern desert.

From the earliest times, the sons of Amalek, Semitic nomads from whom the Israelites and Canaanites were descended, lived to raise their flocks, harvest their dates, race their camels, drink and gamble on proceeds gained by looting each other and their more sedentary cousins in the fertile lands. When the soldiery of the civilized nations were too occupied warring against each other to patrol their frontiers adequately, the Amalekites swooped in on their camels to pillage farms and settlements and then vanished again into the desert laden with spoils. Fear and hatred of Amalek formed perhaps the only common bond between Israelite and Philistine. In Achish's case specifically, with scores of his troops now occupied in operations against Israel, the outlying settlements of Gath lay open to Amalekite depredations. An alliance with David might provide a not unattractive arrangement for Achish, particularly since the formidable enemy warrior would be collaborating with him, rather than warring against him.

Though he could ill afford it, David amassed an impressive tribute – skins of wine, flasks of the purest olive oil, mules, donkeys, sheep, and fine linen of the rich purple for which the dyers of Canaan were renowned. These David's emissaries bore to Achish, together with urgent instructions to reach an agreement with the *sereno* of Gath as quickly as possible.

In the interim, David had literally been forced to begin extorting supplies to maintain his fighting force. His victims were enterprising semi-nomadic chieftains, ruggedly independent Israelite traders, as coarse-grained as the rock of the Negev uplands in which they grazed and sheared their flocks. Sheep were as much valued in Israel for their meat as for their wool. They produced vast wealth for their owners, who were regarded with envy by the small farmers and peasants of Israel as the exploiters of their day. Thus they made highly suitable targets for David. Yet David was discontented in his role and impatient to strike a bargain with Achish, for the vocation of robber baron hardly suited him. He had not been trained to join combat with fat old men on donkeys. He could entertain the notion of living as an outcast, but not an outlaw.

One Israelite gambled intuitively on David's discomfiture. Abigail was the beautiful and aristocratic daughter of a merchant. She had gotten the worst of a bad business arrangement negotiated by her father, who had betrothed her, in settlement of a business debt, to a citizen of Maon in the Negev named Nabal. Nabal's standing as a trader of wealth and substance (he owned three

David (left) at the court of Achish, from the St Louis Bible

thousand sheep and goats) was exceeded only by his reputation as a reprobate. He was a ruthless and unyielding bargainer, and his slaves cowered in fear of him. It was said that Nabal could turn a profit from a stone. Even Abigail was unable to warm the heart and soul of the old curmudgeon; the couple was childless. Abigail complained little of her drab existence. There would have been no point. It was not an enlightened age for its outlook on the role of women. They were chattel – the property of their husbands. It was through the male that their existence acquired any meaning. They had no rights, only duties.

When scouts of David reached the area of Carmel, just north of Maon, where Nabal's flocks were grazed, several of his shepherds asked to desert their master and join David's ranks. They spoke of Nabal's cruelties and excesses and reported in detail on the extent and disposition of his wealth. Within a few days, David's young lieutenants were paying a call on Nabal. The thrust of their proposition was quite plain: provide the insurgents with supplies, and in return David's men would protect Nabal's herds and flocks – from themselves! Most other victims had quickly capitulated. But Nabal's reaction to what in our day is euphemistically called the 'protection racket' was both demonstrative and emphatically negative.

David ordered his men to prepare for the raid. They would simply take what Nabal would not 'volunteer' to provide. Hearing of this, several of Nabal's loyal overseers fled in desperation to Abigail. She had often been their last resort in situations in which generous portions of tact and diplomacy were required – neither of which Nabal possessed in the slightest. 'Consider what you should do,' they told her, 'for David has embarked on a course of evil against our master and his holdings, and Nabal is so ill-natured that we cannot speak to him.'

In later years, Abigail would wonder what truly lay behind the impulsive action upon which she embarked, and she would frankly admit to herself that what she did went far beyond loyalty and duty to her husband. There had been a fascination and curiosity about David, whom she had long worshipped for his exploits and about whom she often fantasized, perhaps in compensation for the barrenness of her own existence. Now she would meet him.

Without consulting Nabal, Abigail ordered the overseers to prepare a generous tribute to David. They issued orders for the baking of two hundred loaves of bread and the slaughter and dressing of five sheep. They collected a generous measure of parched grain, two large skins of wine, a hundred clusters of raisins and two hundred fig cakes and ordered it all loaded on the backs of

mules and donkeys. With Abigail at its head, the caravan moved slowly up the road along which David was advancing towards Carmel.

David had worked himself into a towering passion against Nabal, whose niggardliness had, as David reasoned, forced him into the awkward role of brigand. But the anger vanished within an instant of his surprised sight of the woman who rode into view. But even beyond her beauty, Abigail's tactics were irresistible. She bowed before David and, in word as well as manner and bearing, comported herself with the deference due not to a brigand, but a sovereign. She argued her husband's cause on the ground of David's interest rather than that of Nabal. He must abandon this expedition, she argued, because he would then be free of any grief or guilt which might later arise from a violent assault against the men and property of Nabal's household. And she implied that such behaviour would not befit a man who was truly destined to become a monarch. Consciously or not, she had tailored her petition perfectly to a man under siege by his conscience. David melted before Abigail, accepted the generous peace offering – amounting to provisions for several days – and ordered the men back to camp. He would never have admitted afterwards that he had been bought off. But this, in fact, is what had been perpetrated upon him by a beautiful lady.

Some time later, word was brought to David that Nabal had died in a fit of overdrinking, and he travelled to Maon, ostensibly to express his personal condolences to the widow. David's actual objective was far more self-serving. When the statutes permitted, he wooed and married Abigail. In time, there would be other wives as well, for polygamy was an accepted practice in the area at that time. But throughout his turbulent life, David's relationship with the wise and comely Abigail would remain a singular source of comfort and strength.

In due course, the embassy to Gath brought good news back to David's camp in the hill country of the Negev. The emissaries reported that Achish had at first been astonished by David's proposition. But after a number of audiences and some weeks of thought and consultation, Achish had expressed his tentative interest in the overture. He proposed a secret parley with David. The Philistine wished to take a personal measure of the man and, in a negotiation as sensitive as this, to have a direct hand in the bargaining.

Hostages were arranged and traded as a guarantee for the safety of the two leaders, and a meeting site was chosen outside Debir, on the rim of the Shephelah. Debir was nominally an Israelite town,

When David's lieutenant approached Nabal to request supplies (shown above in an illustration from the 14th-century Wenceslas Bible), he was summarily rejected. But when David personally led a raid to steal what he could not acquire by nonviolent means, he was met by Nabal's wife, Abigail (left, in a painting by Jacob Cornelsz), whose beauty and charm instantly subdued his anger

but it lay so close to the territory of Gath that it belonged to the Philistine economic and political sphere of interest.

There is a singular bond between military adversaries unknown beyond the battlefield. With David and Achish, the shared respect of chivalrous men quickly matured into trust, and mutual admiration ripened into friendship. They worked out in relatively short order the details of a covenant. David vowed to forswear all and any aggressive designs against the confederation of the Philistines. He and his men pledged their loyalty to Achish and agreed to serve as mercenaries in the service of Gath, employed to protect the southern frontier of the territory against Amalekite incursions. In exchange, David would be given as a fief the area called Ziklag in the southern Shephelah on the edge of the coastal plain, one of the last fertile enclaves north of the wilderness. The siting of Ziklag offered excellent communications with Judah.

Achish also reluctantly accepted David's demands that his men be fully equipped with the iron weapons of the Philistines, in place of their own less-durable implements of bronze, and that they be trained by officers of Achish's army in Philistine military organization, strategy and tactics.

On the appointed day, units of David's insurgents reluctantly filed out of the hills into the land of their lifelong enemy. Maturity is in part an acceptance of life's ironies. They would never forget that day; they would never be the same. In those barren hills east of Philistia, they had been hunted mercilessly by a half-crazed king. And yet their sense of loss at the leaving of Judah was beyond description. For at the foot-hills, where they crossed the frontier into Philistia, they left the dominion of Yahweh for the realm of the Philistine deity Dagon. To die and be laid to rest in the land of a foreign god was a fearsome prospect. For it was believed that the sway of a deity could not transcend the sovereign boundaries of the people who worshipped him. Such was man's conception of the divine in David's day. In a way, it was certainly a speculation no less tolerant than that of our own age, in which dozens of creeds, each with its claims of exclusivity upon salvation and truth, wage holy war in the name of One God.

So a final prayer to Yahweh was on the lips of many of David's warriors as they filed out of the Shephelah and onto the broad and fertile plain of Philistia. Yahweh would neither hear their prayers nor control their destinies again, until they should return to His land. Would Dagon heed their supplications? Would he choose to care about creatures from an alien land who were once arrayed against his people? And how, how could one bring himself to speak to this deity through a piece of stone, this graven image

Teshoub, the god of the Hittites, one of the many deities of the Near Eastern pantheon in biblical times. Like the Philistine and Israelite deities, Teshoub was believed to hold sway over only the territory in which he was worshipped

In Carmel, David acquired not only Nabal's supplies, but the merchant's wife, Abigail, whom he later married. Their wedding ceremony is depicted in this painting by the Dutch artist Hugo van der Goes (1440–1482)

exposuim' ouginem psalmox 7 m̃ exponamus quom̃ hebrei li
brū psalmox in quinq; diuidant libros. id est quatuor itaq; libri
finiunt in fine. fiat fiat. Quinq; autē omiis s̃p̃s laudet dñm;

BEATUS VIR QUI NON ABIIT

in consilio impiox 7 in uia peccatox non stetit. 7 in cathedris derisox
non sedit.       S ; in lege dn̄i uoluntas eius. 7 in lege ei̇ meditabitur
die ac nocte.  E t erit tanq̃ lignū t̃ñsplantatū iuxta riuos aq̃rū.
qd fructum suum dabit in t̃p̃r suo.  E t foliū ei̇ ñ defluet. 7 oĩe
d fecerit p̃sp̃abitur. N on sic ip̃ii. s; tanq̃ puluis quē p̃c uentus.
p̃opt̃a ñ resurg̃nt ĩp̃ii in iudico. neq; peccatores in cõg̃r̃e

before whom the men of Philistia prostrated themselves? The journey conjured frightful spiritual prospects for the insurgents, David included. Of all the injustices done him by Saul, David would always hold this to have been the most grievous – an enforced exile from the land of Yahweh for the home and service of a strange god.

For well over a year, David and his men served the Philistines. Under the tutelage of their employers, they developed into a crack military corps whose skills in the science of war matched their audacity and courage. They applied what they learned in a running series of pre-emptive raids on the encampments of the Amalekites to the south. Achish was content; and David was freed from the day-to-day concerns which had so plagued him. At every opportunity, he covertly sent a portion of his Amalekite booty to tribe and clan leaders and to the elders of the towns and settlements in Judah. David hoped to remind them that his exile was only temporary, to maintain their past loyalty and, by making at least symbolic restitution, to rekindle those friendships cooled by his transformation into a somewhat unattractive soldier of fortune.

David's short-term preoccupations were now replaced by a more profound concern. There seemed no prospect that his exile might soon come to an end, no omen in the wind that offered promise of any change. Had he purchased a form of servitude in the land of his enemies for but a mess of bread and pottage?

In due course, the fateful chain of events was precipitated by the Philistine *serenos*. In deliberations with his colleagues, Achish made much of the fact that he had succeeded in neutralizing David as an effective military opponent. His defection, coupled with King Saul's deterioration and the schism between the king and his son Jonathan, led the *serenos* to the unanimous conclusion that conditions were right for a decisive campaign against Israel. Her disarray offered Philistia the best opportunity in years to re-establish her former holdings in the hill country.

Achish summoned David to Gath for a parley and made a stunning offer. If David agreed to renounce his vow never to serve the Philistines against his own people, Achish would propose that David be elevated to the throne of Israel to rule in the *serenos'* name. Would he and his men march with Achish in the coming campaign?

Achish's motives were clear. The Philistines had ultimately been driven from Israelite territory because they could not commit the resources needed to police and subjugate it completely. The Israelites were a fiercely independent, spirited people who could

A Philistine bronze sword, similar in design to swords of other Sea Peoples

David mourning the death of Saul, from the 12th-century Souvigny Bible never be expected to submit directly to the authority of the *serenos* and their god-idol. But if their own former champion, David, were installed over them, the new Philistine dominion could surely be made more secure.

For David, the choice was equally clear. He could either remain a Philistine mercenary, an alien and an outcast, playing lion to the Amalekite gazelle for the rest of his life; or he could gamble upon Saul's defeat by the Philistines and his own succession – the prize he had sought for so long and for which he had sacrificed so much. Once the throne was his, he could then turn his thoughts to the problem of dealing with the Philistines. And so, David agreed to march with Achish and then set out on the delicate task of winning the support of his men.

The Philistine strategy was far more ambitious and sophisticated than the Aphek campaign many years earlier. The *serenos* would avoid a direct assault into the heart of Israelite territory. Instead of moving in strength up the narrow mountain passes, the Philistines would use as their invasion highway the broad valley called the Jezreel, farther to the north. Israel had repeatedly struggled to gain control of this valley, with only limited success. Whoever controlled the valley controlled the movement of the caravans which bore the wealth of the Near East between Egypt and the city-states of Syria to the north and Mesopotamia to the east. The valley was also the essential link between the Philistine coast and the majestic garrison of Beth-shean – the inland fortress of the Philistines which protected the Jezreel Valley against incursions from the east or from the Jordan Valley.

In one stroke, the Philistines would again secure the Jezreel Valley, begin the process of encircling Israel, drive a wedge between Saul and the Israelite tribes of the Galilee and draw Saul and his army onto terrain which favoured the more conventional set-piece strategy of the *serenos* and their chariotry. Beyond that, if Saul moved north to meet them, his lines of communication and supply would be lengthened intolerably and be exposed to interdiction.

The Philistines, on the other hand, had unchallenged mastery of both the coastal and sea approaches to the western Jezreel and were immune from flank attacks. Their ships and armies, David's men among them, moved northwards from the five cities of Philistia and assembled at the port of Dor. From there, the Philistine columns, spearheaded and flanked by the chariots and cavalry, marched inland unopposed past the fortresses of Megiddo and Taanach – among the last great enclaves of the Canaanites, who, in their decline, had effectively become vassals to the Philistines.

Spies sent word to Gibeah of the mobilization measures and troop movements in Philistia, and Israelite scouts reported daily on the march to the Jezreel Valley. The news shocked Saul into a semblance of reason. In a moment of clarity, he saw what he had wrought: David deserted, Jonathan disowned, Michal alienated and distant and the political landmarks of his stormy career reduced to mocking mounds of rubble and dust. Within Saul, the instinct to lead strived to martial him. But his will and energy were hobbled by despair, his spirit all but suffocated by a sense of loss too great to bear.

Saul ordered Abner to mobilize the army and summon the

A view of the Plain of Jezreel from the fortress of Taanach

tribal levies for the march northwards. And he made a tearful peace with Jonathan. As the two rode again side by side at the head of the army, Saul could not dispel a hobbling premonition he was embarking upon a battle he would not win.

The Philistines massed for battle at Shunem, a village which lay in the valley at the foot of the hill called Moreh. Across the valley rose a spur of Mount Gilboa, where the forces of Saul began to mass.

Grave doubts plagued David as he observed the Israelite array from the summit of the Hill of Moreh. Could anything – power, the throne, anything – justify his spilling the blood of countrymen? Discontent spread among David's men, as well. Many could justify to themselves their acts of disobedience against Saul, but never their treason against Israel.

Again, it was the Philistines who made a fateful decision, perhaps more decisive to the career of David than any other. Achish was accosted by his confederates, who were deeply troubled by the presence of the Hebrew mercenaries, as were many of their officers and men. They could not forget how many of their own Hebrew mercenaries turned against them in the crucial battle of Michmash. Could a former Israelite champion like David be trusted within their ranks when Michmash was finally about to be redressed?

Achish replied: 'David has been with me now for some time, and since he deserted to me I have found no fault with him. But the others could not be mollified and prevailed over the king of Gath. Reluctantly, Achish ordered David to return to the south. David barely managed to suppress his overwhelming relief, or the cheers of his men when he ordered a withdrawal. The following morning, the Israelite mercenaries, with David at their head, departed from camp before first light, anxious to be as far away as possible before Israelite and Philistine clashed in the valley below.

After three days of nearly unbroken marching, they reached Ziklag in the Negev only to find it all but devastated, whisps of smoke still rising from the ash of roofs and beams. An Amalekite band had taken advantage of David's brief absence. It had swept against the town on camels and horses, surprised and overcome the small rearguard David had left behind and raced unopposed from house to house, looting and burning. The women and children were herded outside and bound, the elderly put to the sword.

The returning warriors were both enraged and distraught, David no less than the others, for his two wives, Abigail and Ahinoam, were among the missing captives. The usual fate of Amalekite prisoners was permanent bondage, either as slaves to their captors or freight for the slave markets of Egypt. Despite their fatigue from the swift march south, the men clamoured for immediate pursuit. David's force raced south-west toward the Sinai, the direction in which they presumed the Amalekites were heading. The raiders could not be many days ahead, for the ashes of Ziklag were still warm. And they were burdened by both a large number of prisoners and a sizable booty of donkeys, sheep and goats. They could not move with their usual speed and would have to keep close to springs and water-holes.

Then, in the wilderness just beyond Gaza, the pursuers came upon a man lying face down in the sunbaked marl, close to death from heat, thirst and starvation. David ordered food and water brought to him. When the man was revived, he identified himself as an Egyptian, a slave of a clan leader of the Amalekite band which had plundered Ziklag. He had fallen ill on the retreat from the Negev, and the Amalekites, fearful of plague, had abandoned him. David guaranteed his freedom, and, in return, the Egyptian divulged the raiders' route. Within a day, David's scouts had located them encamped at a desert water-hole, revelling in a victory feast. When sated, they slept where they fell amid the mutton bones and the empty wine skins, the loot of Philistia and Judah; and they awakened to a crazed world of fearsome shrieks, the grotesque, helmeted faces of Hebrews limned in the waning light of the acacia fire and the throttled gasps of dying men. The slaughter was nearly complete. Only a handful of Amalekites on the edge of the camp managed to reach their camels and escape.

The women, sons and daughters of Ziklag wept, cheered, prayed, clung to their men and returned with them to the Negev. David had also acquired an enormous spoil – not only the loot of Ziklag, but of other settlements in Philistia and Judah upon which the Amalekites had fallen. And when the booty was apportioned among his men and himself, David scrupulously set aside the customary share for the elders of the major towns of southern Judah. Once these had been delivered, he set about to rebuild Ziklag.

Then David learned of the disaster at Mount Gilboa. He had been expecting some word, with a conflicting mixture of anticipation and anxiety. But he was still emotionally unprepared to cope with the news. An Israelite survivor was brought before him – dishevelled, distraught, his eyes brimming – and he fell to the ground before David in homage.

He told David that the Israelites had been routed and many slain. The remnants, including Saul and his four sons, had been forced to fall back upon the high ground on the flanks of Mount

Gilboa, with Philistine cavalry wheeling and closing in about them. Then Saul was struck by an arrow and gravely wounded. Fearing capture, he fell upon his own sword and died. His sons Abinadab and Melchishua also fell. Abner, Saul's commander, now devoted his flagging energies to saving the two remaining heirs of the House of Saul. He implored Jonathan and Ishbosheth to break off the fight and flee the battlefield. But Jonathan had been mortally wounded and refused to withdraw. He died protecting the retreat of Abner and his last surviving brother.

The Philistines marked the watershed victory with a singular display of barbarity. They mutilated the corpses of Saul and his sons, cut off their heads and carted their bodies in a victory procession to Beth-shean. The royal armour was dedicated to the temple of Astarte, the patron goddess of the city. The bodies were nailed above the gate of Beth-shean, where they might be abused, stoned and gawked at by the masses.

A courageous band of Israelites from Jabesh-gilead, across the Jordan River, recovered the torn bodies at night, while the citizens and soldiers of Beth-shean were occupied in a tumultuous victory feast. Saul had always occupied a unique place in the memories of the people of Jabesh-gilead. For he had broken the Ammonite siege of the town some twenty years earlier – his first historic achievement as king and the victory which had renewed Israel's faith and spirit after the original Philistine occupation. Saul and his sons were buried with honour under a tamarisk tree in Jabesh-gilead, and the citizens of the town mourned and fasted for a week.

It was in Mahanaim, in the rocky heights some 20 miles southeast of Jabesh-gilead, that Ishbosheth established an official court of sorts. But it could not claim effectively to be more than a government-in-exile. Once again, the Philistines virtually controlled all of Israel. They encircled the heart of the hill country to the west and the north. The Israelite union had been sundered.

David grieved for Israel, for Jonathan and, strangely, for Saul. He saw them linked with him in some way quite beyond their control, in a relationship of grotesque ironies. And he wondered ever so briefly whether this might in some way define the permanent condition to which Yahweh had consigned his quite absurd creatures. Kings and princes, indeed, with their battered heads spat upon and kicked, rolling in the dust; their gory bodies hung on spikes to be fingered and jeered at by louts and peasants. Suddenly, David wept for Saul, for his tragedy and the conceits of glory. David had not composed upon the lyre for some years, but now he was driven to take it up, and its notes became his tears:

The death of Saul on Mount Gilboa, by Peter Bruegel

How are the mighty fallen,
and the weapons of war perished.

(II Samuel 1 : 27)

As imperialists, the Philistines had become adept since their earlier occupation. Now they imposed a divide-and-conquer policy upon Israel. A division of sorts could be said to exist between the Israelite tribes to the north and south of the Jebusite city Jebus – a demarcation both geographical and cultural in nature. Aiming to exploit this, the Philistines may well have undertaken diplomatic initiatives to both Ishbosheth in the north and David in the south. The former, as the legitimate heir of the vanquished royal house, could only hope to rule by sufferance of the Philistines. If they offered to install Ishbosheth over the north as the recognized successor to Saul, he, in exchange, would have had to agree to recognize the hegemony of Philistia over his land and people.

In much the same spirit, the *serenos* would have offered to support David's elevation to the kingship of Judah in the south. He would be monarch of half a nation. And, quite predictably, he and Ishbosheth would be at each other's throats, freeing the *serenos* from the considerable burden of having continually to pacify this troublesome people. David considered the cleverness of it. Yet what choice did he have? Like Israel, he lacked the power or leverage to haggle over terms. It were far better to be the *de jure* leader of a demi-nation than none at all. Judah could be fashioned into a reliable political and military base, from which David could realistically contemplate the possibility of re-unifying the country and of then finding the means to deal with the Pentapolis.

David's cosseting of the elders of Judah had not been a wasted exercise. They succeeded in overcoming what resistance there was – based mainly on David's collaboration with the Philistines and his somewhat sordid career as a fugitive – to his assumption of the throne in Judah. Hebron was the largest and the most important city of Judah, its history pre-dating Abraham. And it took very little imagination for the Hebronite establishment to foresee the possibilities, still, of Judah's ascendancy to 'tribe of tribes' under the leadership of David. The elders of the south gathered in Hebron to crown David king and declare their fealty to him.

David, of course, made Hebron his seat. But he wasted little time in bidding tacitly for the allegiance of the north. He dispatched an embassy to Jabesh-gilead commending its citizens for their bravery and loyalty in recovering the bodies of Saul and Jonathan. David's implicit message was clear. He was extending his royal favour to the people of Gilead, the seat of his rival Ishbosheth, if and when they chose to accept it. And he was directly challenging Ishbosheth's ability, if not right, to rule.

Ishbosheth was furious. And when he later learned that David had dispatched his commander, Joab, and a body of men to the territory of Benjamin, the tribe of Saul, to sue for support, the king's son and heir was provoked to action. He ordered his commander, Abner, and a force of picked men to expel Joab's embassy from northern territory.

The two parties met at Gibeon, not far from Ramah, the home of the late prophet Samuel. The confrontation took place at the enormous cylindrical pool on the northern side of the city which was the heart of Gibeon's water system, one of the most revolu-

The pool of Gibeon, where the armies of the rivals for the Israelite throne met for a duel that escalated into a battle

Abner slaying Asahel,
from the St Louis Bible

tionary engineering developments of the age. In the name of the House of Saul, Abner demanded that Joab withdraw to Judah. Predictably, Joab refused, and the two sides prepared for battle. As was the custom in those times, Abner suggested that picked men on both sides engage in a series of duels whose outcome would decide the encounter. But the outcome was indecisive, and the confrontation at the pool of Gibeon escalated into a serious battle. Abner and his men were routed by David's force; and in the pursuit that followed, Abner turned about and slew Asahel, a brother of David's commander Joab, who made a vow that he would someday avenge the slaying.

It was as the Philistines had hoped; the civil war was a protracted one. In the long struggle of some seven years, the balance began swinging decisively towards David's army. His cadres had been hardened in the Negev days, then trained in the science of war by the Philistines, while the cream of Saul's army had been decimated in the battle of Gilboa.

In terms of popular appeal, Ishbosheth was no match for David, either. He confronted a growing clamour in the north to step down in favour of the champion whose name conjured popular memories of Israel's brighter days. Along the border between north and south, there were significant defections to Judah. Ishbosheth could not stand without Abner. And Abner slowly became convinced of the inevitability of David's ascendancy over all Israel. Self-interest dictated that he consider what steps should be taken to assure his presence on the winning side. Matters came to a head when Ishbosheth jealously denounced Abner for winning the favours of a concubine who had formerly belonged to Saul and should, therefore, properly have been property of the king.

Abner began conspiring with the elders of the northern tribes in an attempt to persuade them to rise against Ishbosheth and accept David of Judah as king of all Israel. He carried much influence with the elders, for it was no secret that the ineffectual Ishbosheth had become a mere figure-head in the court at Mahanaim, where the power and influence lay with Abner. And there was a growing consensus that only under David could Israel decisively deal with the Philistines.

Once Abner mobilized impressive support in the north, he secretly petitioned David for a parley at Hebron. Abner wanted to conclude the detailed agreement by which he would overthrow Ishbosheth and deliver the north. Not the least important detail was the reward Abner might expect, the role he might play in a new administration of national unity. David responded through a messenger that he was prepared to treat with Abner on condition that Abner arrange for a reconciliation with Michal. David's love for Saul's daughter had long since waned; but it was important that the marriage be reaffirmed in order to legitimatize David's ties to the House of Saul.

This was accomplished; but when Abner arrived in Hebron to undertake the negotiations, Joab, who not only had sworn vengeance upon him for the death of his brother, but had grown jealous and fearful of Abner's importance to David, approached him and stabbed him fatally.

David was beside himself with rage when he heard the news. Joab had seriously jeopardized, if not totally wrecked, the delicate arrangement for which he had laboured so long. Yet David could not move against his cousin. He was unexpendable – immensely popular with the army, of unrivalled excellence as a commander, essential to the struggle that clearly lay ahead.

Nonetheless, it was desperately important that David dramatize to the northern tribes his own innocence in the assassination of Abner. David called for full state honours for the former commander, personally followed his bier to the grave, delivered the funeral oration and undertook a fast of mourning to dramatize his professional esteem for the slain man. Not only was his behaviour towards Abner, and thus the northern tribes, impeccable; it was clear to all that his feelings for Abner were deeply genuine.

Still, Joab's bloody blunder might have been irretrievable had it not been for two officers of Abner's army, Benjaminite brothers named Baanah and Rechab. Distraught at the prospect of service under a totally impotent monarch and hopeful of winning favour from David, they assassinated Ishbosheth as he slept in his bed at Mahanaim.

The House of Saul perhaps deserved better of history than it received. There were those in Israel utterly opposed to the ascendancy of David. They thought him disloyal, opportunistic, completely amoral and treacherous. Yet he understood the uses of power and the influence of charisma. And there was no one else.

Two things weighed heavily upon David's mind as the time approached to receive the elders of the north at Hebron – and to be anointed king of all Israel. The first was the words of the lamentation he had composed for Saul: 'How are the mighty fallen.' He wondered if it might be so with him. He wondered, too, at the price he would be asked to pay for the glory of kingship. But David also pondered a more immediate and pressing question: how would Achish and the Philistines react to the political developments in Mahanaim and Hebron?

David receives the news of Abner's death, detail of a brussels tapestry entitled 'The Story of David' (1515)

# 5 The City of God

To outward appearances, David had every reason to rejoice. Elders and loyalists from every level of Israelite society were streaming toward the ancient shrine-city of Hebron. Each clan and tribe in the land was represented in the streams of pilgrims converging on the city. The civil war was over, and an ennervated people had found new cause to form a consensus around the charismatic figure of David, who, after seven years as king of Judah, would be acclaimed sovereign of all Israel, to reign as the anointed of the Lord. There would be a coronation feast unparalleled in Israelite memory.

The vagaries of a turbulent life had seen David a common shepherd, soldier, singer of psalms, confidant of kings and princes, national hero, outlaw, deserter, mercenary and, now, king by popular acclamation. He had survived the worst to experience the best – the attainment of a life goal. Six devoted women now graced the royal harem, and all had given him healthy sons.

But at the very time of his elevation to the throne of the Twelve Tribes, David's joy had already been dissipated by the nagging cares of the new office, pressing and immediate cares directly related to his enthronement. There was, for instance, the problem of Israel's national aspirations. During seven years of intermittent civil war, Israel in the north and Judah in the south had grown accustomed to separate states of development, to a set of differing historical experiences. The sense of union, of nationhood, of a patriotism surmounting tribal or regional allegiances, had never fully evolved. There had not been the tranquillity or time for the development of national consciousness. How was he, David, to encourage north and south to bury their differences? Here ultimately lay his greatest challenge. For the king knew that the success or failure of his reign would in large part hinge on his ability to weld twelve disparate tribes into a fabric, an experiential essence, indivisible. Where should he begin?

David triumphant, king over all Israel, by Raphael

Furthermore, David appreciated at this moment what most of his subjects did not. A critical time was swiftly approaching. The rejoicing at Hebron would be transitory. When the dancing ceased, and the last of the wine had coursed through the veins, David's first act would be to summon Israel to war.

David had never encouraged any pretentions about the circumstances of his stewardship of Judah; he had reigned with the explicit endorsement and support of the Philistines, as a vassal of the king of Gath. And there was no doubt in David's mind that Achish and his fellow overlords would view the new Israelite union, and the establishment of David at its head, as conflicting with their policies, hostile to their interests.

David's first move had been an act of courtesy. He had sent a special emissary to his liege at Gath inviting him to attend the coronation at Hebron. The *sereno* was quick to take note of one essential omission, as indeed David had fully intended. The

The Cave of the Machpelah in Hebron, where prayers were held at the traditional tomb of the Patriarchs after David's coronation

Israelite had not felt obliged to seek Achish's *imprimatur* – either to his elevation or the act of political reunification implicit in it.

In a peremptory response, Achish did not stand upon ceremony. David was informed that his failure to consult was viewed by the Pentapolis as a provocative act. David's enthronement would be taken as a breach of their covenant, an act of war.

David had not deceived himself about the nature of his challenge to Philistia. Like Saul before him, his would be a martial reign, an era of unceasing battle. His place would be at the head of his troops. For Israel's struggle for life was far from over. Even if Yahweh saw fit to grant him victory over the Philistines, other battles still lay ahead. The unfinished conquests of Joshua must be made complete, and Israel's eastern and northern borders must be made inviolable against hostile neighbours. Only then would the nation know stability and peace.

David was duly crowned at Hebron; and then, accompanied by

The coronation of David, from the 12th-century Léon Bible

Baanah and Rechab, the assassins of Ishbosheth, carrying out their bloody deed

his family, his comrades, counsellors and elders, he prayed at the Cave of the Machpelah, the traditional tomb of the Hebrew Patriarchs Abraham, Isaac and Jacob. When the ceremonies of sacrifice and of obeisance were over, the fatted lambs roasted and eaten, the music of the lyre and cymbal stilled, David summoned his elders and chieftains to council.

In a gesture of conciliation to the north, David announced that he had summarily ordered the execution of Baanah and Rechab, the assassins of Ishbosheth. He dedicated his reign to the deliverance of all Israel from her enemies. And then he described the critical state of relations with Philistia. In all likelihood, war was imminent. For too long had the Philistines drained the very life-blood of the Hebrews. David vowed to seize the initiative and to carry the war deep into Philistia until the strength of the *serenos* was decisively and permanently broken.

The burden of the operation fell upon the army of Judah, supported by levies from the southern tribes. The joint forces were commanded by an élite group of officers whom David had come to call 'The Thirty'. They were honoured veterans who had risen to command under David in the days of Adullam and Ziklag. They had first whetted their swords on Philistine bones and later, as mercenaries, had been trained to fight by and for the Philistines against the Amalekites. Thus their knowledge of the enemy was an incalculable asset on which David intended to capitalize.

The period of service with the Philistines had produced another priceless benefit. David's artisans had quietly observed Philistine smithies at work and had mastered the secret techniques of smelting and shaping iron. A Philistine technological monopoly of nearly three centuries had decisively been broken. The Israelites could now match their enemy weapon for weapon.

Even while Achish, who would bear the burden of the Philistine campaign, had begun to mobilize for a flank assault against Hebron, David left a small residual force in the capital and marched the main body to the fastnesses of Adullam, the barren region overlooking southern Philistia which he had come to know so well as a fugitive. From here, David mounted surprise raids in strength deep into enemy territory. The raids created panic and consternation, for the Philistines had considered the lands of the Pentapolis impervious to attack.

Achish was desperately anxious to avenge the defeats and bring David to heel. The leader of Judah was clearly more of an embarrassment than Achish could tolerably bear – a former ally and associate in whom trust had been misplaced. The Philistine council understandably expected Achish to handle the turncoat smartly and

A portrait of David in stained glass from the gothic Cathedral of Strasbourg

decisively. And so, his attention diverted from Hebron, Achish dispatched a major expedition into the heights towards Adullam. The rugged terrain made the use of chariotry and cavalry impossible, depriving Achish of the mobility upon which Philistine tactics depended.

As the forces of Gath moved into the mountains, David's troops, mounting only token resistance, feigned defeat and drew back towards the rocky defile to the south of Jerusalem called the Valley of Rephaim. The army of Gath pressed forward. By the time Achish realized that he had unwittingly been manoeuvred into a trap, David had made retreat impossible. When the last of the enemy entered the valley, a detachment of Israelite troops appeared at the Philistine rear, blocking Achish's escape route. From the precipitous sides of the valley, a shower of stones and arrows rained upon the Philistines. The valley offered no natural cover, and they were badly mauled. Then, hundreds of Israelites with spears and bows seemed to erupt from the hillsides. It was a classic ambush, resorted to by Hebrews since the days of Joshua and the Judges. And when, at the call of the rams' horns, the Israelites melted back into the hillsides, the army of Gath, to all intents and purposes, ceased to exist.

Achish's forces were trapped and destroyed by David's army in a steep-sided valley south of Jerusalem

News of the annihilation stunned the *serenos* of Ekron, Ashdod, Ashkelon and Gaza. Gath had served as the anchor of Philistia's south-eastern flank, and suddenly David had laid it bare. The *serenos* hastily mounted a second expedition against the Israelites, but it fared no better than the first.

For the first time the balance of power shifted decisively to Israel. All of Philistia, except the great fortified cities themselves, was now effectively vulnerable to Israelite attack. David aggressively ordered 'The Thirty' to follow up the double victory by seizing the Shephelah and as much of the coastal plain as possible, short of the major cities. Despite their brilliance in the field, the Israelites, as we shall see, still lacked the capability to conduct a major siege.

David's northern armies were mobilized, strengthened and trained. The king ordered these forces to concentrate on liquidating or isolating the few Philistine garrisons remaining in the heights. The key target was to be the Philistine base at Bethlehem, just 5 miles south of Jerusalem (also known as Jebus). The Jebusite rulers of the city had, at the time of Saul's defeat, also submitted to the hegemony of the Philistines. The *serenos* had based a strong force at Bethlehem both to ensure the loyalty of the Jebusite city and to lend it assistance in the event of danger.

David needed Bethlehem because he wanted Jerusalem. The city was the key to a strategic conception of which he had long dreamed. It was, of course, an alien enclave which had been a

Jerusalem crowning the Hills of Judea

bone in the Israelite throat since Joshua had first led his invaders into these mountains. Jerusalem intruded between the Israelite tribes of north and south, though as a practical matter the leaders of Jerusalem had rarely sought to exploit the situation.

But David's conception went far beyond the elimination of a potential irritant. It was, in fact, the central thread of his design to replace the dual chauvinism of north and south and the traditional sense of tribe with a permanent sense of nationhood. David was convinced the way to union lay within the gates of Jerusalem. Hebron was a southern city. It clearly could not serve as capital of the Davidic nation, for it would have been unacceptable to the people of the north, as the choice of the northern city of, say, Gibeon would have been angrily repudiated by the south. But the site of Jerusalem lay between the two regions and belonged to neither. Thus both north and south could easily accept the city as their common capital, without the slightest loss of pride. Jerusalem would be the heart of the country, figuratively as well as geographically.

The king's conception went even further. Jerusalem was a legend even in David's time. It sat, like a crown upon the head of a giant, atop the massive bulwark that formed the backbone of the land. Jerusalem seemed as one with the clouds and the firmament. The magic of the city in part resided in this. For the ancient peoples traditionally looked to the rocky summits as the homes of their deities. The name Jerusalem (Yerushalayim) went back to a misty time beyond memory. It meant 'the foundation of the god Salem, or Prosperor'. Jerusalem had long been considered a holy city, not only because it dominated the lofty spine of Canaan, but because the site culminated in a summit-like table of rock called Moriah, which had been revered as most sacred by the people of both the city and the region. Here Canaanites had come to honour their principal gods. Salem had in time given way to the head of the Canaanite pantheon El, and he now reigned as the unchallenged deity of Jebusite Jerusalem.

But David also knew from the oral tradition of his own people that Jerusalem had figured heavily in the lives and travels of the Hebrew Patriarchs. As the towering shrine of the holy rock upon which Abraham prepared to sacrifice Isaac, Jerusalem was more than worthy to become the sacred citadel of Yahweh, the Lord Most High, El Elyon, who would depose the inferior divinities of the Canaanites and reign forever supreme in His holy city. Jerusalem would be the religious as well as the administrative capital of Israel, and, thus, doubly demanding of the allegiances of all Israelites.

Surprisingly, however, Jerusalem was not a city of exceptional wealth. Most cities of its size and times lay astride great trade routes, which pumped the wealth of the Near East into their market-places, the coffers of their burgeoning merchant classes and the treasuries of the local princes. Jerusalem, on the other hand, lay slightly apart from the well-travelled arteries of commerce. The lure of riches rarely drew men to Jerusalem in those days.

However, what Jerusalem lacked in wealth, it more than made up for in another essential quality. It was all but impregnable, and this aspect of the city very much appealed to the martial instincts of David. The city site lay on a narrow spur of rock which jutted from the main ridge line of central Canaan. The spur was bounded by precipitous ravines on the west, south and east. Many an army exposed on the slopes below had been torn to pieces by withering fire from the great towers which rose over the walls or had dashed itself hopelessly against the great honey-pale walls of the local Jerusalem stone, founded as they were in solid rock. It was a fitting

Remains of a wall dating from the period of David's capture of Jerusalem from the Jebusites

The scale armour used by the Philistines was one aspect of the advanced military skills and weaponry that allowed them to resist the territorial ambitions of the Israelites under David's rule

quality for the City of the Lord. Like Yahweh and Jerusalem would the new state stand majestic and invincible.

To realize his conception, David, of course, confronted a fascinating paradox. He would have to find the means of bringing the invincible city to heel. The problem was greatly compounded by the Israelites' lack of experience in the martial art of reducing great fortified cities, for the siege of a great fortified city was a feat of the highest order in ancient times. The Israelites' battle experience had been in the open – the desert, field or mountain. It had been based upon guile, stealth, innovation and surprise. But the techniques of investing and reducing a great walled city were of a far different order of difficulty. One's forces were ranged about the perimeter in full view of the defenders. Manpower requirements for a static siege were overwhelming, and losses could be expected to be heavy, for the besiegers often presented clear targets to the defending bowmen and slingmen above.

The Israelites were without the great armoured siege engines needed to crack, buckle and breach the massive blocks of a monumental bastion. And the masonry of Jerusalem was too well founded to permit its manhandling by simple levers or pikes. Walls might also be mined, but mining, too, required a knowledge of sophisticated engineering techniques which the Israelites did not possess. And, even had they the sappers to tunnel a passage beneath the walls, Jerusalem's ramparts, for the most part rooted in foundation trenches hewn into solid rock, defied attempts to undermine them by tunnelling.

If an attacker could not move through or under the walls, he could theoretically climb over them using scaling ladders, which required little technical competence to build. But massed assaults of this kind were tremendously wasteful of human lives. A storming operation could only be undertaken as a complement to the use of the siege engines; nor did the Israelites have the intricately devised suits of scale armour in the numbers needed to provide adequate protection for sizable numbers of storming parties. For all these reasons, most of the great lowland cities like Gezer and Megiddo, Gaza and Ashdod had until now defied the territorial ambitions of the Israelites.

There was yet another option to which David could resort. The city could be surrounded for an indefinite period of time and with its lines of supply interdicted, might be starved into submission. But Jerusalem was said to be well supplied against such an eventuality. A deliberate siege of attrition could drag into months, perhaps years, tying down an even greater number of men and imposing an open-ended burden of logistics upon the attacker that impoverished Israel could not sustain. Furthermore, the besieger was in some ways as vulnerable to attrition as was the besieged. Sanitary conditions in siege camps were minimal, at best, and diets were unsatisfactory. As many investments were broken by plague as by the valour and endurance of the beleaguered. And besides, the static nature of an investment held no attraction for David, whose disposition and experience led him towards more aggressive tactics.

Then how could the city, ringed on all sides by natural defences and imposing fortifications, be taken? And what effective means lay within the capability of the Israelites? Again, David reasoned, the answer must lie within the realm of the unorthodox, the unexpected.

Somewhere, David told his lieutenants, at some point along the great sweep of Jerusalem's walls, there lay a weakness, a flaw which could be effectively exploited and could deliver the city into their hands. David dispatched spies to Jerusalem to seek out such a 'back door' which could assure a maximum degree of surprise together with a minimum number of casualties.

The Israelite spies, commanded by Joab, entered the city individually, disguised as traders, beggars, religious pilgrims. It took only a few days of judicious reconnaissance for them to confirm what they had long feared and intuitively known. The stout walls and the ravines which sheered away deeply from them made Jerusalem an all but impossible objective. Yet there remained one avenue of hope – perhaps. The curiosity of several of the Israelites had been drawn to the principal source of Jerusalem's water supply – a natural spring the Israelites later came to call Gihon, which bubbled and welled from the foot of the precipitous slope that comprised the city's south-eastern flank. The Gihon Spring had originally presented two fundamental problems to the Jebusites. It was sited too low to be included within the city walls, for defenders on such a rampart would have been within easy view and bow range of an enemy disposed higher up on the hill opposite. Secondly, the walk up the steep slope from the spring to the city above was exhausting at best, hazardous at worst. Women had to struggle upwards bearing the enormous weight of filled jugs upon their shoulders, risking a serious fall with each uncertain step.

Joab and his men marvelled at the solution devised by the Jebusites. Like the great pool at Gibeon, the Jerusalem water system was a brilliant engineering feat. Canaanite engineers had hollowed out a horizontal tunnel into the rock behind the crevice from which the spring issued. Thus the water of Gihon was made to flow along this tunnel under the hill. High above, within the walls of the city,

The Pool of Siloam, which collects the water of the Gihon Spring. The spring itself was located outside the walls of the Jebusite city, and the shaft which gave access to its waters also provided Joab and his men access to the city

the engineers then sunk a sloping passageway which terminated in a precipitous vertical shaft. This shaft, by some means unerringly surveyed, debouched into the roof of the horizontal water tunnel below. The women of Jerusalem could easily walk down the sloped tunnel within the city, lower their water jugs down the vertical shaft on ropes to the water tunnel and gently draw them back up again when they were filled. The arduous journey to and from the spring itself had been eliminated.

After a closer examination of the water system, Joab wondered whether the Jebusites themselves might have provided the 'back door' which David sought in this very monumental project. Might agile men find enough hand- and foot-holds in the hewn rock of the vertical shaft to climb it? If so, Jerusalem *was* vulnerable. Late one night, Joab took a torch and risked a lone reconnaissance of the Gihon tunnel. He waded through the water, moving slowly with the gentle current deep inside the hill, until, in the rocky ceiling above him, an irregular aperture appeared. Joab thrust the torch toward it as high as he could reach. Its gleam reflected dully from the rough-hewn surface of the shaft. A climb would be difficult – so difficult, in fact, that the Jebusites had left this access unguarded. But it must be tried. When he reported to David, Joab ventured that trained climbers might possibly succeed.

Joab's opinion triggered the first phase of David's plan. The king ordered his northern command to move against the small garrison settlement of Bethlehem, and the Philistines readily abandoned the town. Maintaining their pressure against the retreating enemy, the Israelites cleared the slopes below Jerusalem to the very walls of Gezer and Ekron. There would be no relief for the Jebusites.

Shortly thereafter, under cover of night, Joab stealthily led a large body of volunteers, several skilled climbers among them, to the spring in the eastern valley below Jerusalem. Within the cover of the water tunnel behind the Gihon Spring, torches were lit and ropes were looped over the shoulders of the agile men upon whom the penetration of Jerusalem depended. They moved upwards with a studied deliberateness that seemed painful for those crouched below to watch. So much depended upon every inch, each cautious movement of hands and feet. Time itself seemed suspended. When the climbers exultantly reached the brink of the shaft, the men stifled an almost overpowering urge to shout. Ropes were secured above and dropped to those waiting below. Before the alarm could be spread through the sleeping city and the troops roused, Joab's men had penetrated the defences, reduced key Jebusite strongpoints along the walls and the main portals and opened the eastern gate from within to David's main force, which had crouched silent-

The capture of Jerusalem by stealth and the opening of the eastern gate to David's army, from the St Louis Bible

ly in the ravine below waiting for the outcome of the initial assault. Jerusalem, which had resisted conquest for centuries, surrendered virtually intact.

David had specifically ordered his warriors not to engage in looting or killing. He required the skills of the more sophisticated Jebusites to maintain the life of the city and its vital services for the time being. And he did not want to tie down large numbers of his men on permanent pacification duty. So he offered these terms to the populace: those who wished to leave Jerusalem would be

The exit to what is believed to be the actual shaft climbed by Joab's men to enter Jerusalem. It is still located outside the city walls in an area known as the Ophel (David's City)

permitted to do so, those who wished to retain their holdings and possessions and remain might do so; those who agreed to adopt the God and creed of Israel in time would be accepted as Israelites. Many accepted. The places of those who left the city were taken by Israelites. Jerusalem emerged from prehistory to be hailed in Hebrew annals as the foremost city of all the Israelites, the House of Yahweh, the City of David.

The king had profited well from Saul's mistakes. The failure of the late and tragic sovereign to maintain a sound relationship with the priesthood had in large part led to his downfall. David now moved to re-establish and reorganize the levitical hierarchy by appointing two high priests: Abiathar, son of the late High Priest of Nob and the sole survivor of Saul's massacre, a descendant of the line of Eli; and Zadok, the former Jebusite king-priest of Jerusalem. Zadok, as spiritual retainer of the legendary holy rock of Moriah (which the Israelites were to rename Zion), had enthusiastically embraced the deity of the conqueror, and David chose to reward him as an example to the Jebusite population. In accepting the posts, both Zadok and Abiathar were tacitly acknowledging the supremacy of the throne. By dividing spiritual authority between the two High Priests, David hoped to prevent the ascendancy of a new all-powerful prophet who, in the manner of Samuel, might choose to challenge the power of the throne. And by installing the new priesthood in Jerusalem, as he now proceeded to do, the king ratified Jerusalem as the nation's religious, as well as governmental, centre.

Amid scenes of rejoicing unparalleled in Israelite history, the Ark of the Covenant – which held the holiest relics of the Israelites, the tablets of the Ten Commandments brought by Moses from Mount Sinai – was borne to its new resting place, Jerusalem, in a lurching ox-drawn cart preceded by a huge troupe of musicians. Melodies of joy and praise were sounded on horns, harps and lyres – a din augmented by the throbbing rhythms of tambourines, castanets and cymbals that reached to the heavens and echoed and re-echoed from the hills. Next in the procession came the dancers, King David himself among them, leaping to the shouts of the ecstatic crowds which elbowed and craned to view the scene along the trail.

This was the very Ark, of acacia wood and beaten gold, that Yahweh had commanded Moses to build in the desert. Borne on its poles by the priestly clans of the Tribe of Levi, it had preceded Joshua's Israelites from the plains of Moab to the walls of Jericho. It had led the Israelites into battle against the Philistines, only to be captured at the battle of Aphek and held for a time when Israel's fortunes were at their ebb.

David leading the procession of the Ark to Jerusalem, by Francesco Pesellino (1422–1457)

Now that the wandering nation had finally begun securing and consolidating itself under David, the portable Ark – symbol of the unique bond between the Children of Israel and their One God – had come to the end of a journey which had begun at Mount Sinai nearly three hundred years earlier. Before the Ark, David sacrificed an ox and a fatling and led his people in a huge feast of thanksgiving. The act sanctified the city. Jerusalem would be, through untold ages, a permanent monument to the genius of David; and the tablets of the Ark, defining the moral relationship among men and between men and God, would ultimately become the basis of the Judaeo-Christian ethic.

But how would the Ark be housed? For David, it was a difficult

The Israelites' neighbours built great temples to honour their deities. *above* The Temple of Luxor. *below* The Temple of Abu Simbel

and complex question. There was, for instance, the matter of prophetic tradition. The mythic memory of Israel's religious origins in the desert, of the essential Hebrew formative experience as nomads, was a particularly tenacious one. Both the central focus and symbol of this experience had been the portable tent of goat's hair, ram's skin, lamb's skin and acacia wood called the Tabernacle. Here, in the Mosaic tradition, had resided the essence of God on earth; here petitions had been offered and assemblies gathered; here the Ark had been housed at each station along the way. Where the Israelites marched, the sacred Tabernacle was there to remind them of Yahweh's all-pervasive presence.

Though David had now dedicated a monumental new 'Tabernacle', a great city befitting a noble and settled nation, the nomadic tradition persisted. The priests Abiathar and Zadok and the prophet Nathan argued impassionedly before the king that no mortal conquest could serve to alter a divine commandment; that the place of the Presence of God on earth, the home of the Ark, must remain the sacred tent, or Tabernacle.

David's aspirations for the Ark had been much more pretentious. The nations round about – the Egyptians, Aramaeans, Assyrians, Canaanites – had honoured their deities with monumental temples of finely dressed stone, cedar, beaten gold and precious stones – temples which dazzled and humbled the beholder, soared majestically toward the heavens, commanded the people's awe and obedience, memorialized the monarchs who erected them for all time as paragons of piety, wealth and power. Surely Israel's God, who had raised his people into a mighty nation, deserved no less. And surely no Israelite monarch was more worthy of the honour of creating Yahweh's temple than himself. David yearned not merely to emulate these sovereigns. He meant to surpass them.

Yet practical considerations, together with the ingrained Israelite distaste for pretentiousness, forced David to curb his ambitions. He complied with the will of the holy men and duly ordered the ancient Tabernacle erected in Jerusalem. As with any wise decision of state, it was dictated by a number of reasons. David's plans to secure and consolidate the nation, both politically and militarily, mandated the maintenance of an atmosphere of national concord. David could not at this crucial stage in his reign risk a cleavage with the priesthood over so emotional an issue. Secondly, a project such as David envisioned required vast resources in both manpower and material wealth. He had more pressing needs to occupy the energies of the former, and the young state lacked the latter.

Finally, Israel was in an embryonic state of development culturally. There was no architectural tradition to speak of in her nomadic

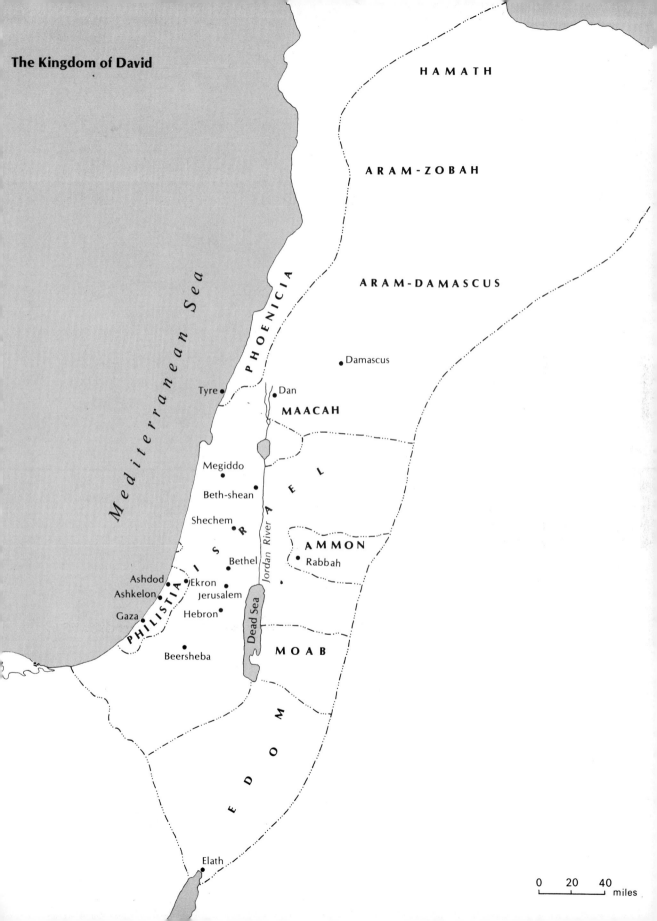

**The Kingdom of David**

HAMATH

ARAM-ZOBAH

ARAM-DAMASCUS

Mediterranean Sea

PHOENICIA

Damascus

Tyre

Dan

MAACAH

Megiddo

Beth-shean

Shechem

I S R A E L

Jordan River

Bethel

AMMON

Rabbah

Ashdod

Ekron

Ashkelon

Jerusalem

PHILISTIA

Gaza

Hebron

Dead Sea

Beersheba

MOAB

E D O M

Elath

0    20    40
└────┴────┘
miles

Detail from the sarcophagus of King Hiram of Tyre, showing a king attending a sacrifice. Hiram contributed his country's knowledge and skills to both David and Solomon's achievements as kings

background, a background as spartan as it had been demanding. The struggle to carve a home in Canaan had diverted Israelite energies from such cosmopolitan pursuits as fine ceramic design and craftsmanship, weaving, carving, metal-work. The sacred stricture against graven images also tended to inhibit artistic expression. Beyond all this, Israel suffered as fundamentally from a scarcity of raw materials, or the wealth to purchase them, as from a dearth of artisans.

It was embarrassingly evident to David that his young nation needed technical assistance. Israel required an ally who might instruct her in the ways of nationhood, as Jethro had counselled Moses in the ways of the desert. Even if the time was not ripe to construct a temple, other great public works were needed in the new capital city. There were permanent defences to build throughout the land. There were borders to secure, Canaanite enclaves to be reduced, the Philistines to humble, expel or assimilate.

One other man of power keenly appreciated Israel's situation, King Hiram of Tyre. He had watched the trials and metamorphoses of the new state with more than passing interest. Under Hiram, Tyre, on the Mediterranean coast, had not only become the most powerful city-state of Phoenicia, but the wealthiest commercial city in the Near East. Hiram had constructed a great merchant navy, and Phoenician expeditions were even now pushing out into the *terra incognita* of the Mediterranean basin to establish trading colonies as far west as Spain, Sardinia and Sicily.

Through geography and commercial contacts dating back many centuries, the worldly Phoenicians had not only become the unrivalled merchants of the Orient, but the mediators of Near Eastern culture – of Egypt and Syria, the high civilizations of the city-states of Mesopotamia and the nation of the Hittites. Phoenician masons and stone carvers, architects and scribes of the new alphabetic writing were sought for the excellence of their taste, craftsmanship and expertise. Phoenician dishware of beaten gold, relief carving upon ivory, jewellery decorated with palms, lion's heads, goats and other natural motifs were coveted by the nobles of many lands. And the aromatic cedar of Lebanon, one of the unsurpassed natural resources of Phoenicia, graced the walls of palaces and sacred temples from the Nile to the Euphrates.

Hiram sought the grain, olive oil and wine of Israel. He wanted to secure friendly relations with the stripling nation which was securing its grip on the strategic cross-roads between Mesopotamia, Anatolia and Egypt. He wanted an *entente* with the powerful young king who had broken the Philistine monopoly upon iron and was now ending Philistia's domination of Canaan. David clearly intended to expand Israel's borders at the expense of those who chose to be her enemies. Hiram wanted no territorial challenges from the south. Most important, he had much to gain from the total liquidation of the Philistine confederacy – the only maritime power which had effectively challenged Phoenicia's control of the sea-coast and sea lanes of the Mediterranean.

David coveted the wealth of Phoenicia, the wisdom of its leader and its sophisticated arts to grace both the new court and the great works he hoped to establish. He wanted to leaven the austere lives and natures of his people. He sought to enlist the Tyrian fleet in his campaign to eliminate the Philistines and to share the counsel of Hiram's civil servants in establishing a central administration at Jerusalem that would cleave the Hebrew to his throne and country for all time.

But David and Hiram were drawn together by more than a mutuality of interest. They were both West Semites, both shrewd and ambitious and, beyond this, both were motivated by a sense of history and of humanity which elevated them above the ranks of petty statesmen. Hiram and David had reached their zenith at the dawning of a new age. Both were in a position to shape that age, and both had the vision to know it.

DAVID
REX

ASAPH EMAN

ETHAN IDITHUN

# 6 When Kings Go Forth

There comes an historic moment in the existence of a young nation when destiny's intentions are written large, when everything appears possessed of heroic dimensions and nothing seems impossible, when all apprehend the essential rightness of the instant and when the ambitions and visions of men are in tune with the order of things. Thus it was with David and with Israel.

The King was infused with an intuitive optimism which seemed to deny the very existence of failure; and his enthusiasm was in some manner felt deeply by each and every subject. The moment had come to complete two essential objectives: to establish firmly the Davidic state as the legitimate successor of the ancient tribal order; and to so enlarge and consolidate the nation that it might come to dominate, and thus control, the affairs of its turbulent region.

The former implied the subtle transfer of allegiance by David's subjects from the tribal authority to the throne at Jerusalem and the incorporation of Israel's ancient and singular religious tradition in the new political order. Yahweh's presence was construed to dwell in Jerusalem, but Yahweh did not rule there. David both reigned and ruled in His name. Zadok and Abiathar, the High Priests, might view with disfavour this revolutionary conception, but David both proposed and disposed. The two High Priests held office at the king's please and could be removed at the king's pleasure.

To David, the challenge of securing both Israel's borders and her place in the international order could be summed up in a phrase – the attainment of Joshua's mission: 'From the wilderness and this Lebanon as far as the great river, the river Euphrates, all the land of the Hittites to the Great Sea toward the going down of the sun shall be your territory.'

King David and his musicians, from a manuscript in the Cambridge University Library

An illustration of David's House of Cedar Wood from a 14th-century German exegesis

And David's musicians and singers prepared the people:
'I will extol thee, O Lord, among the nations . . .'

David commanded that Jerusalem be made worthy of her role as the seat of the monarchy, the seat of the Lord, the heart and soul, the focus of Israel's national and religious aspirations. King Hiram the Phoenician had sent to David Tyrian architects, engineers and masons, and Phoenician ships had delivered supplies. The first monumental project was to create in the finest Phoenician manner the royal palace within the precincts of Jerusalem just to the south of, and below, the sacred summit of Mount Zion.

The second monumental work was the repair and expansion of the Millo, so that the city might be further enlarged. The Millo merits some comment. The original limestone spur on which the Jebusites created their Jerusalem is no more than 8 or 9 acres in area. Precipitous ravines on three sides of the spur circumscribed the city site, yet the population continued to grow. To provide additional living space, Jebusite engineers conceived of the Millo, a series of terraced platforms composed of ramparts of rock foundations and earth fill which clung to the precipitous eastern slope

above the Gihon Spring. On these terraces houses had been built, and men viewed this architectural wonder with awe.

Understandably, the Millo was vulnerable to erosion in torrential rain and to the danger of eventual collapse due to the shifting of the earth and the normal weathering of the stone support walls. Thus the Millo was in need of constant repair. With Phoenician technical supervision and Jebusite labour, David set out to improve and enlarge the terraces, so that more buildings might be erected to house the new Israelite population and the growing apparatus of government.

For Israel was already tasting the consequences of success, of growth and change. When David decisively defeated and contained the Philistines, the cities of the northern coastal plain had also capitulated to him. A number of Canaanite settlements and city-states which had resisted the early Israelite invaders, only to become subject to the Philistines – like Beth-shemesh and Debir on the fringes of Judah – now submitted to the overlordship of Israel. Beyond this, there was Jerusalem, the new capital. These were the responsibility or property of no Israelite tribe, but accretions to the central authority, the personal fief of David. These

A section of steeply terraced houses on the same hill as the ancient Millo. This part of Davidic Jerusalem was built up, with the aid of Phoenician expertise, to accommodate more housing and the expanded royal establishment

acquisitions alone mandated the need for a strong centralized authority and enlarged the wealth, prestige and power of the throne.

The musicians of David would memorialize these events, as was the oriental custom:

> Thou didst deliver me from strife with the peoples;
>   thou didst keep me as the head of the nations;
>   people whom I had not known served me.
> Foreigners came cringing to me;
>   as soon as they heard of me, they obeyed me.
>                               (II Samuel 22:44–5)

But there was still more to do. The prophet Nathan shared the king's vision of a greater Israel still, an Israel no longer passive and helpless before the aggressive appetites of other nations, other rulers; an Israel that would fulfil the partriarchal promise: 'For all the land which you see I will give to you and to your descendants; and your descendants shall be like the dust of the earth . . .'

Nathan's oracles were the drumbeats to which the legions of Israel marched, the fire in the veins of David himself:

> And I will appoint a place for my people Israel, and will plant them, that they may dwell in their own place, and be disturbed no more; and violent men shall afflict them no more . . . Moreover the Lord declares to you that the Lord will make you a House! (II Samuel 7:10–11).

To David, Nathan's promise seemed the promise of immortality. The House of David, the Rock of Israel, forever guardian of the destinies of a unique nation whose One God towered so nobly above the complex families of warring semi-divines worshipped by the nations round about; whose people, the people of Zion, were thus singularly blessed and unlike any other people beneath the firmament. In the name of Yahweh and His Chosen, the sword of David would now realize the territorial designs of Joshua.

The historical moment David chose to enlarge his domain was significant. For centuries the region between the Mediterranean and the Euphrates had served as an arena for the confrontation of great powers perched on the periphery. The people of Syria-Palestine had traditionally been vulnerable to military incursions and endless exploitation by the Egyptian empire to the south, the Hittite kingdom to the north, the conquerors of Mesopotamia to the east. In the time of Moses and Joshua, the thirteenth century

BC, the great powers had simultaneously begun to founder through military excesses, barbarian invasion and internal disruptions. Their decline left Canaan, Syria and the area of Transjordan free of external domination for the first time in hundreds of years. This development coincided with the arrival of waves of nomadic migrants who established footholds and chose to settle in the area – the Philistines on the southern littoral, the Israelites in the highlands, a succession of other Semitic peoples on the fringes. They began to contest the Canaanite inhabitants and each other for supremacy, attempting to fill the void left by the 'super-powers'. They created their own rudimentary political organisms, mobilized and skirmished for territory and coalesced into independent kingdoms.

The Philistine bid for supremacy had failed. With his own house in order, David now intended it should be Israel's hour. There was peace with Phoenicia, but east of Hiram's domains dwelled a congeries of competing Syrian city-states populated by Aramaeans, Semitic people who were occupied in allying with, intriguing against, or warring upon one another. There was Maacah in the southern foot-hills of Mount Hermon; the wealthy trading city of Damascus; powerful Zobah to the north, whose territory stretched from the Anti-Lebanon range to the Syrian desert, and whose nominal influence extended even farther eastwards to the banks of the Euphrates; and Hamath, which lay to the north of Zobah along the Orontes River.

To the east of Israel, in Transjordan, ranging from north to south lay the Semitic states of Ammon, Moab and Edom. Israel had first collided with the peoples east of the Jordan River early in her history, on the historic folk migration into Canaan. To Israel's south lay the boundless desert quarter of the Negev and Sinai, the home of the nomadic Amalekites and nominally the fief of Egypt but in fact vulnerable to any nation possessing the strength to lay claim upon it. To David, an Israelite presence in the barren south meant not only control of vital trade routes but a defensive screen of frontier posts against the depredations of the Amalekites, and also a protective buffer against any future expansionist tendencies by the once-vaunted pharaohs.

David's territorial ambitions would have to be at the expense of all these. The king enlarged and trained his professional army corps, strengthened his internal administration and waited for the opportunity to launch his campaign.

David's geopolitical conception was simple and sound. The great powers at the extremities of Canaan would not remain in eclipse forever. They would surely once again come to contest

Control of the Negev Desert, to the south of Judah, was among David's territorial ambitions because of the area's strategic importance for trade and as a buffer zone against the hostile Amalekites

for this land as part of their rival spheres of influence, unless Israel were sufficiently strong to retain its independence. If Israel were weak, it and the neighbouring local peoples would again be swallowed.

National strength stems basically from economic soundness, and Israel was a poor country. It had few indigenous resources, save the produce of its fields and farms – grain, olives, olive oil, and wine. Yet there remained an untapped source of wealth here. Israel lay at the very centre of the commercial and communications arteries linking the great eastern empires. And tremendous riches flowed through those arteries.

Specifically, two great caravan routes passed through the area. One was called the Way of the Sea (Via Maris). It ran north from Egypt along the rim of the Mediterranean to the coastal plain of Phoenicia. Smaller routes branched off to the east from the Plain of Sharon and the Jezreel Valley, guarded by mighty Megiddo, to Damascus and Mesopotamia.

The second caravan highway, called the Way of the King, ran from Egypt to the Negev, turned east of the Jordan, ran through Edom, Moab and Ammon to Damascus and Mesopotamia. Other intermediate branches traversing the mountain passes of Israel completed the network by linking the Way of the Sea to the Way of the King.

Command of both highways would allow David to impose taxes upon the merchants and their goods as they passed through his domain. These considerable revenues would in turn help support an army powerful enough to prevent the exploitation of the two roads as invasion routes by great imperial armies. And control of these most important commercial arteries would grant Israel a political and strategic importance far beyond her wealth or size.

Beyond this, Israelites might, in emulation of the Phoenicians, serve as merchants and transporters, as intermediaries between the great markets of the East. The House of David would, in the long run, convert the region's curse into its blessing; would assure Israel's continuity through commerce, not war.

The eclipse of Philistia gave David partial mastery of the Way of the Sea. Ammon, directly east of Jerusalem across the Jordan River, gave him the pretext for gaining the rest. David had maintained friendly relations with Nahash, sovereign of the Ammonite people, who reigned in Rabbah (Rabbath-bene-Ammon), the site of modern Amman. But Nahash died, and his son Hanun perceived correctly that David meant to establish Israelite hegemony over the Way of the King.

Hanun formed an alliance with a league of Syrian city-states – including Aram-damascus, Maacah, Tob, Rehob, and Zobah. The leader of the Syrian league was the king of Zobah, Hadadezer, named for the Aramaean god of storms, Hadad. When David chose to send an Israelite embassy to Rabbah gingerly to test Hanun's intentions, the new Ammonite king quickly and unceremoniously made them apparent. He grossly humiliated David's emissaries, shaving off half the beard of each and mutilating their garments. The gesture was clearly designed to be seen as an affront to the national honour of Israel, a calculated insult to the House of David, a declaration of war. David ordered the army

An Assyrian stele on the Way of the Sea (Via Maris), the ancient trade route from Egypt up the coast to Phoenicia

fully mobilized and directed that Joab lead it against the Ammonites.

As the army of Israel approached Rabbah, Joab's scouts reported the alarming news that the army of the Syrian confederacy under Hadadezer had suddenly materialized at the Israelite rear. Joab had no choice but to divide his forces. One detachment of picked men under his personal command would attempt to beat off the Syrians, while the remainder of the army under Joab's brother Abishai proceeded as planned against the Ammonites, who were now deployed outside the main gate of Rabbah. If one or the other adversary proved too strong, the Israelites could shift units to the salient where they were most urgently required. If both Syrians and Ammonites prevailed, Israel was lost.

An essential part of David's military philosophy was resort to the offensive as the most effective defence. Retreat had no place in the Israelite lexicon. Israel's only path of retreat led into the sea. Joab now applied the maxim against the Syrian league. On horse and on foot, his forces charged the combined armies of Hadadezer. Caught off balance by the unexpected attack, they fled in disorder. The Syrian rout demoralized the Ammonites, and they melted before Abishai, fleeing inside the gates of Rabbah to prepare for a long siege.

Hadadezer wisely retreated, salvaging the Syrian forces that remained. He had lost a battle, not the war. The Syrians withdrew to Helam deep in Bashan some 40 miles east of the Sea of Galilee. Here Hadadezer regrouped and mobilized reinforcements, some from among the nomadic Aramaean peoples dwelling in the Syrian desert and along the western bank of the Euphrates. Again, David decided to seize the initiative before Hadadezer had a chance fully to reconstitute his forces. David personally led his army across the Jordan and surprised the Syrians at Helam. Before they could mount an effective defence, a phalanx of David's warriors penetrated to the Syrian rear and slew Shobach, the commander-in-chief of the Syrian league. The rout was total. Thousands of Aramaeans were killed or injured. The remainder fled or surrendered. David ordered the horses of Zobah's crack chariotry hamstrung. Zobah had twice challenged Israel. There would be no third time. David's actions ended for all time the dominance of Zobah as the foremost military power in Syria.

The vanquished monarchs of the Aramaean confederacy acknowledged the supremacy of David. They dispatched emissaries to his camp bearing lavish tributes. From the king of the humbled forces of Aram-damascus, David exacted greater tribute still. Israelite garrisons were established in the mighty commercial

King David with Abishai, the commander who led the Israelite army against the Ammonites at Rabbah, in a work by the Swiss painter Konrad Witz (1400–1445)

city of Damascus itself, which now became the administrative capital of the province of Syria and a part of an Israelite empire which stretched east to the Euphrates.

Rabbah, the capitol of Ammon, fell after a long siege, and was annexed as an Israelite province. With the Syrian-Ammonite collapse, the last great fortified Canaanite city, Beth-shean, capitulated, together with the cities and settlements of Galilee. In rapid order, David's forces also scored decisive victories over the Moabites and Edomites in Transjordan. With stunning abruptness, David had transfigured Israel. He had succeeded in making it the foremost power of the region between Egypt and Mesopotamia. The domain under David's direct rule now stretched from the barren desert in the south to the snow-crowned heights of Mount Hermon in the north, from the Mediterranean to the lands far east of the Jordan. The southern boundary followed the line of the great Wadi El Arish in northern Sinai. The northern border followed the flanks of the Lebanon range opposite Phoenicia.

> Thou hast given me the shield of thy salvation,
>   and thy help made me great.
> Thou didst give me a wide place for my steps under me,
>   and my feet did not slip;
> I pursued my enemies and destroyed them,
>   and did not turn back until they were consumed.
>
> (II Samuel 22:36–8)

Over 250 years after a homeless group of Semitic outcasts from Egypt had crossed the Jordan and entered Canaan, Israel was a vaunted nation. Philistia was vanquished, Canaan absorbed. The charismatic judge who had sprung to the forefront of the tribes in time of need had given way to the *melekh*, the king – and his subjects were legion.

His coffers were also full to overflowing. Much booty and lavish tribute had been exacted from Israel's vanquished neighbours; and more tribute still was bestowed upon David from other nations which now sought his alliance or protection, such as the northern kingdom of Hamath. There were precious objects of silver and gold, jewels and other treasures. From Hadadezer's kingdom, where it was mined, came large quantities of copper ore. In David's mind, another great design had begun to take shape, and these riches would be earmarked for it. In a service of tribute, the great portion of the wealth not diverted to the national treasury or selected to grace the royal apartments were proffered as an offering to the Lord. Then storehouses were built for it. The people, historically conditioned to poverty, spoke with wonder of the spoils and of David's frugality. But his intentions for the treasure remained a mystery.

The administrative outlines of David's kingdom were based in part on the counsel of his Phoenician advisers, in part on the unique nature of the Israelite nation and in part on the governing structures he had observed as a mercenary chieftain in Philistia. As a first step, it seemed essential to David that he number the people. A census was the necessary prelude to a workable system of taxation, conscription, national labour service and the division of Israel into provincial administrative units. Corvées would be needed to carry out the ambitious public works David envisioned; levies were required to help underwrite the costs of expanded government, national security and the maintenance of the annexed and conquered territories. The draft would replace the uncertain tribal militia system with an enlarged standing army and a reliable system of mobilization in time of emergency.

David ordered his army commanders to carry out the census. For over nine months, military teams roamed throughout the new empire numbering the people and dispatching census lists to the capital.

The census provoked the first serious political opposition to the king's policy. The tribal elders obviously had a vested interest in opposing it, for they correctly saw in the census a further shift of power from the tribal councils to the state. Zadok and Abiathar made common cause with the elders. The tribal outlook, the nature of Israelite monotheism and the essentially democratic structure of the theistic state had instilled in the Israelite psyche a brooding suspicion of temporal leadership. Samuel had exploited these anti-royalist tendencies effectively in his struggle against Saul. They had lain dormant in David's reign.

But now the propagandists of the anti-census coalition invoked the ancient admonishments of Samuel: '[The king] will take your sons . . . take your daughters . . . take the best of your fields and vineyards . . . take the tenth of your flocks . . .'

The elders and priests found a supporter in no less a personage than Joab, David's military commander. When the king consulted Joab on the census, the loyal veteran objected: 'May the

Harvesting the produce of the ancient Near East as depicted in a wall painting from the Tomb of Nakht in Egypt

A woodcut by Julius Schnorr von Carolsfeld of the pestilence which afflicted Israel after the census

Lord your God add to the people a hundred times as many as they are, while the eyes of my lord the king still see it; but why does my lord the king delight in this thing?' David persisted. The census was essential not only to the national welfare, but to the designs which he intended for Israel. The tribal structure was no longer germane to Israel's future. David prevailed. The king needed only to invoke the debt of blood over the affair of Abner to insure Joab's loyalty and compliance.

In later ages it would be recalled that a great epidemic fell upon Israel after the census, and, as was the ancient way, the misfortune would be attributed to God's wrath over the numbering of His people. The census was the first step toward the ultimate 'disappearance' – the assimilation – of the twelve 'lost' tribes of Israel. For over the men of Judah, of Dan, of Benjamin, Manasseh, Reuben and the rest, David imposed a new set of loyalties.

At the apex of the pyramid, of course, was David himself. To insure his own control over the burgeoning bureaucracy, David appointed no prime minister, no vizier, but retained the duties both of head of state and government.

On particularly sensitive or difficult questions, however, David often consulted with his personal counsellor, Ahithophel, a dis-

Egyptian hieroglyphics (above), from the Temple of Abu Simbel, contrasted with early alphabetic writing (below) in the form of an Aramaic inscription on a stone jar found in Ein Gev

tinguished elder of Judah from the town of Gilo, whose son Eliam was one of the king's trusted officers, a veteran of the days of Adullam. The royal establishment was administered by a *mazkir*, a royal herald. The herald supervised palace ceremonials, served as a sort of appointments secretary, arranging royal audiences and acting as liaison between the king and lesser officials. This herald, Jehoshaphat, was also in charge of protocol, was responsible for the maintenance of the royal household, issued all royal proclamations and supervised the office of annals and archives.

Under Jehoshaphat, David established the post of royal scribe. It would prove an epochal act. Until this time, Israel's was a largely oral, rather than written, tradition. The record of the Hebrew origins, historical and religious, had been passed by word of mouth from generation to generation. The Phoenicians, as cultural intercessors with the Canaanites, had wrought a miraculous achievement. From the absurdly cumbersome hieroglyphic system of the Egyptians, with its thousands of symbols, centuries earlier Canaanites had begun deriving a limited number of crude symbols which might be used in writing in rudimentary form their Semitic speech. Under the Phoenicians the system was sophisticated, enlarged and brought to a high state of development. We call the revolutionary concept the alphabet. Using a syllabary of some twenty symbols, an infinite number of Semitic words could be written, representing an infinite number of meanings and shades of meanings.

To David, the written signs of the Phoenicians – whose language was virtually identical to Hebrew – seemed a gift from God. Man's memory was imperfect at best. It was no longer a suitable storehouse for the complicated business of government and commerce. Alphabetic writing provided the tangible and immutable record that was now needed. King David was quick to appreciate the profound implications of the Phoenician achievement. There were, as we have seen, the census records, which scribal skills made possible. The official record of his reign – the record of his acts as the steward of Yahweh – could also be preserved for all time. But beyond that, the adventure of the Hebrew people, from the most ancient of days – the acts of Yahweh made manifest through the children of Israel – could be compiled, fixed, and disseminated. It could be taught to the populations of the occupied territories who had chosen to adopt the Hebrew faith. With chisel on stone, or quill on potsherd or parchment, the legal statutes of Yahweh could be codified and made known to all.

> For all His ordinances were before me,
>    and from His statutes I did not turn aside.
>                               (II Samuel 22:23).

The *sopher*, the scribe or royal secretary, was personally proffered to David by Hiram the Phoenician – a gift of fire! The scribe's name was Sheva. His father was a native of Egypt who had been brought to Tyre to assist in the refining of the alphabet and to establish a class of Phoenician scribes trained in their use. Now Sheva would do the same for David and Israel. In addition to maintaining the royal archives and handling David's missives and dispatches, Sheva instructed military officers in the new art of writing. He also taught the priests. Sheva's pupils would in turn help found Israel's scribal tradition both to serve the bureaucracy and to spread the gift of literacy to the cities and settlements.

> For this I will extol thee, O Lord, among
>    the nations . . . (II Samuel 22:50)

In David's pyramid of power, the priestly hierarchy in Jerusalem was dominated, of course, by Zadok and Abiathar. As the ideological and moral preceptor of Israel, the prophet Nathan was attached to both the court and the levitical establishment; but in a quite indefinable way, Nathan stood apart from both. He was totally independent of any temporal institution. His ultimate loyalty was to the sovereign Yahweh.

To circumscribe the power of the High Priests, David appointed another priest, Ira the Jairite, who tended to the spiritual needs and observances of the court. The king eventually entered several of his sons into the priesthood to strengthen the crown's links to the secular establishment and oversee the throne's interests within it.

David's cousins, Joab and Abishai, served as commander and chief of staff of the army, respectively. But in the oriental manner, the king also recruited quite independently a detachment of foreign mercenaries to serve as his household guard. Another of David's veteran officers, Benaiah, was placed in command of the mercenaries. Foreign soldiers did not aspire to the throne because they could not rule. Thus, as regards the safety of their own persons, sovereigns understandably felt a degree of confidence and security among hired mercenaries which the proximity of their own armed subjects failed to inspire. Ironically, David's picked guard was composed in large part of Philistines! They personified the radically changed historical fortunes of Israel and Philistia. And David, the former mercenary of Philistine Gath, derived quiet pleasure from their presence.

David's establishment contained a harem of impressive proportions, and a burgeoning 'king's table' attended regularly by a growing number of guests upon whom David chose to bestow his generosity, grace and favour. One of these was the sole surviving heir of the House of Saul, Jonathan's son Mephibosheth.

It had come to David's attention that Mephibosheth was living in a settlement in Gilead north of Mahanaim, where his uncle Ishbosheth had long ago established his ill-fated government in exile. Mephibosheth was lame. To David, the son of Jonathan posed a paradox. As the son of his martyred companion, Mephibosheth was due a debt of loyal love in the name of a father who might himself have worn the royal crown. But Mephibosheth was also the last legitimate issue of the House of Saul. Crippled and seemingly unfit to reign, he might still become a convenient rallying point for factions bent upon overthrowing David.

David ordered Mephibosheth to be escorted to Jerusalem; and the only survivor of Saul's line arrived understandably expecting the worst. Mephibosheth fell and prostrated himself before David. But the king bade him rise and said: 'Do not fear; for I will show you kindness for the sake of your father Jonathan, and I will restore to you the land of Saul your father; and you shall eat at my table always.'

Detail of a painting by Konrad Witz showing Benaiah, the commander of David's personal guard of mercenaries

David receiving petitions
from his subjects, detail
of the 16th-century
'Story of David' tapestry

From that time on, Jonathan's lame son became a permanent
retainer in the court of David, and was treated as nobly as one of
his own sons. The full restitution of Saul's properties made Mephibosheth independently wealthy for the remainder of his days. In
one stroke, David had both repaid an oath of blood, and removed
a potential symbol of opposition. The act pleased him. It set a
number of matters right. The court spoke well of it. David had
lived too long with power to find discomfort either in adulation
or vanity. They were anodynes which allayed the endless cares and
tensions of office.

Power is most merciless to those who dispense it. As time went
on, the crown seemed to weigh more heavily upon David's head.
The zest of victory soon gave way to a surfeit of administrative
burdens which seemed only to increase with time. The king often
found himself recalling with nostalgia the spontaneity and peace
of mind of an earlier, a simpler age.

More and more did David turn to the prophet Nathan for
counsel and comfort as his own resilience and spiritual resources
seemed to wane. The words which the prophet dispensed were
neither sycophantic, ingratiating nor palliative. In the tradition

of Hebrew prophecy, Nathan served as the nation's social and spiritual conscience. He was not intimidated by royalty or rank. He was an independent spirit, outspoken and direct, whose sole concern was the maintenance of Yahweh's moral order and the admonishment of those who strayed from it. And in the Israelite order, the king was not to be exempt. There could not be one law for the monarch, another for his subjects. In this manner Nathan served David, and often his words could be as thorns. But David trusted Nathan implicitly.

Change came to dominate David's life. Even before Ammon had finally capitulated with the surrender of Rabbah, the king's energies were totally monopolized by the multiplying demands of statecraft. He was tyrannized by them – consolidating the conquests in Transjordan and Syria, establishing Israelite authority in the annexed and occupied lands, approving and supervising new public works and military fortifications, planning civic improvements for Jerusalem and the newly acquired Canaanite cities, creating and overseeing the new bureaucracy, as well as the machinery of diplomatic relations so essential to international commerce. All the while, David remained obsessed by the siege of Rabbah, the first of any consequence ever carried out by an Israelite army. Static sieges were not David's kind of war. The indecisiveness of the investment of Rabbah troubled him.

Above and beyond all this, David was expected to receive personal petitions from his subjects at regular periods, adjudicate major disputes between the tribes and clans, and maintain a watchful eye on the activities and observances of the priesthood.

David was at the zenith of his career; yet, never had he been so tired, so lonely, so confounded by the growing sense of personal powerlessness that comes to afflict the powerful. The king was a captive of the new state and felt he was stagnating as a man, that he had been forcibly stripped of his right to personal fulfilment. No king had achieved more; but it ceased to satisfy him. The intervals between David's visits to his harem lengthened. There was less and less time for his children. David's family was Israel.

He might love his nation, but he could not possess her, find solace or escape in her. He could not share his essential feelings with his subjects, confide in them, be himself with them. His role was that of king; he could never for a moment be seen to step out of the role. It was suffocating to him. Yet David's humanity would not be submerged. He was a lusty, passionate man; a man of enormous character and power. They magnified his appetites, his desires, his needs, as they had also magnified his capacities for greatness. The hungers within him only drove David more ferociously into his labours – and his loneliness.

# 7 Fathers and Sons

Late one afternoon of a spring day in Jerusalem, with Joab and his army still encamped before the walls of Rabbah beyond the Jordan, David sought momentary release from his cares. He climbed to the roof of the palace and looked down upon Jerusalem. The stones of the city seemed suffused with golden light in the slanting rays of the new sun. David turned to the east, toward the Millo and the rolling terrain beyond, to the jagged cleft which dropped steeply away to the Jordan Valley far below Jerusalem. Rabbah lay behind the range of distant hills across the Jordan. Where Jerusalem began to give way to the wilderness of the Jordan cleft, normally barren earth was matted with a carpet of desert flowers, the issue of the late winter rains. Soon, the sun of summer would parch them, and they would turn to dust, the garden of the desert spring again paling to wasteland.

David walked to the western parapet of the palace which over-looked the city. Immediately below his glance lay the rooftops of his city, now washed by deepening lavender shadow. David detected a brief movement on one of the house tops. He looked intently and saw the stooped figure of a maidservant filling a broad-mouthed pottery basin with water. The servant retreated, and moments later the figure of a young woman appeared. Like David, she looked out upon the city in the waning light, unaware that she was being observed.

Then she turned gracefully towards the large basin and loosened her long, dark hair. With natural modesty, the woman bathed her face, then raised the hem of her insubstantial robe above her knees and began laving her feet and limbs. The perfectly sculpted outlines of her leg and thigh shone ivory against the darkening shadows. Then, with a naturalness more provocative to David than any studied gesture, she loosened the upper portion of her

View (from foreground) of the landscape around Jerusalem, the Judean Desert, the Dead Sea and the hills east of the Jordan, beyond which lay the Ammonite capital of Rabbah

137

robe, brushed it from her shoulders, and gathered its folds at her waist. David saw the strong but delicate lines of her back, the upthrust roundness of her breasts as she turned to bathe her neck, her bosom, each outstretched arm.

Then, a gentle, satisfied toss of her head, and she was finished. She let the breeze caress her body to dry her. Suddenly the woman was gone behind the gently rounded dome of the rooftop. David called a servant to him, pointed to the now-empty rooftop and asked if he knew the woman's identity. The servant replied: 'Is not this Bathsheba, the daughter of Eliam, the wife of Uriah the Hittite?'

Bathsheba's grandfather was David's counsellor Ahithophel of Gilo, the renowned elder of Judah; her father and husband, both members of the legion of David's most honoured officers, 'The Thirty'. Uriah was a foreign mercenary from the northern lands who had joined David in the days of Adullam and had remained in his service, adopting the religion of Yahweh. At this time, David knew, both Eliam and Uriah were with Joab before the gates of Rabbah. The lady was too intimately connected to the royal establishment for David to risk a flirtation. And yet he was recklessly oblivious to the danger.

Man's role is to tread an agonizingly narrow path between temptation and restraint. His choice, conscious or unconscious, is whether and when to cast forbearance to the winds. He is, in fact, an inveterate gambler. But he has not the stomach to envision losing. If he is a king, he cannot imagine losing.

David sent servants to bring Bathsheba to the palace. She was startled by the unexpected summons, but would never have dared spurn it. On the contrary, on this still spring evening, there was every reason why she should have gone, and so hastened to dress with mixed feelings of expectation and dread. Her father and husband, both favoured officers, were in battle. Perhaps one of them had fallen: perhaps this was the news the king intended personally to convey.

But to her surprise, David wished only to dine with her, to bathe her in flattery a trifle too self-conscious in its ardour; quite obviously, to seduce her. The prospect was a shocking one. Even more shocking to Bathsheba was that she did not feel shocked but rather a trifle pleased. To be desired by the most renowned figure of Israel, a man so revered, so honoured, so beloved of herself and her people was singularly gratifying. It is not an easy thing to reject the advances of a king. But to accept them was to place herself in fearful jeopardy. Did not Yahweh's statutes impose a sentence of death upon adulterers? As David's personal servant

Bathsheba bathing, by the Flemish painter Hans Memling (1430–1495)

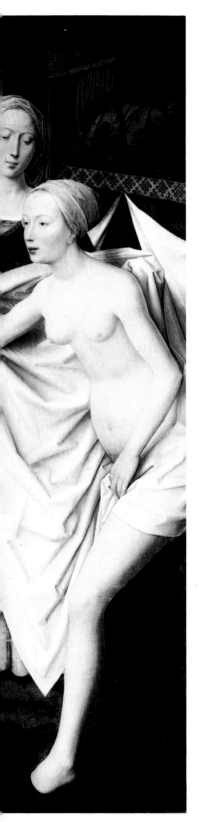

and bodyguards knew of her presence, Uriah and Eliam were surely bound to learn of it. Ahithophel knew of all that occurred within the royal precincts, and this would hardly escape him. Yet Bathsheba had quietly nursed pretensions for herself, ambitions for Uriah, that David now stirred. And physically he was not displeasing to her. She could not bring herself to reject him.

David called for food and wine. He spoke freely of his life, his burdens and his cares. They savoured the heady wine of Carmel, and it stirred both wonder and desire in her. She pondered the contrast between the seeming unapproachability of the monarch and the vibrant humanity of the man himself. The air was resonant with the fragrance of a Jerusalem night, crystal with the white flame of moon and stars. David rose and drew her to his couch. There was no resistance in her. They made love throughout the long night, and, spent and glowing, slept in each other's arms at dawn.

In the time that followed, desire was transformed into love. But when, after a night of lovemaking, Bathsheba awoke and confessed 'I am with child,' David reacted with ambivalence. He was determined to have Bathsheba within his harem. Yet he was horrified at the complications a child would bring them both. He was the Lord's anointed, sworn to uphold the statutes of Yahweh; yet he had broken a cardinal commandment. Bathsheba would be seen to have been unfaithful to a husband who, in his long absence, clearly could not have been the father of the child. And the secret of their liaison could not possibly be kept. Servants knew, and servants gossiped.

David conceived of a desperate plan. He dispatched a messenger to Joab at Rabbah, hastily summoning Uriah back to Jerusalem. When the warrior arrived, David seemed unusually solicitous, but vague as to the reason for Uriah's recall. A sumptuous meal was laid before the warrior. David questioned him intently about the siege, the enemy, the army, his own adventures. He commended Uriah for his valour before Rabbah, proclaiming that this brief leave in Jerusalem was to be his reward. This made the matter no clearer, for Uriah well realized other warriors were no less deserving of such treatment. David brought the bizarre audience to a close, saying to the warrior: 'Go down to your house.' David understandably assumed the abstinence of the battlefield would surely propel Uriah into Bathsheba's bed, and into a ready acceptance of her pregnancy some months hence.

But Uriah, a foreigner, had accepted the faith of Yahweh with the zealousness of the committed convert – he was more Hebrew than most Hebrews. There was a custom which forbade an Israelite soldier from engaging in intercourse in the midst of a campaign.

The purpose of the taboo was in all likelihood to keep concubines from the camps, given the rigidity of the Hebrew attitude toward adultery. Uriah meant to observe it. Despite David's urgings, his clumsy male insinuations, the warrior declared forthrightly that it was his intention to spend a chaste night in another lodging, rather than submit himself to the temptations of Bathsheba.

Uriah's puritanical zeal vexed David, all the more so in contrast to his own behaviour with the warrior's wife. Concealing his irritation, David summoned Uriah to the palace the next day and again urged him to go to Bathsheba. 'Have you not come from a journey?' the king asked. 'Why do you not go down to your house?'

Uriah replied: 'The ark and Israel and Judah dwell in booths; and my lord Joab and the servants of my lord are camping in the open field; shall I then go to my house, to eat and to drink, and to lie with my wife? As you live, and as your soul lives, I shall not do this thing.'

David was baffled and angry. But he had little option other than to continue acting the magnanimous commander. To Uriah's growing annoyance, David repeatedly extended his leave, summon-

Bathsheba's husband, Uriah, met his death during an attack on the Ammonite capital of Rabbah. These attacking soldiers on the march are from the palace of Sennacherib in Nineveh

ing him continually to the royal apartments, clumsily repeating himself in boring, distracted conversation, plying Uriah with ever more liberal portions of his finest wines. The warrior resisted even drunkenness.

The king was driven to a last, desperate act. He wrote a sealed order for Joab, and, giving it to Uriah for delivery, ordered the Hittite to return to the field. In effect, the order was Uriah's death sentence. It read: 'Set Uriah in the forefront of the hardest fighting, and then draw back from him, that he may be struck down, and die.'

Joab did as the king ordered. He placed Uriah in command of a detachment positioned before the main gate of Rabbah, through which starving groups of defenders often sallied, trying frantically to break the siege. Here casualties were the heaviest; and here, as the king intended, Uriah was eventually killed.

David exulted when the messenger bore him a dispatch from Joab containing word of Uriah's death. But his relief was shortly replaced by a sense of deep revulsion and, beyond that, anxiety that Joab might perhaps be driven to disclose the secret. So David sent this sealed missive to reassure his commander: 'Do not let this

matter trouble you, for the sword now devours one and now another; strengthen your attack upon the city, and overthrow it.'

David had no need to be unduly concerned about Joab's trustworthiness. He was far too mindful of both blood ties and ancient debts to David to compromise either. But the fact of David's trysts with Bathsheba became common knowledge in Jerusalem, and after a respectful interval, the king formally took Bathsheba as a wife. There would, at least from one quarter, be fateful repercussions in time; but few, not even Bathsheba, accepted Uriah's death at the gates of Rabbah as anything other than the fate of a brave soldier in combat.

Yet three men were sorely troubled by these events. One was Ahithophel. Deeply devout, a zealous adherent of Yahweh's statutes, the sage was outraged by the scandalous behaviour of both the king and his granddaughter. He concealed his feelings, but discreetly sought out the details of Uriah's death. Another was the prophet Nathan. He had often reprimanded the king for his excesses, for his tendencies both toward profligacy and despotism – for the keeping of concubines, for his teeming harem, which had come to include the irreligious daughters of neighbouring kings. All these Nathan had vehemently denounced as idolatries, heretical indulgences unworthy of the anointed of Yahweh. Nathan had often warned David that his behaviour was rapidly becoming a source of discontent among the devout. The affair of Bathsheba could now only exacerbate their resentment.

The third man was David himself. The king was in torment, his conscience flayed by the enormity of what he had done. For David was a complex and sensitive man. His love for Bathsheba was deep and genuine. But, in its name, he had committed first adultery, then murder. How could a man capable of fielding thousands of warriors at a single command also prove incapable of commanding his feelings? David ordered his chamber cleared, and the prophet summoned. For long moments, the two men faced each other in silence. David could not speak.

Nathan knew the king's soul was convulsed, and he intuitively divined its cause. Without preamble, the prophet began to relate a parable. The king listened with mounting horror, for it constituted his condemnation. Thus Nathan spoke:

There were two men in a certain city, the one rich and the other poor. The rich man had very many flocks and herds; but the poor man had nothing but one little ewe lamb, which he had bought. And he brought it up, and it grew up with him and with his children; it used to eat of his morsel, and drink from his cup, and lie in his bosom, and it was like a daughter to him. Now there came a traveller to the rich man, and he was

While David was courting Bathsheba (above), he called her husband back to Jerusalem (below) in the hope of concealing the true paternity of Bathsheba's child. This portrayal of the episode is from the 16th-century 'Story of David' tapestry

unwilling to take one of his own flock or herd to prepare for the wayfarer who had come to him, but he took the poor man's lamb, and prepared it for the man who had come to him (II Samuel 12:1–4).

David feigned innocence, affected great indignation and thundered self-righteously at the prophet: 'As the Lord lives, the man who has done this deserves to die; and he shall restore the lamb fourfold, because he had no pity.'

Nathan in his prophetic wrath had no patience to indulge David's evasions. He raged:

You are the man. Thus says the Lord, the God of Israel, 'I anointed you king over Israel, and I delivered you out of the hand of Saul; and I gave you your master's house, and your master's wives into your bosom, and gave you the house of Israel and of Judah; and if this were too little, I would add to you as much more. Why have you despised the word of the Lord, to do what is evil in his sight? You have smitten Uriah the Hittite with the sword, and have taken his wife to be your wife, and have slain him with the sword of the Ammonites. Now therefore the sword shall never depart from your house, because you have despised me, and have taken the wife of Uriah the Hittite to be your wife.' Thus says the Lord, 'Behold, I will raise up evil against you out of your own house; and I will take your wives before your eyes, and give them to your neighbour, and he shall lie with your wives in the sight of the sun. For you did it secretly; but I will do this thing before all Israel, and before the sun' (II Samuel 12: 7–12).

David trembled, and wept and confessed to Nathan: 'I have sinned against the Lord.'

The prophet replied: 'The Lord also has put away your sin; you shall not die. Nevertheless, because by this deed you have utterly scorned the Lord, the child that is born to you shall die.'

In Israel alone at this time could a hierophant so address himself to a monarch with impunity. Not even David could diminish the authority of the prophetic figure in the theocratic order. As the balance of power shifted from the spiritual to the temporal establishment, the prophet assumed the compensating role of sublime conscience, moral bulwark, social revolutionary. A prophet drew his strength from Israel's special view of its one God, who devised not only the rules of Nature, but the ethical system by which men conducted their lives. In political terms, the prophet drew his power from the faithful, and, in return, became their ombudsman – perhaps the first in history. Thus Nathan could speak to David as he did and remain untouched and untouchable.

As Nathan had predicted, Bathsheba's child, a boy, was feeble and sickly at birth, and the royal midwives held out little hope that

The death of the son of
David and Bathsheba
shown in a woodcut by
Julius Schnorr von
Carolsfeld

he would survive. When the news was given him, David fell to the ground and began to pray passionately for the infant's life. His servants tried to comfort him, but the king could not permit himself to be consoled. He had heard Nathan pronounce sentence, and he knew that sentence was fitting. His abrogation of the statutes demanded an act of contrition, of penitence. But he would ask Yahweh to spare the child. He would neither eat nor drink until its fate was known. More than this he could not do, either for the child's life or his own redemption.

After David fasted for a week, the newborn died. The servants who had come with the news huddled anxiously at the chamber entrance, hesitant to approach the distracted king. From their bearing and their agitated whispers, David knew what had happened. He nonetheless asked, 'Is the child dead?' And they answered: 'He is dead.'

Then David rose, for the first time in seven days, with a feeling akin to liberation, to relief. He did not prepare for the customary rites of mourning. Instead, he washed, changed his clothes, went to the royal chapel and prayed, then asked that a meal be prepared for him. Somewhat amazed, one of the servants boldly asked him: 'What is this that you have done? You fasted and wept for the child while it was alive; but when the child died, you arose and ate food.'

The king was not offended. He explained: 'While the child was still alive, I fasted and wept; for I said, "Who knows whether the Lord will be gracious to me, that the child may live?" But now he is dead; why should I fast? Can I bring him back again? I shall go to him, but he will not return to me.'

It was the better part of a year after this that the siege of Rabbah took a dramatic turn. Joab's forces broke the long stalemate by isolating and capturing the source of the city's water supply. Once the water stores inside the walls were depleted, thirst became the Israelite's irresistable ally. Joab dispatched a messenger to Jerusalem. A levy of additional forces was needed for the decisive assault, and Joab invited David to lead them to Rabbah and so be present when the city fell. Otherwise, the commander explained, history would record that it had fallen not to David, but to Joab.

The defenders were faint with thirst, hunger, exhaustion and ravaged by illness. They fell back as a massive Israelite assault succeeded in breaching the gates. The fall of Rabbah brought David not only more spoil, but possession of Ammon and a firm anchor east of the Jordan.

And, in Jerusalem, Bathsheba again presented David with a son. The event was noted by few. David's harem had been industrious supplying him with potential heirs. There was understandably little reason why a latecomer named Solomon should disturb either the routine of the court or Jerusalem.

David's first-born was Amnon, born of Ahinoam of Jezreel, whom David had married in the days of refuge from Saul; and David had accordingly recognized Amnon as his successor and heir. Chileab, David's son by Abigail in those same years, would have been next in the line of succession, but he had died as a youth. Therefore the princes Absalom and Adonijah followed Amnon in precedence. In the matter of royal primogeniture, Nature has so often seemed to delight in ironic jest. The House of David was no exception. Amnon had inherited David's sensual appetite, but neither his ambition, his capacities for leadership, nor his physical beauty. These qualities had fallen in abundance to Absalom, the prince who was forced to dwell in Amnon's shadow. Absalom was David's favourite, for in him David recognized so much of himself. All that we know of Absalom's appearance is the brief description which tells us he was heralded for his beauty, as David had been, that from his head to his feet he was a man of physical perfection, and that he was renowned for his flowing mane of hair. Absalom was the son of Maacah, the daughter of the king of Geshur in the heights of Golan above the Sea of Galilee. David had wed Maacah when he ruled Judah from Hebron. Macaah had also borne David a daughter – Tamar – whose radiant beauty complemented that of her brother Absalom. The pair was renowned throughout Israel. And yet, to the consternation of many of his subjects, David's respect for Amnon's birthright was in no way lessened by the deficiencies of his eldest son. Amnon would be king. Absalom found this situation intolerable and resented both Amnon and his father because of it.

This domestic conflict was to be resolved in a terrible way. As though bent on his own destruction, Amnon had an insatiable sexual appetite and was now obsessed with the desire to make love to his half-sister Tamar. Amnon hungered for Tamar with an intensity that could only be understood as a kind of madness. He fantasized about Tamar, conjuring mental images of their feverish love-making, of her total compliance to him.

Amnon's closest friend was his cousin Jonadab, the son of David's brother Shimeah (Shammah). Jonadab sought far more than companionship from Amnon. He was hardly indifferent to the privileges of being boon companion to a future king and was anxious to do whatever he might to enhance the crown prince's dependence upon him.

It was to Jonadab that Amnon confessed his desire to make love to his half-sister. To the Israelites, incest was one of the most

Akhenaton and Nefertiti, the Egyptian rulers who were brother and sister, husband and wife, king and queen. Unlike their neighbours to the south, the Israelites considered marriage to siblings an abomination

reprehensible of sins – an abomination. Specifically mindful of the pharaonic practice of choosing a queen from among the sisters of the sovereign, and probably of the genetic dangers involved, the sacred statutes enjoined Hebrews from doing 'as they do in the land of Egypt'. Yet the artful Jonadab was neither shocked by Amnon's craving nor possessed of the good sense to counsel him against the likely consequences. Instead, Jonadab suggested to Amnon how he might lure Tamar to bed.

'Lie down on your bed,' Jonadab counselled, 'and pretend to be ill; and when your father comes to see you, say to him, "Let my sister Tamar come and give me bread to eat, and prepare the food in my sight, that I may see it, and eat it from her hand."'

Amnon did as he was advised and took to his bed as though dreadfully ill. The king was informed, and he rushed at once to Amnon's bedchamber. His parental solicitude was compounded by official concern for the general welfare of the heir apparent. In this event, David was mystified, for Amnon seemed less afflicted with physical anguish than a bizarre preoccupation with his appetite. When David asked him rhetorically if there was anything more he might do, Amnon replied: 'Pray let my sister Tamar come and make a couple of cakes in my sight, that I may eat from her hand.'

Had the king paused to consider fully Amnon's request, he might intuitively have spotted trouble – the anxiety in Amnon's voice, perhaps, or the feverishness in his eyes. But David was far too occupied with his own concerns and anxieties to notice. He could easily rationalize Amnon's request. Tamar was the delight of David's household; her characteristic aura of cheerfulness was infectious. She was beloved and sought after. And her cooking skills were legendary. Amnon cherished her. Her solicitude would surely make him well. David sent word to Tamar to minister to her half-brother.

With her servants at her side to assist, Tamar patiently kneaded a fine dough of wheat and barley, then baked the cakes to a turn in the oven of Amnon's house and served them with the purest of honey and goat's milk. But before Tamar fully understood, Amnon had commanded: 'Send out every one from me.' The servants scrambled to obey his order leaving the prince and princess alone. Then, from his couch, Amnon beckoned to Tamar and said quietly, 'Bring the food into the chamber, that I may eat from your hand.' Despite a feeling of vague disquiet, Tamar obeyed, because of the awe in which she held her eldest brother.

Amnon interpreted her compliance as surrender. He had ceased differentiating between reality and fantasy, convincing himself that Tamar longed to possess him as passionately as he dreamed of ravishing her. Amnon was a vain and brutish man. He had neither the patience nor capacity for subtlety. He lunged from the couch, grabbed her arm, and dragged her to him. 'Come, lie with me, my sister,' Amnon said. To his amazement, Tamar resisted; seemed, in fact, both stunned and repelled; raked his arm with her nails as he threw her upon the couch and thrust himself upon her.

'No, my brother, do not force me; for such a thing is not done in Israel; do not do this wanton folly. As for me, where could I carry my shame? And as for you, you would be as one of the wanton fools in Israel.' But Amnon would not be put off. In desperation, Tamar cried out: 'I pray you, speak to the king; for he will not withhold me from you.' Amnon was beyond listening. He had gone too far. He would taste his fantasy, now!

But when he had spent himself, all too quickly, and Tamar had withdrawn to a corner of the couch, breathless, hysterical, with her clothing ripped and her fair skin bruised, Amnon suddenly knew that his lust had deceived him. What he had convinced himself he sought was unobtainable. It had been a crude affair. But Amnon lacked the integrity to blame himself. Instead he projected his intense self-loathing outwards upon the raped girl, and he shouted at her, 'Arise, be gone!' Tamar was inconsolable: 'No, my brother; for this wrong in sending me away is greater than the other which you did to me.'

But there was now no room in Amnon for compassion. He could not bear the sight of her. He called a manservant, and rasped: 'Put this woman out of my presence, and bolt the door after her.' The servant rudely thrust Tamar outside.

Tamar tore her long robe, and cast dust upon her face and head. It was for herself she mourned. Then she stumbled toward the chambers of her brother Absalom, under the searching glances of the courtiers and domestics who happened by.

Tamar was half-crazed with shame. Absalom gave her shelter. She had become the living, breathing symbol of his hatred and loathing for Amnon. The sin upon his sister cried out for vengeance. And Absalom vowed to extract it – to the fullest measure – in time, and in his own way.

David reacted to news of the deed with disbelief and self-reproach. Not only had he served as an unwitting agent of Amnon's assault upon Tamar, but his own sexual excesses had served as a model for Amnon's behaviour. Like David, Amnon had come to believe that he was somehow excused from the statutes of conduct to which the common folk of Israel were expected to adhere. But Amnon went beyond his father in the degree to which he pursued his monstrous fancies. He saw himself free to rape, free to commit incest in the

*overleaf* 'Amnon and Tamar', by the Dutch painter Jan Steen (1626–1679)

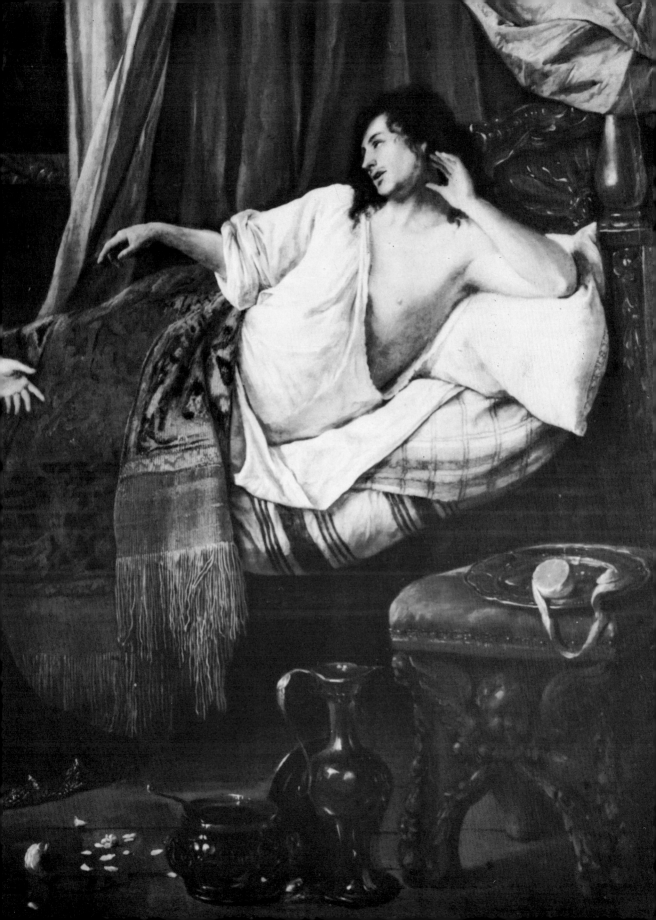

royal chambers, free to violate the chastity of a sister, free to violate the integrity of the royal house.

David vented his anger upon Amnon and disgustedly sent him away. But the king knew the act was a feeble one; for he was powerless to hurt Amnon in the only way he could be hurt. Much as he now wished, David could not possibly disown the crown prince in Absalom's favour. Neither politically nor psychologically could he risk tarnishing the name of the House of David. Suckled on glory, David now choked on scandal and sordidness. If he proclaimed the truth about Amnon's deeds, the adherents of Yahweh would rightly demand his death. Influential elements within the priesthood, as well as opponents of the royal house, were already stirring up discontent over excesses within the courtly establishment. To confirm their accusations, to provide still more grounds for grievance was a step fraught with peril for both the king and the country. On the other hand, David could not permit Amnon to succeed him now. Amnon had compromised himself beyond recall.

David was perplexed over what to do – and, consequently, did nothing. Outwardly, at least, little seemed to change. Amnon went unpunished, appeared still to retain his father's confidence and blessing. Yet each pilgrim to Jerusalem returned to his village, vineyard or farm bearing a version of the dark events; and the tale grew more sordid with each telling. Absalom, seemingly resigned to the uneasy *status quo*, continued to nurture a double grievance – his sister's and his own. Vengeance and ambition fed upon each other and were further attenuated by a deep, brooding hurt over the apparent unwillingness of David to grant him the patrimony of which Amnon had proved unworthy. In time, Absalom's enmity became an all-consuming obsession. He conceived a plan.

It was the custom for the owners of the great flocks to celebrate the time of the annual sheep shearing with a festival of thanksgiving. As they came of age, David had granted his sons portions of the flocks he had acquired through both taxation and conquest. Absalom's were grazed at Baal-hazor in the country of Ephraim, 15 miles due north of Jerusalem. To his festival at Baal-hazor, Absalom invited all his brothers, carefully anticipating the suspicion that would have attached to a summons to Amnon alone. Absalom also invited the king, knowing full well that David would refuse to go in person, both because of the pressure of state business and his growing fondness for seclusion. Absalom reasoned that, as was the custom, the king would ask Amnon to attend in his stead. As Absalom expected, the king gracefully demurred – but failed to make mention of Amnon.

Absalom coolly pressed the point: 'Pray let my brother Amnon

go with us.' David's suspicions were aroused: 'Why should he go with you?' Absalom artfully pressed for Amnon's presence. David could easily convince himself that two years had now passed since the rape of Tamar, and, outwardly, relations between the two brothers had remained correct, albeit cool. Surely the appetite for vengeance had by now abated. David consented to Amnon s attendance and gave his blessings to Absalom's festivities as well.

Absalom commanded several of his most trusted servants to fall upon Amnon with their knives, but only upon his signal. For the crown prince would be under the watchful gaze of his personal retainers – that is, until the wine had flowed sufficiently to dull their senses as well as their single-minded sense of duty.

At the height of the merrymaking, Absalom's assassins did as they had been ordered, attacking Amnon and butchering him. In the confusion that followed, Absalom and his servants escaped; and, among the stunned guests, the cry went up that all the royal princes had been killed. This was the first word borne to the king at Jerusalem. He rent his garments in the customary outpouring of

The murder of Amnon by Absalom's assassins, by the 17th-century painter Bernardo Cavallino

grief, and fell to the floor in misery, suffocated by the sense of unspeakable horror over what he had been told.

Moments later, Jonadab, the dead prince's close companion, arrived from Baal-hazor and corrected the initial report: 'Let not my lord suppose that they have killed all the young men the king's sons, for Amnon alone is dead, for by the command of Absalom this has been determined from the day Amnon forced his sister Tamar.'

The news hardly mitigated David's grief. He was a king, and the heir was dead; he was a father, and his eldest son was dead. In his grief, Amnon's sins were forgiven and forgotten.

But David grieved for Absalom, too, who was both a murderer and a fugitive and was now riding hard for Geshur, east of the Sea of Galilee, many miles from Jerusalem. With Talmai his grandfather, king of the Geshurites, he would find asylum and sympathy. Moreover, David grieved for himself. His destiny was to be deceived by sons in whom he had reposed his love and trust. Yahweh was surely making sport of him now, as he had Saul.

As the months passed, new doubts came to tyrannize David. The succession had passed to a renegade, a man who bore the mark of Cain upon his forehead. It was in David's power to forgive Absalom. Should he do so? Should he rather turn to Adonijah? Where, in fact, did his duty lie? The conflict tormented the ageing king. He reacted by withdrawing further – from the court, from his friends, from the nation. David became apathetic, indifferent toward his duties. Affairs of state ceased to consume him. Increasingly, he found comfort from his anguish in the momentary distractions of the harem. Petitioners found him unavailable. Petty bureaucrats were left to deal as best they could with urgent matters of policy and administration.

Exacerbating the crisis of leadership, the winter rains were insufficient, and famine produced great discontent among the people. They muttered of David's indifference and relished in both relaying and magnifying the gossip of the goings-on within the palace compound in Jerusalem. Taxes grew more burdensome. Cases of maladministration abounded. Ancient grievances found ready expression. Priests again intoned the maledictions of Samuel and retold the tragedy of Saul. Israel grew restive and impatient with its monarch.

Seeing all this, Joab began to fear for both his own welfare and the well-being of the monarchy. The times were fraught with peril. Joab believed it essential to win the dilatory king's pardon for Absalom, to press for a reconciliation, to bring Absalom home. This Joab persistently tried to convince the king to do, but without success. With advancing age and mounting travails,

'The Toilet of Bathsheba', by Rembrandt

David was given more and more to wildly fluctuating moods. Sheer caprice moved him more frequently than reason. Joab decided to exploit these bouts of temperament. He enlisted a wise woman from Tekoa in his plot, and persuaded the king to grant her a rare audience as a personal favour. After she did obeisance to David, she arose and told this tale:

Alas, I am a widow; my husband is dead. And your handmaid had two sons, and they quarrelled with one another in the field; there was no one to part them, and one struck the other and killed him. And now the whole family has risen against your handmaid, and they say, 'Give up the man who struck his brother, that we may kill him for the life of his brother whom he slew'; and so they would destroy the heir also. Thus they would quench my coal which is left, and leave to my husband neither name nor remnant upon the face of the earth (II Samuel 14:5–7).

The wise woman of Tekoa assisted Joab in his plot to bring about a reconciliation between David and Absalom. This Phoenician ivory shows a woman of the times

David, clearly moved by the tale, as Joab had gambled he would be, said indignantly to the woman, 'As the Lord lives, not one hair of your son shall fall to the ground.'
And now, the woman seized the point:

Why then have you planned such a thing against the people of God? For in giving this decision the king convicts himself, inasmuch as the king does not bring his banished one home again. We must all die, we are like water spilt on the ground, which cannot be gathered up again; but God will not take away the life of him who devises means not to keep his banished one an outcast (II Samuel 14:13–14).

The woman's courage and eloquence affected David deeply, but he was also shrewd enough to suspect the ruse. 'Is the hand of Joab with you in all this?' David asked. The woman answered forthrightly without pause, for she knew Absalom's cause might be seriously compromised by evasion:

As surely as you live, my lord the king, one cannot turn to the right hand or to the left from anything that my lord the king has said. It was your servant Joab who bade me; it was he who put all these words in the mouth of your handmaid. In order to change the course of affairs your servant Joab did this. But my lord has wisdom like the wisdom of the angel of God to know all things that are on the earth (II Samuel 14:19–20).

David had been angered by the revelation of Joab's deviousness. But as his commander had gambled, her words had been as a sudden shaft of light illuminating a murky recess of his soul; and David was ashamed. He beckoned Joab, who, expecting to feel the king's wrath, fell to the ground and repeatedly prostrated himself. To his amazement, Joab heard David: 'Behold now, I grant

The aged King David, by Rubens

this; go, bring back my son Absalom.' Joab prepared for an immediate departure.

But while Joab was in Geshur preparing to escort Absalom home to Jerusalem, David's mercurial temperament overwhelmed his good sense. He grew fearful of the impending reunion, of the seeming emotional price he must pay. He was pridefully reluctant to be seen granting paternal absolution to a son who not only had openly deceived him, but stained his hands with the blood of a brother. But there was in all likelihood far more. David feared Absalom – the radiance of his youth, his unalloyed beauty, his profound popularity with the people, which had grown rather than diminished with the murder of Amnon. The dual tyranny of pride and envy condemned David to a fateful mistake. When Joab entered the royal chamber in Jerusalem to inform David of Absalom's return, that he was waiting outside to be reunited with his father, David rasped: 'Let him dwell apart in his own house; he is not to come into my presence.'

Absalom was first stunned, then speechless with humiliation and rage. He had come joyfully from Geshur, believing that he had been vindicated, to be returned to his rightful station in Israel. Instead, he had been tricked into abandoning exile for eternal disgrace – at the hand of his father and in the very sight of his people. His soul was indelibly scarred with what he construed as the treachery of David. And a form of treachery perhaps it was. We have witnessed, in the fate of Amnon, the consequences of Absalom's brooding sense of outrage. Now, as he tried fruitlessly through Joab and others to obtain an audience with the king, to intercede for him in the name of fairness and justice (elusive then as now), Absalom for the first time began concretely to contemplate rebellion.

Undoubtedly, there were those self-serving intriguers within the ruling establishment, or on its fringes, who tried cleverly to insinuate the idea of revolt into his mind. But Absalom needed no one to provide him with cause, no one to make him aware of the temper of the times and of the climate for change it offered, no one to remind him of how an ageing and somewhat careless king has grown neglectful of his duties to his nation. David's operatives constantly brought reports of the civil unrest to the counsellor Ahithophel, who diplomatically but forcefully tried to arouse David's concern. To Ahithophel's mounting distraction, David would not heed him.

It is not certain when Absalom fully committed himself to the scheme of overthrowing his father. But this is because he was not reckless. He fully realized the implications of this extreme course of action, the need to plan covertly, slowly and well, and to begin constructing a reliable base of support within the establishment, the army, and the people. In order not to arouse official suspicions, Absalom continued to press for a reconciliation with his father. But his efforts repeatedly failed. Two full years had passed since his disastrous return from Geshur. Joab, embarrassed by the way in which David had compromised him in the affair and irritated by Absalom's persistence and the king's obstinacy, ceased to have anything to do with the prince.

But Absalom's plan to depose David now depended basically upon first extracting a modicum of legitimacy from his father. Joab owned a large field of barley beside property belonging to Absalom. The prince ordered his servants to set fire to Joab's field when the barley was ripe and to take no pains to conceal their identity. Predictably, the blaze brought Joab rushing to Absalom's house demanding an explanation: 'Why have your servants set my field on fire?' And Absalom icily replied: 'Behold, I sent word to you, "Come here, that I may send you to the king, to ask, 'Why have I come from Geshur? It would be better for me to be there still.'"' Now therefore let me go into the presence of the king; and if there is guilt in me, let him kill me.'

Absalom's shock treatment worked. Joab urgently carried the prince's suit to David and argued it eloquently. Joab suddenly

Absalom had Joab's field burned in an attempt to incite his father's captain and bring Joab to him. The harvesting of barley in biblical times as shown in a wall painting from the Tomb of Menna, Thebes

found his argument vigorously supported by old Ahithophel. The counsellor's actions were animated by motives that would have astounded Joab, had he but known. For Ahithophel had been recruited covertly to the cause of Absalom, after having reluctantly concluded that David was no longer fit to rule. Ahithophel might have spared David with more charity, but for the fact that he had never forgiven the king for his scandalous conduct with his granddaughter Bathsheba.

David was convinced by his two trusted aides that he had sorely mistreated his son. Overcome with guilt and longing, he immediately summoned Absalom to him. They passionately embraced, and David wept. His emotions were heartfelt, if somewhat belated. But Absalom's were not. The reconciliation had come too late.

Through Ahithophel, Absalom had begun to acquire significant support among the tribes by exploiting their fear and suspicion of change, as represented by the central authority in Jerusalem. And now that he had succeeded in regaining the king's favour, Absalom could operate more openly in his bid to widen his popular following. He acquired a magnificently wrought chariot and an official escort of fifty retainers. Wherever Absalom travelled throughout the country, the bodyguards heralded his coming by preceding the chariot on foot. The populace was suitably impressed.

Of all the official lapses for which David was accountable, the most serious, perhaps, was neglect of his duty to dispense justice – to serve as the ultimate magistrate in cases involving petitions of grievance, disputes between clans and tribes and interpretations of the civil statutes. A steady stream of petitioners came to Jerusalem from all parts of the kingdom seeking the king's judgement, only to learn that he had cancelled all public audiences and had established no surrogate tribunal to hear their cases. Such reports were scarcely believed when they were carried home, but Absalom exploited this.

He would frequently station himself on a seat in the broad plaza before Jerusalem's main gate, his impressive retinue at hand. When travellers announced themselves to the guards as seekers after the king's justice, Absalom would hail them in a moving display of solicitude, ask of their cities and tribes and then utter a self-serving speech which, with minor variations, hewed to this basic form: 'Your claims are good and right; but there is no man deputed by the king to hear you. Oh that I were judge in the land! Then every man with a suit or cause might come to me, and I would give him justice.'

The men so addressed would respond to Absalom's attentiveness as might the politically alienated among us respond to a demagogue sensitive to the passions of the populace. They paid obeisance to the young prince who so readily espoused their grievances, prayed fervently as they kissed his hand that he might soon assume the throne, and promptly carried glowing tales of Absalom throughout the land. When reports of these patently seditious activities reached Ahithophel, he conveniently neglected to forward them to the king.

In time, Absalom was convinced all was in readiness. All that remained was to signal the rising and provide sufficient evidence to would-be supporters that he could confidently carry it off. He approached David and asked permission to visit Hebron. The ostensible purpose was a religious pilgrimage. Hebron still retained its traditional importance as a cultic center and its prestige as the former capital of Israel. Hebron was surely the ideal site from which to challenge the authority of David and Jerusalem. Under Ahithophel's prodding, David gave his blessing to the pilgrimage, as he had blessed the festival of the wool shearing some six years earlier.

Two hundred supporters marched south with Absalom to Hebron, where other conspirators had prepared to help him take control of the city. Once ensconced there, Absalom sent messengers to his principal supporters throughout the land, with a single message: 'As soon as you hear the sound of the trumpet, then say, "Absalom is king at Hebron!"'

Ahithophel slipped out of Jerusalem secretly and rode swiftly to Hebron, where he openly declared his allegiance to the son of David. Soon, similar declarations of support were winging to Hebron, borne by rebels prepared to fight for Absalom. Some army units mutinied and went over to his cause.

A messenger was brought before David. His brief report was paralysing: 'The hearts of the men of Israel have gone after Absalom.' Reports of mass desertions now began to reach the palace in Jerusalem. Both the speed and magnitude of the uprising overwhelmed the old king, who had refused to be stirred earlier. He called for Ahithophel. His counsellor was nowhere to be found. Absalom was now reported martialling his forces for an assault on Jerusalem.

'Arise and let us flee,' David told his court, or else there will be no escape for us from Absalom.'

As the court prepared to evacuate the capital, it was being said that the king had panicked, that all was lost. But a former fugitive does not easily abandon his instincts for the first principles of survival.

# 8 Into the Hands of Solomon

Royal messengers sped through the narrow lanes of David's city; heralds proclaimed the message at the city gates, the market, the water shaft of the Gihon Spring, the Pool of En-rogel. Their words could scarcely be believed: the king and court were evacuating the capital, withdrawing east of the Jordan. At the prescribed hour, all loyal soldiers and citizens were to gather beyond the gates on the highway to the east, the Way of the Arabah. The crisis would surely be dealt with. Jerusalem would be regained.

One can now only try to imagine what lay behind David's startling decision to abandon Jerusalem. In and of itself, word that Absalom was marching from Hebron would not have seemed sufficient cause. A ruler is not easily persuaded to forsake his seat of power.

But the king was suddenly confronted with a number of things. The early developments all seemed to indicate that Absalom's challenge was a grave one. Consider the news that David's most senior official, Ahithophel – a statesman so universally respected throughout Israel that he was considered virtually a prophet – was a party to the revolt. With the anguished recognition of hindsight, David could now recall Ahithophel's strident warnings about the seriousness of public disaffection. Surely it would be safe to assume that Ahithophel would not have deserted the king had he not been reasonably confident of Absalom's ability to exploit that disaffection.

But that is not all that Ahithophel's defection would have signified to David. Ahithophel would surely have carried a significant amount of tribal support with him – including the king's own tribe, Judah. Ahithophel was perhaps the most influential elder of Judah—the largest of Israel's tribes, with a virtual monopoly on the southern portion of the country. David had risen from

David with his court singers, dancers, musicians and jugglers, from an illuminated Latin psalter

161

Judah; Judah could pull him down. Hebron, Judah's capital, was in Absalom's hands; surely, so was Judah.

Absalom had most probably secured the allegiance of important tribal elements in both north and south with a pledge to restore to the tribes much of the power and authority which David had gradually pre-empted for Jerusalem. Thus Absalom had come to represent the last desperate hope among older, conservative elements for a restoration of the old order, in which the social, political and military structure would again devolve upon the tribes.

Then, too, it was an age of primitive communications, in which rumour and fact were so often inseparable, and the obtaining of accurate information required precious time. David could not have had the intelligence information in those early hours to know, for instance, the extent of Absalom's support in depth; where the majority of the armed forces stood, with the aristocracy, the provincial bureaucracy, the priesthood. Whom would the people follow when the chips were down, David or Absalom? Surely, much of the apparatus that might have produced rapid answers had been controlled by Ahithophel, and he was gone. David, who had been indolent for so long, would have to find other ways of getting the information he needed.

Age, however, had apparently not impaired David's capacity to adapt to sudden change, to respond when gravely challenged. His was a temperament which fed upon contention, and languished when it was not being tested. David was clearly in command again, and his penchant for the unorthodox speedily reasserted itself. Given the dearth of raw information, he must have considered that if Absalom had martialled sufficient strength to mount an effective siege, a king locked within the walls of Jerusalem like a bird in a cage would be worse than useless – cut off from his people, his administrative apparatus, his army. David reasoned that if he were not now able to remain highly visible, were not effectively *seen* to be in command, all would be lost. And he could not wait until the rebels arrived at the gates to assess Absalom's fighting strength. It might then be too late to leave.

The essential credo of David's strategic thinking had always been to retain the essential capacity of manoeuvre. He had fought as a tiger, not an elephant. Set-piece warfare was anathema to him. In our day, conventional generals fight to capture places. But places which are abandoned today can be regained tomorrow. David fought not for places, but for advantage. Room for manoeuvre, once lost, could never be retrieved again. And there were phases of a struggle in which the gaining of time was more vital than the holding of territory. Jerusalem was David's city, not his coffin.

He would leave it today to return and reclaim it tomorrow.

But before leaving Jerusalem, David required an immediate inventory of his strength, a separation of loyalists, opportunists and traitors within his own establishment. So he ordered all who chose to follow him to muster and pass in review before him as they embarked upon the road to the east. If, as David gambled, large numbers of Jerusalemites marched with him, Absalom would find himself in effective control of an all but empty city.

The resounding blare of the rams' horns signalled the appointed hour of the evacuation. David and his official retinue passed beyond the eastern gate of Jerusalem. Once again the dust of the highway clung to the feet of a fugitive. The thought of it might have shattered him. He might well have been paralysed at this moment by the utter somberness of abandoning without a struggle the city which had come to be a living monument to his reign, or by the prospect of a struggle with a son who sought his life as well as his throne. But, as intelligence is measured by one's ability to adapt, strength is the capacity to confront the possibility of failure or tragedy. They were the source of David's enormous resilience.

David stood at the outer threshold of the gate and watched the procession issue from the city. He was noting faces and counting heads, and he was elated by what he saw. The servants of the royal household were there to a man. Ahithophel had taken few of the lesser court officials with him. Bathsheba, David's favoured wife, preceded the other women of the harem and the daughters of the king, while Adonijah led the young men of the House of David, Solomon among them. None had followed their brother Absalom to Hebron.

With them trooped the large Philistine mercenary force under the command of Benaiah, which constituted David's sizable household guard. The question of their loyalty had been crucial. Numbered among the mercenaries were the several hundred veterans whom David had brought from Gath when he ascended the throne of Judah at Hebron. And David, deeply moved by seeing them, now honoured the Gittites by beckoning to their commander, the Philistine Ittai.

'Why do you also go with us?' David asked him. 'Go back, and stay with the king, for you are a foreigner, and also an exile from your home. You came only yesterday, and shall I today make you wander about with us, seeing I go I know not where? Go back, and take your brethren with you; and may the Lord show steadfast love and faithfulness to you.'

It had not escaped Ittai's notice that David had referred to Absalom as king; he would never know whether he was being tested or whether in fact David had unintentionally revealed his own inner doubt about the outcome of the struggle. Ittai left no doubt where he stood: 'As the Lord lives, and as my lord the king lives, wherever my lord the king shall be, whether for death or for life, there also will your servant be.'

Behind the large military contingent marched the two High Priests of Israel, Zadok and Abiathar, and a host of Levites, the priestly tribe, bearing the Holy Ark. Three centuries earlier, the Ark had preceded their ancestors as they marched west with Joshua across the Jordan. Now it was retracing the way that it had come. The thought seemed distasteful to David. It occurred to him that the Ark and Jerusalem were now inseparable, that it must never leave – not now or ever. It was the Ark which gave Jerusalem its unique religious character and meaning. The presence of the king in the view of history was irrelevant. But the presence of Yahweh could not ever depart these gates.

In this way David ratified the singular nature of the Holy City, and, in theocratic Israel, the subservience of the king to the changeless, the immutable authority of Yahweh.

David summoned his High Priests and commanded them: 'Carry the Ark of God back into the city. If I find favour in the eyes of the Lord, he will bring me back and let me see both it and his habitation; but if he says, "I have no pleasure in you," behold, here I am, let him do to me what seems good to him.'

Before releasing Zadok and Abiathar, David made it clear he also intended to derive some worldly benefits from their return to the city, so as not to leave the course of events totally in the hands of the divine. He ordered the priests to coordinate spying activities during Absalom's occupation, using their sons Ahimaaz and Jonathan as couriers. David intended to march eastwards along the Way of the Arabah until he reached the western bank of the Jordan. He intended to await word from the High Priests as to Absalom's intentions in Jerusalem before committing himself to a decisive crossing of the river.

David marched to the east for a number of salient reasons. The bulk of his professional military force was east of Jordan, engaged in occupation duties in the conquered territory. The king judged that his élite soldiery would remain loyal to the crown and spearhead his return to Jerusalem. He also counted upon the loyalist tendencies of the Israelites of Gilead, that ancient and vulnerable Israelite salient on the heights east of Jordan. Because of its isolation, Gilead was always the first to suffer from external predators when Israel was weak. The men of Gilead found little virtue in separatism. Their safety and welfare lay in a strong central

When David fled Jerusalem, he refused to remove the Ark from the city and diminish his capital's status as a holy place. Cherubim and seraphim guarding the Holy Ark, from an illuminated Latin manuscript in the Vatican Library
*overleaf* A 16th-century stained-glass window in the King's College Chapel, Cambridge, illustrates Shimei taunting David

government. For this reason, they had never abandoned Saul; nor would they abandon his successor.

One more vital arrangement remained to be made. When he heard of Ahithophel's defection, David had prayed that Yahweh might 'turn the counsel of Ahithophel into foolishness'. To that end, he had arranged a rendezvous with one of his most valued confidantes, Hushai of the Archites, the clan which dwelled on the border of the lands of Ephraim and Benjamin. He commanded Hushai to meet him upon the summit of the Mount of Olives, which commanded the eastern approaches to Jerusalem. Here the road east ascended, as though to offer the sojourner a last spectacular view of the Holy City, before it plunged downward into the cleft of the Jordan. Atop the summit stood a high place to Yahweh, an altar of unhewn stone before which pilgrims sacrificed to invoke divine protection for their journey. But the history of the site as a holy place stretched back into the mists of antiquity, before men had given names to their gods.

David guided his multitude to the high altar. As they gathered at the summit, they turned towards the city. It lay beneath them across the Kidron Valley, its dun-coloured stone burnished to a golden hue by the light of the sun. A green mantle of forest lay upon the shoulders of the hills. The emotional impact of their swift departure overwhelmed them. Men and women cried. They grieved for themselves, their city and their king. It was noted by many that David, too, wept, and displayed the ritual signs of mourning.

The elder Hushai, a man numbered among the wise and revered in Israel, greeted David before the altar. A servant bore Hushai's belongings, for he had intended to follow David from Jerusalem. But the king ordered the old man to turn back in haste before Absalom's arrival: 'Return to the city and say to Absalom, "I will be your servant, O king; as I have been your father's servant in time past, so now I will be your servant." Then you must defeat for me the counsel of Ahithophel. Whatever you hear from the king's house, tell it to Zadok and Abiathar the priests. Behold, their two sons are with them there, Ahimaaz, Zadok's son, and Jonathan, Abiathar's son; and by them you shall send me everything you hear.'

With a rudimentary but highly trustworthy intelligence apparatus now hopefully penetrating to the inner councils of the enemy, David's preparations were complete, and he led the long procession briskly down the eastern slope of the Mount of Olives towards the wilderness. Waiting for him was Ziba, the old retainer of Mephibosheth, the son of Jonathan, with a welcome gift of provisions

— bread, wine and fruit. David understood the gift to be from Mephibosheth, who had merited the king's grace and favour for so long. But where was he? Why had he not joined the royal party? The servant looked troubled and his words tore at David's heart: 'Behold, he remains in Jerusalem; for he said, "Today the house of Israel will give me back the kingdom of my father."'

Mephibosheth's loyalty, too, had proved fragile. He was both a traitor and a fool, accepting the king's favours while hating him, dishonouring the very covenant which had given him any claim to privilege. He had somehow convinced himself that a schism within the House of David might convince the nation to turn again to the House of Saul. David ordered that Mephibosheth be dispossessed. The remnants of Saul's property and wealth were awarded to the servant Ziba.

One last humiliation awaited David on that long day's march to the river. A kinsman of Saul, a Benjaminite named Shimei, stood by the side of the road openly exulting at David's misfortune. Shimei flung stones and handfuls of dust, heckled the marchers and shouted at David as he passed: 'Begone, begone, you man of blood. The Lord has avenged upon you all the blood of the house of Saul, in whose place you have reigned; and the Lord has given the kingdom into the hands of your son Absalom. See, your ruin is upon you; for you are a man of blood.'

Abishai, Joab's chief of staff, reached for his sword and asked David's leave to silence Shimei on the spot. But the king stayed Abishai's hand. 'Let him alone, and let him curse,' David said. There would be blood enough before the struggle with Absalom was resolved. The spilling of Shimei's blood would resolve nothing; it would only be as senseless as Shimei's taunts had been cruel.

David was upon his mule, and the procession marched on behind him, descending into the oppressively hot valley of the Jordan. By the banks of the river, a camp was erected. Before fording the river, David would await word from Jerusalem.

As the king expected, Absalom was unnerved when he found the city half-deserted, a climactic showdown deferred, a king who would not be forced into a confrontation, abdication or surrender. For the first time Absalom's confidence and composure were shaken. It can be understood, then, why he disregarded any grudging suspicions he may have entertained and readily accepted David's friend Hushai into his service. Hushai had couched his offer to Absalom in the most statesmanlike terms. He had explained that his loyalty was not to David, but to the royal office itself. Thus, he told Absalom, 'As I have served your father, so will I serve you.' Absalom needed reassurance. Hushai seemed prepared

A view of the arid Jordan Rift Valley, to which David and his procession turned on their flight from Jerusalem

to supply just that to his new sovereign in unlimited amounts.

The wise Ahithophel quite correctly counselled Absalom to press his advantage against David, while the king was still in retreat, while the loyalist forces were still too disorganized to fight, and before David could place the defensive line of the Jordan behind him. Ahithophel argued: 'Let me choose twelve thousand men, and I will set out and pursue David tonight. I will come upon him while he is weary and discouraged, and throw him into a panic; and all the people who are with him will flee. I will strike down the king only, and I will bring all the people back to you as a bride comes home to her husband. You seek the life of only one man, and all the people will be at peace.' The advice was sound. Had Absalom accepted it, the outcome would have been different.

But instead he said: 'Call Hushai the Archite also, and let us hear what he has to say.' Hushai knew he had to shake Absalom's confidence in Ahithophel, and that the prince's mounting self-doubt was his most potent ally. He argued persuasively that David's battle-hardened veterans had never lost a major fight,

and would hardly be defeated now by a hasty, ill-conceived attack; that David had in all likelihood already slipped away from the main group to a place of safety; and that Absalom's time would be better spent consolidating his position in Jerusalem and mobilizing as powerful a striking force as possible for a decisive confrontation with his father. Hushai thereby forced Absalom to entertain for the first time the possibility that he might be beaten.

Ahithophel pleaded passionately against the counsel of Hushai. Caution, he argued, had fathered the revolt. But caution now could spell its doom. Revolts are the work of giants and gamblers. Absalom was neither. He accepted the advice of Hushai. Ahithophel was humiliated. He well knew that David had gained a priceless reprieve – the gift of time. He knew, too, that David would exploit it to the fullest. Sadly, without fanfare, Ahithophel withdrew and rode alone slowly to his home in Gilo of Judah. *He* had been a gambler. He had lost.

Through the priests Zadok and Abiathar, the exultant Hushai sent word to David at the fords of the Jordan that he had won a pause. There would be no immediate pursuit; but Absalom would now martial a sizable force for a conventional military campaign against him. Acting on this intelligence, David withdrew in order across the Jordan and proceeded north to Mahanaim in the territory of Gilead, north of Ammon. It had been in Mahanaim some two decades earlier that Ishbosheth had formed his government in exile after Saul's death at Gilboa. As David had hoped, the Israelites of Gilead proved loyal to the monarchy again. They supplied provisions in generous amounts for the camp of the king and provided an impressive levy of men to complement the crack force of regulars that had accompanied the king, as well as those David now summoned from occupation duties in Ammon.

David organized his striking force into three major elements, based on the original organizational formula employed by Saul. Joab commanded one, Abishai a second, Ittai the third. Two elements could act frontally in tandem, one could be detached to defend a flank, while the third served as a blocking force. As David was completing his preparations, word arrived that Absalom's army was marching north into Ephraim and would shortly turn eastwards across the Jordan and move directly against Mahanaim.

Characteristically, David refused to let the enemy dictate the time and place of battle. He ordered his three commanders to proceed swiftly towards the Jordan to surprise Absalom as he moved through the rock-strewn hill country of Ephraim. None present at that final meeting would ever forget the poignancy of David's final order to his commanders. 'Deal gently for my sake with the young man Absalom.' Joab thought David a sentimental fool.

Absalom's was a raggle-taggle army – a collection of tribal militias and untrained volunteers bolstered by a relative handful of regular units brought over by Amasa. Despite their anti-Davidic fervour they were simply no match for David's élite force. The loyalists had a monopoly on experience and professionalism, and having seized the initiative, they never lost it. The slaughter on the field of Ephraim that day was frightful. Thousands were slain. Those of Absalom's army who survived simply melted into the hills and returned to their homes.

When Absalom fled the site of his army's defeat, his head was caught in a tree, and he was found by David's forces and was executed by Joab. 'The Escape and Death of Absalom' by Francesco Pesellino

Absalom himself tried to flee the battlefield on a mule, intending to make his way back to Geshur, where he would find asylum. But he was captured by a patrol of Joab's troops. A soldier was dispatched to inform Joab and to seek further instructions. Joab demanded to know why they had not killed Absalom at once. He was reminded of David's order to deal gently with his son. But Joab on this day was not to be hobbled either by royal sanction

iocem

omin'

ncam

omem

t contur

ter oms

uerta

ualde

t filio

i.

pma

mper

oum.

Eati quorum
remisse sunt u
quitates et quorum te
ta sunt peccata
Beatus uir cui non
impurauit dominus

or fatherly sentiment. Absalom had endangered the state and would have dealt summarily with Joab had their positions been reversed. There was no need to consider the problem further. With his retinue, Joab was led to the spot where Absalom was being held. Joab told him simply: 'I will not waste time with you.' He stabbed the prince, and his armour-bearers ran him through with their swords. Absalom's death was strikingly like that he had arranged for Amnon some nine years earlier.

The king had been sitting in the cobbled plaza of the double-gate at Mahanaim across the Jordan awaiting word of the outcome. The watchman in the tower above caught sight of the messengers racing swiftly toward the city. But after they had given David the news of the great victory, he would not yield to exultation. 'Is it well with the young man Absalom?' he asked. And when he was told, David slumped upon the stone bench and wept bitterly, heedless of the many who looked on. They heard him intone repeatedly in his grief: 'O, my son Absalom, my son, my son Absalom! Would I had died instead of you, O Absalom, my son!'

Joab had ridden swiftly to Mahanaim with his men expecting both praise from the king and rewards from the king's purse. But Joab's jubilation turned to incredulity when he learned that David was presiding over a lamentation, not a triumph. There is no simple explanation for what Joab now set out to do. Certainly, his was the mentality of the dedicated soldier – only victory counted; all else was secondary. Perhaps, he was animated by guilt at having disobeyed the king and was attempting to conceal his fear. It might have been that Joab could not bring himself to be tolerant over the sentimental maunderings of a lion who had grown too old. Certainly, as the military leader he would have been deeply upset by the demoralizing effect of the king's conduct upon troops who had risked their lives for him, only to receive a dole of royal tears for their sacrifice.

Joab burst in upon David like a fury:

You have today covered with shame the faces of all your servants, who have this day saved your life, and the lives of your sons and daughters, and the lives of your wives and concubines, because you love those who hate you and hate those who love you. For you have made it clear today that commanders and servants are nothing to you; for today I perceive that if Absalom were alive and all of us were dead today, then you would be pleased. Now therefore arise, go out and speak kindly to your servants; for I swear by the Lord that if you do not go, not a man will stay with you this night, and this will be worse for you than all the evil that has come upon you until now (II Samuel 19: 5–7).

An illumination of David and Joab from the Duke of Berry's Book of Hours (15th century)

That such words tumbled from the lips of a confederate of long standing was shock enough. But Joab had savagely murdered a son, enemy or no, in defiance of his wishes. There was truth in what Joab had said about the troops, but this failed to mitigate the rest. Somehow David mastered his emotions, choked back his grief and anger and let himself be guided back to the gates of the city to put things right with his worn army. But after a collaboration of forty years, David would never forgive Joab.

He chose to remain at Mahanaim for a time. The ordeal of putting down the rebellion, coupled with the tragic death of Absalom, had all but consumed him emotionally. He needed to rest. He needed time to heal. The nation needed time for reconciliation. And David would have to make peace with himself before he could bring himself to make his peace with others. In that dark and brooding time at Mahanaim, David was perhaps forced to accept that he had been in large part responsible for having driven his son to rebellion; and for having permitted the conditions to flourish in which the seeds of rebellion could find sustenance.

In binding the nation's wounds, the king embarked upon a calculated policy of leniency. There would be no reprisals at this time, tempting though it would have been to the old man's ego to settle his personal grievances with the likes of Shimei and Mephibosheth. For the settling of old scores would only create new ones. What was required was unity; vengeance was an indulgence that could not be afforded now.

But generosity would be tempered with firmness. Before taking up his burdens again in Jerusalem, David would expect a demonstration of support from a penitent nation – most particularly, a reaffirmation of fealty from the errant tribes.

Perhaps David's deepest disappointment was the behaviour of his own tribe, Judah. From the beginning of the affair to the end, Judah had offended him. It had reared him, elevated him to the throne of all Israel, then abandoned him for the shoddy blandishments of Absalom. Delegation upon delegation arrived in Mahanaim to render tribute, to demonstrate submission, to implore the king to return to Jerusalem. But Judah did not come. Instead, word was sent that Ahithophel, in disgrace, had taken his own life at Gilo. But David did not require scapegoats now. He sought consensus and, also, personal reconciliation with Judah. He could not, would not, return to Jerusalem without Judah.

Personal honour, of course, was involved, and pride. But there was far more. Judah accounted for nearly half of all southern

King David enthroned, a
Carolingian ivory plaque
decorated with gold

Israel. Without it, the Israelite union would exist in name only.
Were the elders of Judah too proud or fearful of David's wrath to
seek forgiveness? Or did they still hope to salvage some modest
political profit from the wreckage of Absalom's rebellion?

We do not know. We are told that David was driven to extraordinary lengths to sue for Judah's return. He dispatched plen-
ipotentiaries of impressive rank, the priests Abiathar and Zadok,
to Hebron bearing a personal plea: 'Why should you be the last
to bring the king back to his house, when the word of all Israel
has come to the king? You are my kinsmen, you are my bone
and my flesh; why then should you be the last to bring back the
king?'

David placated Judah in other ways. He stripped Joab of his
command of the royal armies and over him placed Amasa, his neph-

ew and Joab's cousin, the defeated general of the rebels. The gesture was not only intended as a display of deference to Judah. It was the most humiliating punishment that could be devised for Joab the professional soldier – the victor made vassal to the vanquished.

In a final gesture, David agreed that he would re-enter Israel proper on his return to Jerusalem by way of Judah, holding his formal triumph at Gilgal. Such cajolery, demeaning as it was, had its desired effect. Judah made its peace with the king. But the affair also generated an unexpected backlash: it rekindled an historic feud as northerners angrily accused David of having become hostage to the south.

There had been sectional difficulties between the two halves of Israel since the earliest days of the monarchy. Recall Judah's displeasure over the crowning of Saul the Benjaminite, a son of the north; and the importance accorded by David to the sensitive question of siting a capital both regions could accept. North and south shared the same God, the same creed, identical traditional sources. But in many ways they had remained two nations.

Many of the northern Semites had settled in Canaan long before the arrival of the Mosaic stream from Egypt. Each region had undergone differing historical experiences under the loose two-hundred-year confederation of the Judges; and Judah had come relatively late to the tribal union. There were differences in speech, in racial origin, in dress and habit. And underlying all this were the more recent stresses of the long struggle between Saul and David, essentially a sectional conflict, which had culminated in the bitterness of a seven-year civil war.

The resulting strains, like a great earth fault, remained dormant while the internal political forces around it were more or less in equilibrium. But David's posturings to Judah had disturbed the sensitive balance. David may well have argued that his concessions to Judah were more than justified by the benefits of national reconciliation. But many of the north did not see it in that light. While Judah tarried after the rebellion, delegations from the north had been the first to proffer their loyalty to David. Yet it had been Judah which reaped the fruits.

There was at Gilgal an influential kin of Saul, Sheba the son of Bichri, a hot-tempered Benjaminite and a demagogue. As the many hundreds of Israelites who had gathered there prepared to escort the king back to Jerusalem in a display of national unity, the animosity between north and south burst into the open. Sheba ordered the sounding of the ram's horn, and convened an assemblage of northerners. Before the bones of one rebellion had been laid to rest, Sheba tried to kindle another. He harangued the northerners to withdraw from the victory procession and return to their homes. He called for secession from the union. 'We have no portion in David, and we have no inheritance in the son of Jesse,' he cried. 'Every man to his tents, O Israel!'

Many northerners followed Sheba, and a weary and disillusioned David was conveyed to his capital by an escort composed for the most part of his recent adversaries, the men of Judah. David ordered his new commander, Amasa, to return to Judah and recruit a loyal militia which, together with the regular force retained in Jerusalem, was to speed north to put down the secessionist movement before it could spread. Amasa departed as he was ordered, but, for some reason, he tarried. We do not know why.

We do know that David, in desperation, was forced reluctantly to turn to Joab. Together with his brother Abishai, Joab proceeded in pursuit of Sheba at the head of a large contingent of loyal troops consisting largely of Philistine mercenaries. We know that the brothers stopped *en route* in Gibeon, north of Jerusalem, where Amasa was. We can only guess why, since he had been dispatched to Judah many miles to the south. It may well be that he had chosen to defect to Sheba in yet another attempt to depose the king. Gibeon was in Benjamin, the tribe of Sheba. On the other hand, it may be that Amasa had already recruited his men from Judah as ordered and was in the process of dealing with the insurgents.

At any rate, Amasa at Gibeon wound up another bloody example of Joabite justice. The former commander avenged the disgrace of his recent demotion by running a sword through Amasa and was restored forthwith by the royal troops to his former office, we can assume, by acclamation. David, still deeply dependent upon his soldiers, grudgingly deferred to their will.

For the second time, the national army spelled the decisive difference for the monarchy, restoring order as it moved north in pursuit of Sheba. His original supporters deserted him, and he was unable to muster sizable replacements. The odds were too great; the example of Absalom too fresh. In time, Sheba found sanctuary in a town of the extreme north called Abel-beth-maacah, beneath the south-western flank of Mount Hermon. When the army of Joab and Abishai surrounded the town, the citizens voted for David by beheading Sheba and throwing his head over the wall.

Sheba had been premature. The venom of sectionalism had been neutralized, but it remained in the bloodstream. In time, it would transform other discontented men into insurgents, and Israel would pay dearly for its bedevilling tendency towards

David before the Lord,
from a 15th-century
hymnal belonging to the
Cathedral of Prato

atomization, a not uncommon characteristic in the history of the
Semite peoples.

With the end of Sheba's rebellion, Israel won a respite of some
years. The nation entered a period of political stability and economic
well-being. Its new prominence on the geopolitical face of the
Orient had begun to bring benefits to David's subjects unknown
in the four hundred years since Joshua established his beachhead
in Jericho. Sectional grievances were put aside as Israelites savoured
a time of prosperity and peace. Living conditions improved
immeasurably. And David finally ruled a tranquil land.

He had reigned now for about thirty years over all Israel, north
and south. While he had experienced too much personal tragedy
ever to know contentment, age and tranquillity seemed now to
surround him with an aura of what, for want of a better phrase,
might be called benign resignation, the singular sense of calm
that derives from a combined sense of achievement and an awareness
of approaching death.

Those about the king, however, knew no tranquillity. The
question of the succession lay unresolved. The universal axiom of
politics is that struggle and intrigue flourish in a vacuum. Adonijah
was the oldest of David's living sons and was accordingly considered
by some as uncontested heir to the throne. These elements, their
eye on the main chance, aligned themselves with Adonijah and
began agitating to win the king's public blessing for him. Adonijah's
chief supporters were Joab, barely tolerated by the king in deference
to the army, but now *persona non grata* in intimate courtly circles,
and the High Priest Abiathar.

We know virtually nothing about Adonijah – except for his rampant ambition, a not unique characteristic of David's sons. And we know, too, that he was at a distinct disadvantage. For there was a far more potent coalition working against Adonijah's interests and in support of the young prince Solomon, now perhaps in his late teens. What Solomon lacked in precedence, he more than made up in the potency of his support. Leading the way was his mother Bathsheba, the last and greatest love of his father David. She was vigorous, compassionate, proud of her place in the Davidic hierarchy and uncommonly single-minded, as her treatment of the late and hapless Uriah attests.

It is safe to assume that, from birth, Solomon was the beneficiary of David's special feeling for Bathsheba. It seems equally safe to assume that from the moment Solomon took his first step, uttered his first word, he was groomed by Bathsheba for the role of David's successor and that this devoted and confident woman never ceased bringing her influence to bear with the king to favour Solomon. She had apparently had some success, for we are told that David privately vowed to Bathsheba that Solomon would reign after him. But David evidently temporized over issuing a public decree to that effect.

The make-up of the pro-Solomonic coalition is a testament to Bathsheba's political acumen. She had gained the support of the High Priest Zadok as a counterweight to Abiathar. Quite amazingly, the prophet Nathan, who had been Bathsheba's most vehement detractor, declared for Solomon. This could, of course, say more for the inherent capacities Nathan discerned in Solomon than for the adroitness of his mother.

The decisive element in the complex equation was, in all likelihood, 'The Thirty', the informal but influential association of David's veteran officers, together with Ittai's loyal corps of mercenaries and their Hebrew commander, Benaiah. The officers, who probably constituted the balance of power within the army and militia, were at minimum in a position to neutralize the influence of Joab; at maximum, to counteract it. Benaiah and Ittai the Philistine were most probably prepared to back their choice with the sword, if necessary.

But David tarried. He was old and feeble. Apparently, as time went on, the Israelites, who believed (along with their neighbours) that the vigour and well-being of the community were directly related to the health of their king, sought out the most beautiful young woman in the land as the king's new paramour. Her name was Abishag. She came from Shunem, in the fertile Jezreel Valley. This exquisite maiden, in expectation of some day producing

*overleaf* 'The Anointing of Solomon', by Raphael

heirs for David's successor, now nursed David and even indulged him by sharing his bed at night. But the man who once ruled the bedchamber as lustily as he dominated the affairs of Israel was now only capable of modest pleasures. He must have displayed his keen appreciation by flattering glances and busy hands. Abishag responded with tenderness and compassion. She could wait.

David, too, waited. He grew weaker by the day, but each day passed without his affirming a successor. The people grew restive; the bureaucrats, concerned over the question of continuity; the plotters, more desperate and audacious. Now, Adonijah secured the critical support of the elders of Judah – at what price, we do not know. Surely, there was again risk of civil war unless the king spoke.

Was David hesitant, perhaps, because of his misplaced trust in the dead Amnon and Absalom? Did he possibly wish as a seasoned politician to encourage competition between Adonijah and Solomon, on the theory that the most able would triumph? Or, as in earlier times, was he simply indecisive on questions related to his personal affairs?

David continued to fail, and Abiathar and Joab deemed the situation critical – somewhat precipitately, as it turned out. They evidently lacked confidence in their ability to carry out a military coup, and so resorted to artifice, based in part on the hope of presenting their opponents and an addled old king with a *fait accompli*, in part on the legitimacy of Adonijah's claim and in part on desperation.

Adonijah summoned those of his party to a secret assembly at a traditional place of worship and sacrifice beside the spring called En-rogel at the southern spur of the City of David. There, Abiathar the priest hastily anointed Adonijah, who, as the self-proclaimed sovereign, sacrificed sheep, oxen and fatlings in the hope of securing Yahweh's blessings for his reign. Messengers were sent throughout the city proclaiming the fact of Adonijah's coronation and summoning the populace to a feast.

The prophet Nathan brought the word to Bathsheba. Surely more than the throne hung in the balance. Were Adonijah allowed to succeed, he would scarcely permit his rivals to survive. Nathan urged Bathsheba to rush to the king, tell him what had transpired and convince him of the need to acclaim Solomon at once. She hurried to the king's bedside: 'My lord the king, the eyes of all Israel are upon you, to tell them who shall sit upon the throne of my lord the king after him.' She reminded David that the alternative would be the death of Solomon and herself.

According to plan, Nathan entered the chamber and, repeating

Bathsheba's essential tale, asked in seeming innocence if David had indeed given his imprimatur to the crowning of Adonijah. The question was calculated to underline the cardinal issue to the ailing man – his authority had been assaulted, defied! There could now be no temporizing. Solomon would have to be crowned co-regent, and the event proclaimed to all Jerusalem in advance of the planned feast of Adonijah.

David beckoned Bathsheba to his bedside, and said: 'As the Lord lives, who has redeemed my soul out of every adversity, as I swore to you by the Lord, the God of Israel, saying, "Solomon your son shall reign after me, and he shall sit upon my throne in my stead"; even so will I do this day.' Bathsheba prostrated herself, saying simply: 'May my lord King David live forever!'

Now the king repeated his decision to the priest Zadok, to Nathan and Benaiah, and ordered that Solomon be anointed at once. David would have time later to instruct his son. And so it was that a very small, quite unregal procession made its way hastily down the steep path on the eastern flank of Jerusalem to the main water source of the city, the Gihon Spring, escorted by soldiers of the household guard – the young Solomon upon the ceremonial mule traditionally reserved for the king, flanked by Zadok, Nathan and Benaiah. Behind them were royal heralds with rams' horns, ready to proclaim the news to the city.

Thus, with a minimum of ceremony did Solomon, son of David, kneel before the aged priest Zadok, beside the water source which remains today the essential symbol of Jerusalem's continuity. 'There Zadok the priest took the horn of oil . . . and anointed Solomon.'

The blare of rams' horns, now in unison, now in sequence, echoed and re-echoed in the Kidron Valley, interspersed with the triumphant cry of the heralds. The chorus of rams' horns formed a rainbow of sound which arced between the summits of Zion and the Mount of Olives. In the city above, the people listened and then took up the heralds' cry: 'Long live King Solomon!'

The cry was heard, too, in the vale by the spring of En-rogel, where all was in readiness for the coronation feast of Adonijah, and where, now, the conspirators furtively departed to contemplate in fear whether Solomon would be a lamb or a lion.

And the sound of the rams' horns penetrated the thick stone walls of the chamber where the king lay slowly dying, and where Abishag heard David pray: 'Blessed be the Lord, the God of Israel, who has granted one of my offspring to sit on my throne this day, my own eyes seeing it.'

SALOMON　　　　BERSABEE

# 9 Solomon the King

A number of ambitious men had reason to fear young Solomon that day. The clique of Adonijah had gambled, and the outcome could not have turned out worse for them. They had actively conspired to deny the throne to the new sovereign and now had little reason to expect that Solomon and his supporters would let them live to plot again.

According to the ancient statutes, Yahweh had appointed his sanctuaries as places of asylum to which fugitives might flee from their enemies, placing themselves under the Lord's protection by seizing hold of the horns which projected from the corners of the altar-top. Adonijah himself sought sanctuary, believing that his brother's first order of business would be his summary execution.

Adonijah's concern proved unjustified. Solomon, Bathsheba and others of their party determined that, perilous though it might be to let their rivals go unpunished, it would be far more dangerous still to purge them. The political climate of Israel remained volatile. Beyond this, Solomon was secure as long as David lived, for the army would continue to enforce David's, will. Then too, Judah had aligned itself with the faction of Adonijah during the struggle over the succession. To deal other than gently with him at this sensitive stage could only risk stirring new secessionist tendencies in the south.

So Solomon found it expedient, for the moment, to follow the path of qualified restraint. He sent a message to Adonijah in sanctuary: 'If Adonijah prove to be a worthy man, not one of his hairs shall fall to the earth; but if wickedness is found in him, he shall die.'

A greatly relieved and penitent Adonijah abandoned the sanctuary and made for the palace, where he at once prostrated himself and, venting a torrent of apologies, affirmed his loyalty to the

Solomon and his mother, Bathsheba, shown in a detail of a 15th-century tapestry of the coronations of Saul, David and Solomon in the Cathedral of Sens

new monarch. Solomon appeared indifferent, unmoved: 'Go to your house,' he commanded. There Adonijah was escorted, and there he was detained.

As for David, he had removed himself from all of this. Liberated after four decades from the tyranny of responsibility and the distractions of statecraft, the ageing king came seriously, for the first time, to assess the content of his unique life, as well as the certainty that it was nearly at an end. He savoured a deep-seated sense of fulfilment. Not only had he successfully surmounted one last great challenge on the fields of Ephraim; he had indeed lived to see the establishment of the Davidic dynasty within a stable and prospering realm. Israel's centrifugal tendencies, of course, had only been neutralized, not eliminated. That problem would devolve upon Solomon.

Yet there was one essential task still to be completed by the old king towards the assured continuity of the Israelite union, towards his own sense of mortality and immortality and towards the institutionalization of the faith of Yahweh, under whose beneficence Israel now prospered. The Ark still remained within its portable tent – symbol of a once-nomadic people. But the desert tabernacle was no longer relevant to Israelite development or consciousness.

For years, David had laid aside portions of his spoils and tribute for one great work: a Temple to house the Ark and to serve as a focus for the devotion of Yahweh's people. The priesthood, Abiathar in particular, had opposed it. But Abiathar was now discredited by his support of Adonijah, and David's control of the levitical establishment had never been more absolute. He alone had the power to commit Israel to the construction of the Temple, even if he could not live to see its completion. The task could not be left to the new king, whose power and endurance still remained untested. Only David possessed the unquestioned stature to launch the project. So he devoted the last of his energies to the creation of the Temple.

It had been the practice of the Semitic peoples, stretching back into the misty corridors of prehistory, to propitiate their deities at so-called 'high places', usually rocky heights or prominences on which rough-hewn altars were erected. They often shared their sites with monumental standing stones which symbolized the divine entity or entities to whom the high place was dedicated. Some of these pre-Israelite high places were specifically intended for commemorative purposes, such as the worship of the spirits of the dead; others as places of sacrificial ceremonies and feasts, where animal offerings might be vowed to a god, slaughtered,

roasted and eaten, and where, often, such abominations as child
sacrifice, as well as male and female prostitution, were performed.

In addition to the stone altar, the high places were usually
equipped with a festal court, a cistern or reservoir for water supply
and, occasionally, seats carved into the rock. In the countryside
the high places might be located on hills or under trees, sites to
catch the cool west wind or offer celebrants shelter from the
burning oriental sun. Certain trees themselves, the *asherah*, were
often considered holy.

In the revolutionary Israelite usage, the high places were re-

Kiriath-jearim, the last of
the high places in which the
Ark was temporarily
located before its permanent
installation in Jerusalem

tained. But whereas the Semitic kin of the Hebrews viewed an inchoate world ruled and influenced by a pantheon of warring, striving, competing gods, the Israelite cosmology was formed upon the concept of the Single Spirit, Yahweh, the architect and ruler of all – on, above and below the earth. And rather than serving literally as a gesture of propitiation to satisfy the all-too-mortal appetites and cholers of the many demon-gods, the act of sacrifice in the Israelite cult came to possess symbolic content based upon the spiritual obligations of man in a material world.

Suppliants in Israel gathered before the altar to sue for divine intercession in their personal lives. They gathered on the sabbaths, the occasions of the new moon, and on annual religious occasions which were mainly based on the agricultural cycle. They sacrificed cattle, goats and sheep or the offerings of the field – grain, wine, oil, olives, figs. Often, as in the case of the high place atop the Mount of Olives, Israelites tended to expropriate for their own use sites considered holy by their predecessors.

A sacred tradition of great antiquity was certainly associated with the gaunt, pitted slab of rock which dominated the skyline immediately to the north of the City of David. Here Jebusites had trooped to honour the father of the Canaanite pantheon, the most holy El. And here the ageing David was now borne to claim formally the sacred site for Yahweh and his Temple. The land roundabout the rock was owned by a Jebusite farmer named Araunah, who used the western slope as a threshing floor because it trapped the breeze from the sea to winnow the bursting grain at harvest time. From the farmer David purchased the site for fifty *shekels* of silver. He commanded Zadok to erect and consecrate a new altar of unhewn stone to the God of the Israelites. And here he was often brought in his final days to make his offerings to Yahweh. His priests and the levitical musicians and singers were in attendance, and, we may also imagine, Solomon the co-regent beside him. So greatly was David now revered by his subjects that the mere act of his frequent devotions here was sufficient to insure the site's sanctification. The high place of Jerusalem came to rival the tabernacle itself as the focus of the Israelite faith.

And David charged Solomon, his counsellors and his high priests: 'Here shall be the house of the Lord God and here the altar of burnt offering for Israel.' He may well have had them seal their compliance in covenant form. The command would come to ennoble and immortalize David in the hearts and minds of people and nations far beyond the borders and the times of ancient Israel.

Yet David was indeed most mortal, fettered by frailties of personality and character, by the myths and superstitions of his age. His conceits were those shared by leaders both before and after him. He often inadvertently came to confuse his own will and wishes with those ostensibly emanating from his God. Though David might defer judgement in the interests of political expediency, he rarely forgot or forgave his enemies. Yet it would not be totally correct to call David a vindictive man. Like all of us, he was in large part shaped and conditioned by the beliefs of his times. His views of justice, for instance, must have been greatly influenced by his conception of the nature of life after death. For one thing, there was no Heaven or Hell in the cosmology of the Yahwists. There was only the underground of Sheol, the common realm of all the dead. The reward for goodness, as well as the punishment for wickedness, was dispensed on earth. The curse of blood–guilt was attached to the descendants of those upon whom the curse had originally been laid, so long as it remained unavenged. As the infirmity of decline hastened David to his couch for the last time, it seemed essential that he remove that curse from his posterity. Solomon was called to the king's bedside, and was there specifically charged by David to liquidate Shimei of the House of Saul, who had so cruelly tormented and cursed him on the long grim march to Mahanaim, and also to execute Joab, who had the blood of Absalom upon his hands. Not all the years of loyal service, not all the thankless tasks Joab had undertaken for his sovereign could eradicate in David's mind the monstrousness of Absalom's murder. 'Act therefore according to your wisdom,' the dying David told Solomon, 'but do not let his grey head go down to Sheol in peace.'

In or about the year 960 BC, some forty years after he had first been elevated to the leadership of Judah, David died and was buried in the great capital city he had claimed for Israel. We do not know exactly where or under what circumstances David was interred. But all Israel mourned for many days and wondered in its awe and fright if young Solomon was worthy to succeed his father – worthy to serve as a vessel of Yahweh's will.

Solomon had scrupulously observed the nature and uses of power. He had been thoroughly schooled under Bathsheba's supervision in the art of leadership. The new king needed no prompting now to realize that his major source of support was gone. It was now time to abandon his policy of restraint and move selectively but swiftly against his enemies. The army still held the balance of power, but the top command was now splintered into two factions: one loyal to Joab, the other to Benaiah. Solomon now had even less reason to wish Joab alive than had David. The

This tomb hewn out of rock is believed to be the burial place of King David. It is located in the area of Jerusalem known as the Ophel (David's city)

commander had cast his lot with the clique of Adonijah and would surely attempt a test of strength against Solomon again, if given the chance. Without advance warning, the king proclaimed Benaiah to be Joab's successor. Caught by surprise, the deposed commander sped to the tabernacle housing the Ark and grasped the horns of the altar, for he knew what his deposition meant. Benaiah had been ordered to arrest Joab and execute him. Solomon was understandably not anxious to see the sentence carried out within the sacred tent. Yet Joab seemed to have left them no other option. For he stubbornly refused to heed Benaiah's order to surrender, proclaiming, 'I will die here!'

It is more than likely that Solomon now sought guidance from the loyal High Priest Zadok, who would have pointed out that the solution to the dilemma lay within Israelite law. In spelling out the rights of sanctuary, the statutes carefully differentiated between accidental or unintentional homicide – manslaughter – and premeditated murder. The right of asylum was only reserved

for those who had killed without premeditation. 'But if a man willfully attacks another to kill him treacherously,' the pertinent provision reads, 'you shall take him from my altar, that he may die.'

Here was the sanction that Solomon sought. The assassin of Abner, of Amasa, of Absalom hardly qualified for the asylum of Yahweh's sanctuary. Benaiah carried out the king's sentence, in the former manner of Joab himself. He approached his erstwhile commander and slaughtered him at the altar.

Now Solomon moved swiftly to consolidate his power. Benaiah and a handpicked guard were sent to carry out sentence upon Adonijah, who was still restricted to his chambers. Abiathar, who had also backed Adonijah's claim to the throne, was summarily banished to his estate in Anathoth a few miles north of Jerusalem, leaving Zadok the sole legitimate High Priest. Only Shimei remained to be dealt with. Solomon apparently failed to see in this vindictive remnant of the House of Saul the grave

Abiathar was banished to his estate at Anathoth, north of Jerusalem, for his loyalty to Adonijah. The site of Anathoth today

threat of which his father had warned. In partial satisfaction of David's wishes, however, Shimei was commanded to take up residence in Jerusalem, to which he was quarantined under pain of death. Thus he might be kept under constant surveillance, lest he choose to conspire against Solomon and thereby satisfy his grievances against the House of David. For three years Shimei observed the edict. But then he suddenly slipped out of Jerusalem and travelled to Gath, a city of the once-powerful Philistines. Upon his return, Shimei was arrested. He claimed he had only gone to Gath in search of two escaped slaves who had fled there. But Solomon clearly suspected far more sinister motives and Shimei was executed.

With Adonijah and Joab dead, and Abiathar banished, the likely agents of any effective challenge to Solomon's authority had been eliminated. Thus, others who might have harboured similar intentions were put on notice of the high risk, as well as the fact of a ruler who, when threatened, had not a jot of meekness in him. Through the new commander Benaiah and Zadok the priest, the essential support of the two main props of the throne, the army and priesthood, was assured. What remained uncertain, however, in these first days was Solomon's ability to lead his people, as well as his grasp of a cohesive role for the monarch.

Clearly David had dominated his times. He had combined the charismatic qualities of the Judges of old with the political vision and realism of a successful warrior-politician. Unlike Saul, he refused to be intimidated in moments of stress, to succumb to the endemic disease of leadership – paranoia. No other person could have succeeded in wielding by sheer dint of will so volatile a people into a coherent nation. But David's dual natures – one spiritual, the other pragmatic and hard – were constantly at war. This duality seems the key to his inherent contradictions and inconsistencies.

David's heightened sense of mortality exaggerated both his weaknesses and his strengths. Thus his subjects could so easily alternate between adulation and anger, as he himself swung from generosity to vindictiveness, from dedication to self-indulgence. Thus, too, a man normally so decisive in command could, when caught in the grip of his conflicting natures, appear so totally indecisive.

A great leader combines the talents of a poet and a hunter. From their very interaction springs the power to command. But David's greatness also stemmed from his essential humanity. All else derived from this – his unique sense of the flow of history;

A bronze figurine from the Phoenician Temple of Obelisks in Byblos

of the relationship between man's aspirations and his fears; and between man, his society and his yearning for belief. But in the final analysis, greatness derives from one's ability to surmount the burden of his imperfections.

David was annealed by struggle. For Solomon, the challenges would be of a totally different order. They would lie not in battle, but in his ability to exploit the successes already achieved by his father. He inherited an empire whose borders, at this stage, were, for the most part, quiet. To the south, Egypt remained in decline, and the pharaohs of the Twenty-first Dynasty sought feebly to recapture their country's earlier greatness. To the east, Assyria struggled for ascendancy against the other powerful city-states of Mesopotamia. Only in the Syrian regions to the north did the Davidic empire face strenuous challenges from local Aramaean chieftains. For the most part, however, Israel dominated her regions and her times. The dominion of Solomon stretched from the littoral of the Mediterranean Sea, where Israel evidently maintained a loose hegemony over Philistia, to the Euphrates River; and from Beersheba on the border of Egypt to the lands beyond snow-crowned Mount Hermon in the north. The subject peoples of the Israelites included the once-mighty Philistines, Aramaeans, Ammonites, Moabites, and Edomites, upon whom Israel heavily depended for her pool of forced labour. From both the occupied areas and from Israel's allies, lavish tribute flowed to Jerusalem.

Whereas David had been pre-eminent in the field of battle, Solomon was to be tested as a statesman, as the organizer and administrator of a proliferating bureaucracy. David's intuitive brilliance and impetuosity gave way to the studiousness and dispassion of his son. David acted; Solomon planned. David was committed; Solomon, detached. David was blunt and direct; but circumstances afforded Solomon the leisure to master perhaps the most admired attribute of statecraft – subtlety. He could bargain, trade, manipulate, consider decisions not in terms of absolute choices but of a range of options.

If Solomon's principle preoccupation might be stated simply, it was likely to be this: how could he, the son of a giant, prove himself the son of David?

Whereas the flow of momentous events had catapulted David into the annals of history, Solomon was aware that the climate of relative peace and stability through which he guided Israel provided few natural opportunities in which a leader might distinguish himself. He would have to create those opportunities. An apocryphal tale, perhaps originally derived from the official

The Lord speaks to Solomon in the king's dream at Gibeon, from a medieval illuminated Latin manuscript

written record of his reign, the Book of the Acts of Solomon, underlines his awareness of the unique circumstances and opportunities he faced. In the tale, Solomon travels to a great high place at Gibeon in the north, where he offers an enormously impressive sacrifice to the Lord, underscoring the affluence of the House of David. While he sleeps at Gibeon, Solomon is asked by Yahweh in a dream what favours he might desire. And Solomon responds: 'Give thy servant an understanding mind to govern thy people, that I may discern between good and evil; for who is able to govern this thy great people?' And the Lord replies: 'Behold I give you a wise and discerning mind, so that none like you have been before you and none like you shall arise after you. I give you also what you have not asked, both riches and honour, so that no other king shall compare with you, all your days.'

To a wise statesman, the primary requirements of enduring peace are enduring alliances and a strong army. Early in his reign, Solomon accordingly turned his attentions to both the reorganization of the standing army founded by Saul, as well as the reserves, and to the conduct of external affairs. The first matter of business was to renew the Davidic alliance with King Hiram of Tyre. Hiram possessed a number of resources of which Solomon

would have need – expertise, raw materials, mercantile experience, unchallenged sea power. From Hiram's standpoint, the decline of the Philistines at the hands of Israel had given Tyre uncontested dominion over the Mediterranean Sea, and, in exchange, Solomon's armies guarded Phoenicia's southern flank. The Solomonic empire helped provide the stability on land which was essential to the continued expansion of Phoenicia as a maritime power. Then, too, Phoenician traders were highly dependent upon the goodwill of Israel for the use of essential overland commercial routes which ran north and south through Solomon's kingdom.

The city of Tyre itself was ideally sited to be the capital of the world's first undisputed sea power. The city sat upon a rocky isle just off the Lebanese coast, all but invulnerable to attack from the landward side. In the characteristic Phoenician manner, the people of Tyre had carved into solid rock a harbour and commercial basin in which their burgeoning fleet could ride at anchor, safely sheltered from the winds and waves. Tyre ruled a domain that stretched some 50 miles southwards to the Bay of Acre.

Hiram was clearly one of the shrewdest statesmen and enterprisers of his time. Over two millennia before Henry the Navi-

Although the Phoenicians had the most impressive fleet in the Near East, they were not the only people to take to the high seas. This Egyptian trading vessel is from a wall painting in the Tomb of Nakht, Egypt

gator, Hiram had moulded Tyre into perhaps the most cosmo-politan trading centre of its place and time, because he was the first in the world fully to appreciate both the commercial and military potential of seapower. He was also, in a quite modern sense, the world's first true colonialist. Phoenician trading colonies were established in such distant places as Spain, Sicily and Sardinia. In time, Phoenician fleets would even exploit the tin mines of Cornwall, navigating such vast distances long before the development of the compass. Without the Phoenicians, Western civilization could not have evolved as it did. In all likelihood, there would have been no 'Golden Age' of Pericles, for it was Phoenicia which carried the civilization of the Orient to an awakening Greece and brought the light of high culture to those rocky shores.

Hiram saw three likely advantages in renewing his association with the Israelite empire: the land-based might of the Solomonic army, a developing new market for Tyre's goods and raw material and, in Solomon's treasury, a source of untapped capital to help finance Hiram's ambitious designs, which called for continued maritime expansion to the south and west.

It was Hiram who took the diplomatic initiative. Hardly had a week passed following the death of David than he dispatched a delegation of high officials to Jerusalem to tender last respects to the memory of the late king and official courtesies, as well as lavish gifts, to the new one. The treaty of friendship between Phoenicia and Israel was quickly renewed, and both sides agreed in principle, pending negotiations to broaden the compact. The treaty of alliance would remain the cornerstone of Solomon's international and commercial policies. From the negotiating process ultimately emerged a far-reaching pact on trade, aid and mutual cooperation from which would stem Israel's first ocean-going fleet.

Solomon's relations with Egypt were far more delicate, far less open. History accords little distinction to the pharaonic dynasty which ruled from Thebes at this time. The rulers of the Twenty-first Dynasty were dominated by the priesthood of the cult of Amon, enfeebled by civil war and other internal disruptions and humiliated by the low state of national prestige in the Asian lands Egypt had once ruled. Two centuries earlier, in the twelfth century BC, under Rameses III of the previous dynasty, Egyptian hegemony had extended northwards to Syria, and eastwards across the fertile Jezreel Valley of Canaan to encompass the great fortress city of Beth-shean. The pharaoh who ruled in Solomon's time, Siamon, shared the dream of his line to restore

Egypt to the rank of a dominant power, to recreate the grandeur and high civilization of former times. Siamon evidently hoped to regain Palestine and Syria as the anchor of a new empire, along with the wealth which flowed along the trade routes bisecting them.

Siamon's one obstacle was Israel, whose strength in relation to the state of contemporary Egypt made her a dominant factor in the region. In slim hope of weakening the Davidic empire, Egypt had aided, abetted, and even given sanctuary to some of the exiled leaders of the conquered territories of Aram and Edom. At any rate, it seems likely that in a somewhat feeble bid to recapture the Palestine coast, Siamon mounted an ill-conceived expedition northwards. It was perhaps more in the nature of a large raiding party than an invasion force. The expedition managed to push its way through Philistia on the rim of Israel proper and topple the last remaining Canaanite enclave in the Shephelah, the fortress of Gezer.

But Siamon was in no position to retain his conquest and was in all likelihood advised that to try to do so would be to court war with Solomon and the almost certain annihilation of the invasion force. It seems likely that envoys from both sides met to work out a peaceful accommodation – the Egyptians in the hope of withdrawing their forces intact; the Israelites in the hope of eliminating the Egyptian wedge with a minimum of bloodshed, while extracting the maximum diplomatic price that could be negotiated to achieve stability on the southern flank.

Given the foolishness of Siamon's adventure, as well as the parlousness of his domestic situation, Solomon must surely have been able to exert tremendous bargaining leverage. In the end, Siamon gave one of his daughters to Solomon in marriage and presented nothing less than the city of Gezer itself to the House of David as the dowry. Other concessions by Siamon may have included the western shoreline of the Gulf of Aqaba, the finger of water leading to the Red Sea. This, as we shall see, would prove to be essential to the joint future schemes of Hiram and Solomon.

Thus a somewhat tenuous alliance with Egypt was sealed by marriage. The daughter of the pharaoh, Solomon's new bride, was treated with great deference and honour in Jerusalem. This is the only recorded instance in Egyptian history in which a monarch violated the cardinal injunction barring foreign marriages for royal daughters of the Nile. The marriage attests not only to the relative weakness of Egypt at this time, but to the stature of Israel and the House of David within the community of na-

*overleaf* Solomon entered into marriages with foreign women as a tool of his international diplomacy. A portrait of Egyptian princesses from the Tomb of Nakht, Egypt

tions. As time went on, Solomon increasingly resorted to foreign marriages as a tool of international diplomacy – a tactic which would ultimately contribute to a fundamental rupture between the monarch and the religious establishment of Israel.

Administratively, Solomon sought to strengthen the nation and buttress his own authority. In addition to reorganizing the military establishment, Solomon developed a system of forced labour among the conquered peoples, as well as a policy of labour drafts from among the peasantry of Israel. He imposed a geographic administrative structure of twelve provincial units upon the country, which was designed to absorb the remaining authority of the tribal régimes and carry forward to their ultimate development the centralization policies of David. All these moves, in fact, were logical extensions of programmes initiated by the late king.

If there was any popular discontent over the actions of Solomon at this stage, especially the imposition of royal corvées, it is hardly discernable. Israel had now crossed the threshold of what in relative terms might be seen as a golden age, whose roots can be traced to the latter years of David. Israel had attained a degree of political unity and material security unimagined in earlier ages. At Solomon's behest, the Phoenicians were to add a veneer of high civilization upon Israelite society. The material culture imported from Tyre would render the ruling establishment of Jerusalem, at least, quite unrecognizable from the nomadic hordes of Joshua which, three centuries earlier, had invaded Canaan and dug crude dwelling pits in the ruins of Canaanite Hazor; or the subsistence-level farmers and shepherds who coaxed a tenuous existence from the rocky slopes and scrabbly earth of Canaan in the days of Saul.

In the earlier stages of Israelite development, the priorities of sheer survival had left little time, energy or resources for raising the level of material culture. Pottery was strictly utilitarian, clumsily and hastily fashioned and fired. The houses were poorly built of ill-fitting stones, set one upon another with sparing use of mortar. Smaller pieces of rock or rounded pebbles were stuffed between them to seal off the chinks. There was no town-planning to speak of, though neighbouring societies had produced remarkable urban schemes. But in the Israelite settlement, passageways and houses mushroomed on a seemingly random, crazy-quilt basis. City walls were thin and weak. In many cases the Israelites had simply made patchwork repairs on dilapidated Canaanite walls, using and re-using them until they fell down or were knocked down.

But under David, and now Solomon, all this was changing, and in surprisingly dramatic fashion, because the economic basis of the state was changing. The farming class of Israel, which formed the larger part of the population, was in the midst of a technological revolution. Since the Stone Age, food producers had been farming their land with crude implements of flint, which were prone to chipping and readily lost their edge. Even though copper and bronze had come upon the scene around 4000 BC, the metal was too costly and brittle to permit widespread use; and the larger percentage of copper ore went to the production of weapons.

But the breaking of the Philistine monopoly on iron technology democratized the availability of the far more plentiful and serviceable metal – for plowpoints, sickles, pruning hooks, axes and mattocks. The productivity of the farmer increased, and with it his prosperity. Putting it in our own terms, there was a dramatic improvement in the standard of living of the average Israelite, which, in turn, produced taxable revenue permitting the maintenance of a stronger centralized bureaucracy and standing army. Security and stability, coupled with material progress, led to a general increase in the population.

Israel now began to witness the realization of the promise of milk and honey. Men were able to accrue surpluses, which came to represent disposable wealth, and the pace of commerce quickened in the land of Solomon. The principal wealth of Israel was the gift of nature: wheat and barley for bread and cakes; the oil of the olive for cooking, cleansing, medicinal purposes and, of course, as a source of light. The vineyards of Israel produced some of the finest wine of the Orient. The incredible number of words in ancient Hebrew used to differentiate among various types of wine and grapes attest to their importance in Israelite life. The wool of the sheep and the coarser goat's hair were used for clothing, as was flax, which was spun into linen cloth, and also cord.

Except during special holiday feasts, meat played virtually no part in the simple fare of the average Israelite. He lived largely upon the produce of his garden, a limited range of vegetables including cucumber, chick-peas, lentils and horse-beans, onions and leeks; fruits such as grapes, supplemented by figs, dates and pomegranates.

The grain was ground into flour in mortars of black basalt. Food was cooked in ceramic cooking pots and flattened trays, which were placed in round ovens made of alternating layers of clay and potsherds. The means of storing or preserving food were

An iron mattock (above) and a ploughshare from the 11th century BC, uncovered at Tell Jemmeh, just south of Gaza

limited. Grapes, of course, could be sun-baked into raisins. There were also dried figs and fig cakes. A fortunate find of wild honey provided the only probable confection.

If the biblical record is accurate, however, Solomon and the court dined far more sumptuously; and, with far greater intake of protein, they must have been far healthier and physically more robust than their subjects. The royal provender included vast quantities of oxen, cattle, sheep and game such as harts, gazelles, roebucks and various wildfowl.

One of the most dramatic artefacts of Israelite agriculture in the time of Solomon is a small limestone plaque – only 4 inches high and 2 inches long – dating from the first millennium BC. The plaque, found in the ruins of Gezer, contains eight lines of archaic Phoeniceo-Hebraic script, and it is evident that other inscriptions were once etched into the soft stone and then obliterated, so that the stone could be re-used – a sort of crude blackboard. The eight lines are thought to be a schoolboy's ditty, a mnemonic device by which to recall the Israelite agricultural cycle, as well as a drill for scribal students. The ditty runs:

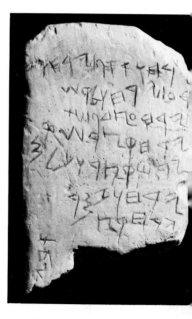

The 'Gezer Calendar', a limestone plaque that records the Israelite agricultural cycle in Phoeniceo-Hebraic script

> Two months of ingathering,
>   Two months [of] sowing,
>     Two months [of] late rains;
> Month [of] plucking [of] weeds,
>   Month [of] harvesting [of] barley,
>     Month [of] harvesting and measuring;
> Two months [of] harvesting produce;
>   Month [of collecting] summer fruit.

It is highly possible that if the Gezer stone does represent a rote drill in literacy for aspiring young students, it is also a testament to the flowering and democratization of the written tradition under Solomon – an early sampling of the same tradition which preserved, then magnified and transmitted the spiritual legacy of Israel to the world.

The biblical authors, viewing the golden time through which Solomon shepherded Israel, could well write: 'And Judah and Israel were as many as the sand by the sea; they ate and drank and were happy. Solomon . . . had peace on all sides round about him. And Judah and Israel dwelt in safety, from Dan even unto Beersheba, every man under his vine and under his fig tree . . .'

# 10 The House of Israel

In or about 957 BC, on the sacred mount north of the city which David had purchased from Araunah the Jebusite, Solomon undertook the building of a great temple dedicated to the presence of Yahweh. The great temple project, which took seven years, was part of an extensive royal complex which comprised the first monumental building enterprise in Israelite history. The aura of brilliance which surrounds the reign of Solomon derives in large part from the construction of the temple, the permanent focus of Jewish faith for all future ages.

Since the time of Moses, over three hundred years earlier, Israelite theology had been dominated by the symbolism of wandering. The portable tent or tabernacle of the Ark had sprung from the nomadic experience, the faith of the desert. To a nation which had now sunk its roots deeply into the soil of Canaan, the tent of animal hide was no longer relevant to Israelite experience, nor to Israelite aspirations. The people of Yahweh shed their tents for dwellings of stone and mortar. So, too, would the priesthood of Yahweh.

The creation of the Temple was also consistent politically with the Davidic development of a Hebrew national essence superseding the tribe, a central authority which would take precedence over more provincial loyalties. From Solomon's point of view, the atomizing tendencies which he strived to eliminate within the body politic were also reflected in the nature of Israelite worship. There was no central seat of religious observance. Men worshipped and sacrificed, as we have seen, at numerous high places – free, we may imagine, to follow varying usages of worship and ritual.

Yet the single essential person in the Israelite cult at this stage was the king. The priesthood derived its strength and authority

The seven-branched candelabrum as shown on a 2nd-century AD Jewish lead coffin. Its design strikingly resembles that of the candelabrum taken from the Temple by the Romans in AD 70 and shown on the Arch of Titus, which commemorates the conquest of Jerusalem

A woodcut of the Ark and the High Altar in the Temple, from a medieval German exegesis

from him. The faith was maintained and defended by him. But the Davidic king was also far more than the protector of the faith. He was the conduit of Yahweh's will. Through David, and now Solomon, the favour of God was projected into the life of His nation and His people. As God's agent, Solomon would also now be God's architect.

Then, too, as the Ark of the Covenant had symbolized the pact of Yahweh with the sons and daughters of Moses, the Temple would ratify David's choice of Jerusalem as the city of Yahweh and permanently affirm God's blessing and protection upon both the Davidic dynasty and its capital.

It is clear that the true father of the Temple was not Solomon but David. His plans for a House of God preceded by many years his purchase of the rocky elevation north of Jerusalem. David had faithfully dedicated substantial amounts of booty and tribute – gold, silver, precious stones, magnificent vessels and other treasures – to the house of worship he envisioned. Also, through commercial transactions, as well as war, he had begun amassing sizable amounts of raw materials – stores of iron, copper, bronze, timber and ivory – against the day when it might be propitious to undertake the project.

Spiritually, with its monotheistic view of the divine order, Israel was far in advance of the polytheistic people around her. But, as we have seen, the material culture of Israel lagged far behind. The arts of high civilization were still beyond her competence. David had sought in Hiram and the worldly Phoenicians both the skills and resources his people lacked. And so it was natural that Solomon, too, should turn to Phoenicia for aid in the great and complex Temple project.

Solomon petitioned the king of Tyre:

You know that David my father could not build a house for the name of the Lord his God because of the warfare with which his enemies surrounded him . . . But now the Lord my God has given me rest on every side; there is neither adversary nor misfortune. And so I purpose to build a house for the name of the Lord my God, as the Lord said to David my father, 'Your son, whom I will set upon your throne in your place, shall build the house for thy name.' Now therefore command that cedars of Lebanon be cut for me; and my servants will join your servants, and I will pay you for your servants such wages as you set; for you know that there is no one among us who knows how to hew timber like the Sidonians (1 Kings 5: 3–6).

The technical assistance pact struck between Hiram and Solomon was a complex one. It encompassed arrangements for vast amounts of material to supplement the stockpiles amassed by David, for skilled and unskilled labour and for terms of repayment by Solomon through barter.

The Temple would consume vast quantities of cedar, as well as fir and cypress, among the most coveted resources of the ancient world, which abounded in the forests of the heights of Phoenicia. It would be embellished by the gold of Africa, the ivory and sandalwood of India, the copper of Sardinia and Spain, all of which were transported to the Orient by the fleets of Tyre. In exchange, Solomon contracted to provide annually to Hiram some 220,000 bushels of wheat and 180,000 gallons of olive oil.

As Solomon's request for Phoenician aid made evident, the skills of Phoenicia were as essential as its wealth of raw materials. Phoenician artisans, masons, craftsmen, architects, engineers and metal workers would be needed to create the Temple, as well as to supervise the Israelite labour pool. In doing so, they were also to teach their skills to the Hebrews in the process. Solomon would cast Israel adrift from her spartan cultural inheritance once and for all, and bequeath to his nation a material splendour to match the majesty of her spiritual achievements.

Phoenicians would teach his workmen to draft and dress blocks of the sun-tinted limestone of Jerusalem, to shape silver and gold, to create magnificent inlays of rare metal and ivory, to cut precious stones, to cast monumental works in bronze, to dye and weave linen and wool fabric of the finest quality, to work the wood of Lebanon.

Solomon raised an Israelite labour force of some 180,000 men for his mammoth construction project. Of these, thirty thousand were sent to Lebanon in rotating groups of ten thousand each month to assist Phoenician foresters in the felling of the timber. The unfinished logs were borne by porters down to the Mediterranean Sea, where they were bound into rafts and floated south to an Israelite port. From there, teams of burden-bearers strained and shouldered the heavy cargo upwards toward the heights of Jerusalem.

The remaining levy of 150,000 worked under Israelite foremen and skilled Phoenician labour toiled in the environs of Jerusalem itself, largely quarrying out the huge blocks of local stone. Jerusalem stone was looked upon with favour by the masons of Hiram, for it was soft in the cutting and later hardened with continued exposure to the air.

In the planning of the Temple structure itself, Solomon also depended heavily upon the architects of Phoenicia. For the material form and symbolism of the House of Israel, we know that Solomon borrowed heavily from Syrian and Canaanite models. The un-

earthing of the remains of several roughly contemporaneous pagan temples, including a Canaanite shrine to the storm god Hadad at Hazor, and a chapel excavated at the site of ancient Hattina in Syria, reveal basic architectural parallels to the fundamental plan of the grandiose Solomonic structure in Jerusalem. But the borrowing by the Israelites was limited to material and artistic forms only. Both the functions and theological conceptions implicit in the Temple remained uniquely Israelite in origin.

The builders' first monumental task at the site of the sacred mount was to compensate for the irregularities of the surface. To accomplish this, they constructed a large platform, or dais, of huge stones finely drafted by Phoenician masons and deeply founded in trenches carved in the native rock. Upon this platform the Temple was erected. The rectangular building stood 45 feet high, 90 feet long, and was 30 feet wide. It fronted upon a large courtyard, and, in the manner of other Semitic temples, it faced east towards the rising sun.

Surrounding the Temple proper on the north, west and south and rising to half its height were so-called side-chambers three storeys high. Out of respect for the sanctity of the Temple itself, the support beams of the side-chambers rested upon offsets, rather than being imbedded in the main walls. Here in the side-chambers were stored the precious vessels and instruments used in the Temple ritual, most notably for the sacrifice; the priestly garments; the store vessels for the pure beaten olive oil which was burned in the holy lamps and for the rare spices from which the incense was compounded. In all likelihood, the Temple treasury was also located in these auxiliary chambers.

The façade, or eastern end of the Temple proper, was bounded by a flight of steps which ascended to the porch, or vestibule, called the *ulam*. Like the porches of many present-day churches, it extended the full width of the Temple. Springing from the *ulam* on either side of the entrance were two monumental free-standing columns of bronze. The columns were over $34\frac{1}{2}$ feet high and fully 18 feet in circumference. They represented one of the greatest creations of Tyre's most renowned foundryman, Hiram, a namesake of the king, who had been dispatched to Israel to supply all of the metalworking requirements of the Temple.

The huge bronze columns were called Jachin and Boaz, more than likely so named from the first words of inscriptions etched upon them. The capitals of the columns were elaborately ornamented with chain-work and intricate rows of lilies and pomegranates. Prototypes of such free-standing columns have been found in the

Cedars of Lebanon, one of the types of trees used to supply timber for the Temple

ruins of other Semitic temples, but their symbolic meaning remains obscure. Some scholars suggest they were huge cressets in which sacred fire or incense burned, perhaps symbolizing the pillars of fire and cloud which led Moses and the Israelites from Egypt. Others argue they were stylized representations of standing stones or the rays of the moon or sun. Still others point to the floral ornamentation as confirmation that their origin lay in the Canaanite religious symbol of the *asherah*, the tree of life. Whatever meaning they may have acquired in the Israelite usage, Jachin and Boaz represented a technical achievement of no small order, and must have deeply impressed, even awed, the Israelites who first beheld them.

As in the scheme of the Canaanite and Syrian shrine, the *ulam* was the first of three sections which comprised the Israelite Temple. Immediately within the entrance beyond the porch was the *hekhal*, or the nave. It was some 60 feet long and was dimly illuminated by the daylight which streamed through a series of windows immediately below the ceiling. The vast amount of cedar used for the beams and panelling, together with the cypress flooring, must have filled the *hekhal* with a rich and fragrant scent.

The decorative embellishments were tasteful, yet elegant. The woodwork of the great doors and soaring walls of the shrine was carved in the Phoenician motif with garlands of flowers, palm trees, gourds and the figures of sphinxes, all generously overlaid with gold and ivory.

At the far western end of the nave lay the innermost shrine, the 'most holy place,' called the *debir*. This Holy of Holies was a perfect windowless cube of 30 feet, lit only by oil lamps. Only the High Priest could gain admittance to this fearful space of awe and silence – the symbolic throne of the Invisible Presence – but once a year, on the solemn Day of Atonement. Here in flickering shadow stood the two sentinels, the cherubim – winged sphinxes with human heads and the bodies of lions carved from olive wood. The cherubim stood 15 feet high. Beneath their delicately carved outspread wings lay the most sacred Ark of desert acacia with its tablets of the Law. The cherubim were of ancient Egyptian derivation, most likely borrowed by Phoenician intermediaries and carried throughout the Near East. In the Israelite usage, it is thought the cherubim represented both the heavenly messengers of the Lord and the eternal guardians of both the Temple and its most sacred artefact, the Ark of the Covenant.

Chains of gold cordoned the *hekhal* from the *debir*. The cherubim were overlaid with gold, and gold was generously used on the walls and even the floors. We are left only with intimations of the

A 10th-century BC Samarian ivory carving of a winged sphinx, one of the motifs used in the decoration of the Holy of Holies

magnificence of this First Temple of the Israelites. For the rest we must depend upon our mind's eye and also imagine an ancient age which, unlike our own, was still possessed of the sense of wonder. Solomon clearly well knew how to invoke it.

Despite the consummate brilliance of the Temple's interior, however, it was the courtyard around which the daily rites of the Yahwists revolved. There stood a tremendous altar, perhaps 15 feet high and 30 feet square, on which centred the ritual of the burnt sacrifice. As the Israelites had borrowed the form of their Temple from the Canaanites and Syrians, they turned eastwards to the ancient Sumerian and Akkadian peoples of Mesopotamia for the altar's form. It was built in a series of three stages, each somewhat recessed from the one below. On the eastern side of the altar, a flight of steps ascended to the top stage, the hearth upon which the offerings were burned.

The symbolism of the altar design becomes apparent when one recalls the plan of the great temple-towers of Mesopotamia,

The design of this Phoenician gold colonette crowned with a floral motif, from the Tomb of King Chemou-Abi in Byblos, may have served as a model for Jachin and Boaz, the two huge columns which fronted the Temple

A horned altar excavated at Megiddo. Altars of this type long predated the construction of the Temple, as we know from the Minoan usage of the horned motif in the 18th-century BC palace of Knossos

of which the biblical 'Tower of Babel' was one example. These great monoliths, called *ziggurats*, were also built in a series of recessed stages, and, as with the much smaller Israelite representation, the *ziggurat* was crowned on each corner of its summit with horn-like projections. Like the great *ziggurats*, the Temple altar rested upon a foundation platform which had originally represented in Sumero-Akkadian usage the bosom of the earth. The original structure possessed the inherent designation of a cosmic mountain on top of which the gods of Mesopotamia were thought to reside. The residue of that belief was evidently carried over into the Israelite name for the uppermost stage of the Temple altar – *har-el* – the mountain of God.

Upon the altar of the Jerusalem Temple was performed the mysterious and complicated ritual of sacrifice to Yahweh – a ritual traceable to dimmest antiquity and man's primordial desire to propitiate the angry spirits of an angry world. Some pagan sects believed that their gods would be satisfied with nothing less than the offering of human life. To the Israelites, however, human

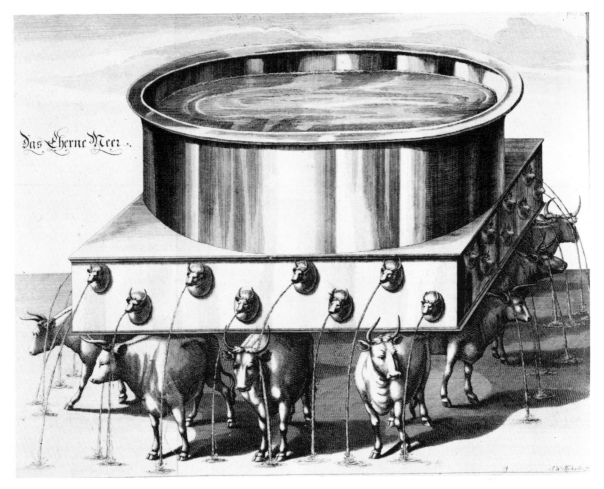

Das Eherne Meer.

An illustration of the bronze Sea on the backs of twelve oxen, from an 18th-century German Bible

sacrifice was an abomination of an order more loathsome than idols. In their observance, the offering came to signify expiation and denial, a symbolic obligation which reminded man that in the midst of his preoccupation with the material aspects of existence, he was a creature of the spirit as well as the flesh.

Before the great altar, Israelites gathered to pray at the twice-daily offering of a year-old lamb. Men brought their measure of barley to celebrate the beginning of the spring yield and the first fruits of the field and orchard to mark the rich harvest of summer. They gathered about the altar in a vast sea each Passover for their portion of the Paschal lamb, commemorating release from bondage in Egypt. The humble came to offer doves or pigeons in atonement or gratitude; the well-to-do, bulls 'without blemish', goats, rams or precious incense.

One other spectacular feature of the Temple courtyard bears mention. There stood an enormous basin of cast bronze some $7\frac{1}{2}$ feet high and about 15 feet in diameter called the bronze or molten Sea. Its brim was wrought 'like the brim of a cup, like the flower of a lily'. The Sea, a magnificent example of ancient metal technology, rested on the backs of twelve bronze oxen, which were arranged in groups of three, each group facing one of the cardinal points of the compass. The molten Sea is said to have held between 10,000 and 16,000 gallons of water. Its use was evidently related to the ablutions and lustrations of the Temple priests and perhaps the ritual cleansing of the implements of sacrifice. Symbolically, there seems a clear connection between the molten Sea and the mythic view of the ocean in Babylonia as the source of all life.

Hiram the metal worker was also charged with creating the bronze vessels and implements referred to above – cooking pots, censers, shovels, libation vases, flesh-hooks and, most central to the preparations of the sacrifice, a series of ten ornately decorated lavers and portable stands for the washing of the animals to be offered. It is estimated that the lavers could each hold 400 gallons of water. They rested in ponderous bases which may have stood as high as 8 feet and were each equipped with wheels. Hiram the craftsman painstakingly ornamented the surfaces and panels of the lavers and basins with representations of lions, oxen, cherubim and stylized palm trees.

In addition, the Temple was equipped with magnificent furnishings in gold – ten large candelabra, oil lamps, tongs, cups, snuffers, incense dishes, and firepans. Even the door sockets of the temple were of gold. Then, too, there was a table of gold for the Bread of the Presence – twelve very large loaves made of flour sifted elevenfold and placed fresh before Yahweh weekly.

The Temple, with its restrained magnificence, was part of a royal precinct which would come to include Solomon's lavish palace complex, a series of walled terraces clustered around the sacred shelf of rock immediately to the north of Jerusalem proper.

The Temple and its royal enclosure rose above the city as a crown. It wrought a spiritual transformation upon Israel. It established for all time the Presence of the Godhead in Jerusalem and imbued the nation of the Israelite people with a quality of immortality which has defied the accepted principles of history. Jerusalem too acquired this aura of the eternal. The city has literally remained the quest of the religious pilgrim to this day.

Israelites turned to pray towards the Temple as they worked in the fields, weaved their garments or journeyed on lonely roads to distant places. So embedded did this city and this Temple become in the Hebrew consciousness that long after the Temple and the kingdom lay in ruins, its people scattered throughout the globe, they oriented their synagogues in the direction of Jerusalem, focussing upon it their aspirations and their yearnings. Jerusalem

This representation of a bronze laver on wheels discovered in Larnaka, Cyprus, fits the biblical description of the ten lavers used in the Temple for animal sacrifices

has remained a folk magnet whose mystical power defies both explanation and expression.

And so, Solomon carried out the wishes of his father. We are told that the Solomonic Temple took seven years to build and that, most likely on the occasion of the autumn thanksgiving festival, Solomon convened a joyous assembly of Israel to dedicate the sanctuary. The leaders of the nation, the tribes, the levitical establishment and their subjects from every corner of the land thronged the capital and rejoiced as the Ark of the Covenant was borne on its poles by the priests from the ancient tabernacle in the City of David to its new permanent shrine within the depths of the *debir*, the Holy of Holies.

When the Ark, with its tablets of the commandments, were set within the Temple, Solomon is recorded as having then proclaimed:

> The Lord has set the sun in the heavens,
>   but has said that he would dwell in thick darkness.
> I have built thee an exalted house,
>   a place for thee to dwell in forever. (1 Kings 8:12–13)

This sarcophagus from the Roman period, a millennium after the golden age of Solomon, shows that the seven-branched candelabrum had become an established symbol in Jewish art

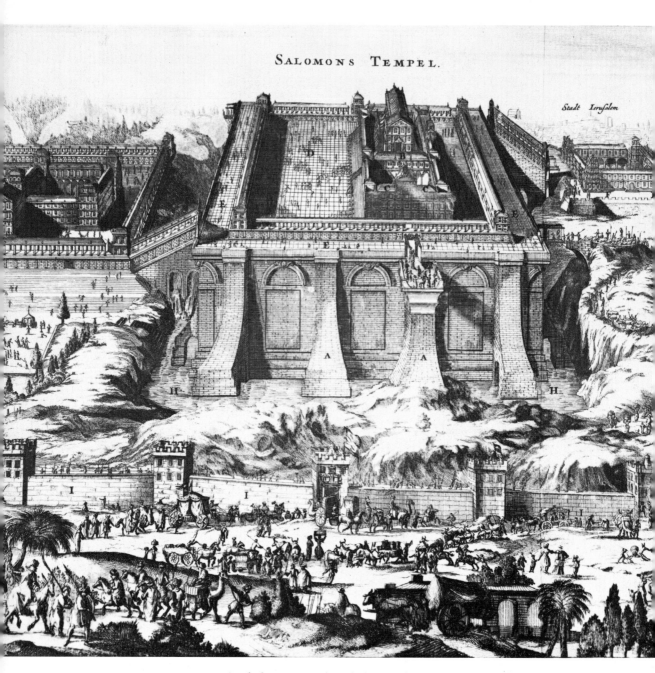

SALOMONS TEMPEL.

A 17th-century
engraving of Solomon's
Temple made from a
model constructed by a
German rabbi

And then it is related that Solomon spoke to the assembly in his capacity as the established guardian of the faith of Israel:

Blessed be the Lord, the God of Israel, who with his hand has fulfilled what he promised with his mouth to David my father, saying, 'Since the day that I brought my people Israel out of Egypt, I chose no city in all the tribes of Israel in which to build a house, that my name might be there; but I chose David to be over my people Israel.' Now it was in the heart of David my father to build a house for the name of the Lord, the God of Israel. But the Lord said to David my father, 'Whereas it was in your heart to build a house for my name, you did well that it was in your heart, nevertheless you shall not build the house, but your son who shall be born to you shall build the house for my name.' Now the Lord has fulfilled his promise which he made; for I have risen in the place of David my father, and sit on the throne of Israel, as the Lord promised, and I have built the house for the name of the Lord, the God of Israel. And there I have provided a place for the ark, in which is the covenant of the Lord which he made with our fathers, when he brought them out of the land of Egypt (1 Kings 8: 15–21).

Before the great altar, Solomon kneeled and raised his out-stretched hands to Heaven. He is recorded as having offered this prayer in the presence of the Assembly of Israel, a prayer which confirmed both the unique theological character of the Temple and the revolutionary faith it enshrined:

O Lord, God of Israel, there is no God like thee, in heaven above or on earth beneath, keeping covenant and showing steadfast love to thy servants who walk before thee with all their heart; who hast kept with thy servant David my father that thou didst declare to him; yea, thou didst speak with thy mouth, and with thy hand hast fulfilled it this day. Now therefore, O Lord, God of Israel, keep with thy servant David my father what thou hast promised him, saying, 'There shall never fail you a man before me to sit upon the throne of Israel, if only your sons take heed to their way, to walk before me as you have walked before me.' Now therefore, O God of Israel, let thy word be confirmed, which thou hast spoken to thy servant David my father (1 Kings 8:23–26).

Then Solomon turned to address the theological quandary which this new shrine of stone and gold posed for the once-portable faith of Israel. Heathen peoples round about, with their teeming pantheons of gods and goddesses, also boasted temples. And in these temples their deities were thought to physically reside. What of the Jerusalem Temple? Would it now be seen to contain the very essence of the One Deity, Yahweh? How, indeed, could the ruler of all that lay above, upon, and beneath the earth be imprisoned within the walls of a structure made by men? The very nature of Yahwism demanded an answer; and, thus, Solomon majestically provided it:

But will God indeed dwell on earth? Behold, heaven and the highest heaven cannot contain thee; how much less this house which I have built! Yet have regard to the prayer of thy servant, and to his supplication, O Lord my God, hearkening to the cry and to the prayer which thy servant prays before thee this day; that thy eyes may be open night and day toward this house, the place of which thou hast said, 'My name shall be there,' that thou mayest hearken to the prayer which thy servant offers toward this place. And hearken thou to the supplication of thy servant and thy people Israel, when they pray toward this place; yea, hear thou in heaven, thy dwelling place; and when thou hearest, forgive.

If a man sins against his neighbour and is made to take an oath, and comes and swears his oath before thine altar in this house, then hear thou in heaven, and act, and judge thy servants, condemning the guilty by bringing his conduct upon his own head, and vindicating the righteous by rewarding him according to his righteousness.

When thy people Israel are defeated before the enemy because they have sinned against thee, if they turn again to thee, and acknowledge thy name, and pray and make supplication to thee in this house; then hear thou in heaven, and forgive the sin of thy people Israel, and bring them again to the land which thou gavest to their fathers.

When heaven is shut up and there is no rain because they have sinned against thee, if they pray toward this place, and acknowledge thy name, and turn from their sin, when thou dost afflict them, then hear thou in heaven, and forgive the sins of thy servants, thy people Israel, when thou dost teach them the good way in which thy should walk; and grant rain upon thy land, which thou hast given to thy people as an inheritance.

If there is famine in the land, if there is pestilence or blight or mildew or locust or caterpillar; if their enemy besieges them in any of their cities; whatever plague, whatever sickness there is; whatever prayer, whatever supplication is made by any man or by all thy people Israel, each knowing the affliction of his own heart and stretching out his hands toward this house; then hear thou in heaven thy dwelling place, and forgive, and act, and render to each whose heart thou knowest, according to all his ways (for thou, thou only, knowest the hearts of all the children of men); that they may fear thee all the days that they live in the land which thou gavest to our fathers (I Kings 8:27–40).

In a most incredible oracle, Solomon is then reputed to have said:

Likewise, when a foreigner, who is not of thy people Israel, comes from a far country for thy name's sake (for they shall hear of thy great name, and thy mighty hand, and of thy outstretched arm), when he comes and prays toward this house, hear thou in heaven thy dwelling place, and do according to all for which the foreigner calls to thee; in order that all the peoples of the earth may know thy name and fear thee, as do thy people Israel, and that they may know that this house which I have built is called by thy name.

If thy people go out to battle against their enemy, by whatever way thou shalt send them, and they pray to the Lord toward the city which thou hast chosen and the house which I have built for thy name, then hear thou in heaven their prayer and their supplication, and maintain their cause.

If they sin against thee – for there is no man who does not sin – and thou art angry with them, and dost give them to an enemy, so that they are carried away captive to the land of the enemy, far off or near; yet if they lay it to heart in the land to which they have been carried captive, and repent, and make supplication to thee in the land of their captors, saying, 'We have sinned, and have acted perversely and wickedly'; if they repent with all their mind and with all their heart in the land of their enemies, who carried them captive, and pray to thee toward their land, which thou gavest to their fathers, the city which thou hast chosen, and the house which I have built for thy name; then hear thou in heaven thy dwelling place their prayer and their supplication, and maintain their cause and forgive thy people who have sinned against thee, and all their transgressions which they have committed against thee; and grant them compassion in the sight of those who carried them captive, that they may have compassion on them (for they are thy people, and thy heritage, which thou didst bring out of Egypt, from the midst of the iron furnace). Let thy eyes be open to the supplication of thy servant, and to the supplication of thy people Israel, giving ear to them from among all the people of the earth, to be thy heritage, as thou didst declare through Moses, thy servant, when thou didst bring our fathers out of Egypt, O Lord God (I Kings 8:41–53).

And finally, Solomon is said to have turned towards his immense congregation and offered this blessing in the newly sanctified courtyard of the Temple of God:

Blessed be the Lord who has given rest to his people Israel, according to all that he promised; not one word has failed of all his good promise, which he uttered by Moses his servant. The Lord our God be with us, as he was with our fathers; may he not leave us or forsake us; that he may incline our hearts to him, to walk in all his ways, and to keep his commandments, his statutes, and his ordinances, which he commanded our fathers. Let these words of mine wherewith I have made supplication before the Lord, be near to the Lord our God day and night, and may he maintain the cause of his servant, and the cause of his people Israel, as each day requires; that all the peoples of the earth may know that the Lord is God; there is no other. Let your heart therefore be wholly true to the Lord our God, walking in his statutes, and keeping his commandments, as at this day (I Kings 8:56–61).

In this manner the Temple of Israel was created. And with vast amounts of sacrifices and the prayers of thousands upon thousands was it sanctified. The lavish feast of thanksgiving lasted for fourteen full days. Thousands of sheep and oxen were offered upon the altar, as a peace offering, together with large portions of grain. Not since David had installed the Ark in Jerusalem had the people of Israel known such celebration or witnessed such spectacle.

This was the final act of the establishment of Israel upon its land, and the first act of the establishment of Yahweh as the master not alone of Israel, but of the universe.

# 11 The Hub of the Orient

Under Solomon, Israelite material culture advanced more in three decades than it had during the preceding two hundred years. We find in Solomonic strata the remains of monumental constructions, great cities with massive walls, the mushrooming of residential quarters with well-built clusters of the dwellings of the well-to-do, a quantum jump in the technical proficiency of the potter and his manufacturing processes. We find, too, the remains of artefacts representing goods made in far-off places, signs of vigorous international commerce and trade.

As seminal portions of the Old Testament attest, the scribes and priests of Israel achieved a quality of expression in style and form that became the classical model for the great Hebrew literary creation which followed. We owe to these sages the preservation in the Pentateuch of the early sagas of Israel's birth, as well as the magnificent chronicles in the Books of Samuel and Kings of the rise and reign of David, and many of the psalms. Like David himself, Solomon is credited with the authorship of verse; and his descendants, in tribute to the explosion of higher culture that occurred in his time, immortalize the wisdom of the king.

Scholars may well contest the accuracy of the portrait of Solomon as classical sage – a portrait recorded several hundred years later. But his political and economic perceptions, his grasp of power, were the epitome of brilliance. Solomon recognized that while his relatively tiny state possessed few unique resources or material advantages, its geographical position offered Israel the way to enormous wealth and influence. All land commerce moving between Egypt or Arabia and Mesopotamia and Asia Minor had to pass through the land bridge of greater Israel. The duties levied upon goods in transit could be enormous, and upon such income an oriental king could flourish.

A 10th-century Byzantine ivory coffret decorated with horses, chariots, camels and traders – scenes from the reign of King Solomon – from the Cathedral of Sens

219

Moreover, Solomon recognized that Israel could well profit as a commercial intermediary, as a middleman among oriental nations and city-states to the north and south. Solomon's conceptions, of course, rested squarely upon David's military achievements. Nonetheless, his vision, his will and his talents for negotiation and organization were the essential complement to David's prowess in war. Solomon maintained unchallenged control of the two major north–south trade arteries, the Way of the Sea along the Mediterranean coast and the King's Highway east of the Jordan River. By dominating the north-western Red Sea coast, the eastern Mediterranean Basin, and the corridor of Transjordan from Edom to Zobah, Solomon controlled the caravan commerce of the Orient.

A shrewd monarch would require little encouragement to exploit such an advantage – for instance, through the establishment of royal monopolies on lucrative and sought-after items of trade. And, we are told, Solomon did this very thing. Cilicia, in south-east Asia Minor, was renowned in the ancient world for its horses. We learn from the historian Herodotus that several centuries after Solomon the Cilicians presented to the Persian emperor Darius 360 magnificent white horses as a coronation gift, and that Cilician horses were used by royal Persian couriers.

Evidently their fame was well established even in the far earlier era of Solomon. He obtained a franchise for commerce in these horses and licensed Israelite traders as his personal agents. The merchants in turn transported the horses to Egypt. Israelite caravans to the Nile evidently also carried to Egyptian craftsmen supplies of hardwood logs from the forests of Syria and Phoenicia. From this wood were fashioned Egyptian chariots, which were internationally renowned. Solomon obtained a franchise on the sale of these chariots to the Syrian and Hittite kings. Solomon's singular prestige among his contemporaries, along with their envy, is thus readily appreciated. He had transformed a tiny buffer state trapped between the great powers of the Nile and Tigris-Euphrates rivers into a trading empire upon which they were dependent – the Egyptian cavalry and chariotry for their horses; the sovereigns of the north for their chariotry. Solomon's traders evidently established a fixed exchange rate of four Cilician horses for one Egyptian chariot. We may easily imagine that the coffers of the king, as well as the purses of his royal agents, were handsomely and regularly filled in the transaction.

Solomon and Sheba shown on a binding inlaid with gold for the Klosterneuburg Bible

The commercial importance of Solomonic Israel, as well as the strategic importance of the land routes which intersected it, may be better appreciated when one realizes that the rise of Israel's

united monarchy closely followed the dramatic expansion of international commerce. We find a hint of this development with mention in the Book of Judges of the Midianites and the Amalekites, with their 'camels . . . without number'. Late in the thirteenth century BC, perhaps about the time when Joshua was leading the Israelites into Canaan, the nomads of the Arabian peninsula were domesticating the camel. The commercial implications were enormous. Prior to the advent of the camel caravan, Semitic traders were hemmed in not only by the relative slowness and limited size and strength of their mules and donkeys, but by the supply of available water. The amount of water which could be carried was limited. Limited, too, therefore, was the distance which could be travelled between distant springs and water holes. The camel, with its enormous capacity for storing water, its endurance and its speed, represented a revolutionary breakthrough. Caravaneers could travel with confidence on a forced march of two or three days without water sources, driving their beasts speedily across the most barren of terrain. And it was this development which eventually led to one of the most celebrated diplomatic events of biblical times – the visit to Jerusalem by the Queen of Saba (the Sheba of the Old Testament).

Saba was one of the jewels of Arabia long before the advent of Islam. For the most part, the Arabian peninsula is one of the most forbidding pieces of geography on earth. It is a vast and inhospitable clot of sun-scorched steppes and deserts, impassable mountains and basaltic plateaus uncut by a single river. Though its coasts border upon five seas, they offered sailors few usable harbours in Solomon's time. Transportation and communication were all but nonexistent throughout most of the peninsula, and commerce consisted of the most primitive levels of barter among nomadic tribes.

The few natural blessings that the peninsula possessed were almost totally restricted to the south-west corner of Arabia, the region bounded by the Indian Ocean and the Red Sea. The first among these blessings was the gift of rainfall, which dramatically demarked the south-west from the vast and arid Empty Quarter and converted that corner of Arabia into a veritable Garden of Eden. Rich soil gave rise to luxuriant vegetation. Fertility, combined with a habitable climate, produced a relatively stable agricultural class among the Arabs of the region, and they prospered.

The symbol of their prosperity was the frankincense tree. South-western Arabia was the sole supplier to the ancient world of incense, the most coveted commodity of the trade of that time. In addition, the favoured land produced myrrh, spices and other

'The Encounter of Solomon and Sheba' by Paulo della Francesca

Ivory and other goods being loaded for their journey to Solomon's kingdom, detail of 'The Meeting of Solomon and Sheba' by Tintoretto

aromatic products for seasoning food and for burning in courtly and religious ceremonials. In addition, south-western Arabia was a hub of international commerce, affording access to the goods and products of remote India and China, as well as Ethiopia and Somaliland nearer at hand across the Red Sea.

The area became the centre of a thriving trade in the swords and textiles of India, the fine silks of China, the ostrich feathers, ivory and gold of East Africa, the pearls of the Persian Gulf. Centuries before the leavening breath of civilization touched the Hejaz, south-west Arabia was an enclave of high culture. Of the principle kingdoms in this quarter, the dominant land at the time was most probably Saba. It lay at the seaward heel of Arabia, where the Red Sea merges with the Arabian Sea.

Here the first Arabic alphabet was most probably in existence in Solomon's time. Art and architecture of impressive quality flourished. Saba was the junction where the trails from the frankincense lands met the principle commercial route which ran northwards along the Arabian coast. The Sabaeans planted thriving colonies along this highway. Sabaeans may have been the very 'Ishmaelite' traders spoken of in Genesis as 'coming from Gilead, with their camels bearing gum, balm and myrrh, on their way to carry it down to Egypt'.

Gold, frankincense and spices constituted the major exports of South Arabia to the oriental world, and it seems clear that Sabaean traders with their camels populated the overland routes. But they are also believed to have dominated the Red Sea trading lanes as well. In the tenth or ninth century BC, South Arabians established

themselves on both sides of the Red Sea, undoubtedly bringing the flame of civilization to Ethiopia. The Sabaeans may also have colonized legendary Ophir, of which more shall be said. At any rate, it seems safe to assume that, as a complement to Sabaean land commerce, the sailors of Saba had helped pioneer sea trade in that part of the Orient. And the queen of that land was in her own right a wealthy and powerful woman.

'Solomon and the Queen of Sheba' by Jan van Scorel (1495–1562)

Surely she would have heard of the fame of Solomon, as we are told, because her caravaneers were most likely forced to pay his officers heavy transit dues for the privilege of transporting their products along the trading highways which he controlled. Commercial interests, in fact, may well have constituted the major reason for the state visit of the queen and her retinue to Jerusalem.

They bore vast tribute to the king of Israel – 120 talents of gold, an amount equal to about a sixth of his reported yearly income; precious stones; and the spices of Saba. It would seem that King Solomon took great pains to impress his female visitor with the power and might of Israel. He honoured her with great feasts within the palace, to which he invited royal officials from throughout the kingdom. He brought her to witness spectacular rites of worship and sacrifice – the priests in their lavish robes, the levitical singers and dancers and musicians with their cymbals, tambourines, lyres and harps. And the king, in turn, presented the Queen of Saba with lavish gifts.

We are told that she was so moved that she said to the king: 'The report was true which I heard in my own land of your affairs and of your wisdom, but I did not believe the reports until I came and my own eyes had seen it; and, behold, the half was not told me; your wisdom and your prosperity surpass the report which I heard.'

Pageantry and spectacle notwithstanding, the queen's mission undoubtedly sprang from matters pertaining to Sabaean trade relations with Israel. It would not be unreasonable to speculate that the queen sought guarantees from Solomon of the right of continued transit upon the Way of the Sea and King's Highway by Sabaean caravaneers, or complained of exorbitant levies. Solomon, too, we may imagine, sought vital trading concessions from the queen which may well have given her pause. He wished to open the shipping lanes of the Red Sea to an Israelite merchant fleet that he was in the process of establishing – a fleet which would extend Israel's commercial links to the East. The sea commerce would clearly compete with the caravans. It would permit Israelite merchants to avoid the perils of nomadic tribes, which often robbed, held to ransom or exacted vast sums of protection money from traders on the Arabian land routes. Solomon may well have chosen to consult the Queen of Saba on his ambitious plans, for she controlled the important Red Sea ports to which he would have wanted access. He controlled the roads vital to Sabaean interests. The prosperity of the two nations were clearly entwined. 'Mutuality of interest' is the appropriate phrase in the diplomatic language of our own day.

Solomon's sea venture was perhaps the most exciting and commercially important dimension of his collaboration with King Hiram of Tyre. Ancient literature contains several other examples of such joint maritime enterprises. Israel had had little experience of the perilous art of seafaring. But, we may assume,

A drawing of a Phoenician merchant ship reconstructed by Björn Landström from a wall painting in the tomb at Drah Aboul Neggah, Egypt

Solomon had been deeply impressed by the experiences and sea-based prosperity of the northernmost Israelite tribes of Asher, Naphtali and Dan, Phoenicia's closest Israelite neighbours. The Song of Deborah speaks of Dan, which 'abides with the ships', indicating that Danites took service as sailors as early as the beginning of the eleventh century BC. The ships were most probably the vessels of the Phoenicians. Sea trade offered Solomon exciting new possibilities for extending his sources of profit and influence.

Since he controlled the territories from Zobah and Damascus south to Moab and Edom, Solomon dominated all the land routes stretching between the Red Sea and Palmyra. Now the Red Sea would be his gateway to the riches of Africa, Arabia, India and China. For Hiram, collaboration with Israel unlocked the portals to a quarter of the world denied to his fleets until now.

Phoenician shipwrights taught their Israelite counterparts how to construct ocean-going galleys. They must have been similar to those Hiram had launched to conduct trade with the Phoenician colonies throughout the Mediterranean Basin. Phoenician mariners taught their Israelite apprentices the secrets of the winds, of navigating by the stars, the signs of good and bad weather, the ways of avoiding reefs, shoals and shallows, of spotting the hazards of roadsteads and harbours and of riding out the storms.

The craft of the Phoenicians were more than likely biremes – crude vessels by later standards – driven by a single broad sail, with staggered sets of oars on two levels for additional power. Their achievements were awesome, considering that they sailed without charts and compass. Mostly they made their transits within sight of land. Navigators learned to pinpoint their locations by topographical landmarks such as mountains, by the types of birds and fish, the colour of the water and estimating the distance travelled (calculated possibly by timing the passage of a floating chip of wood from stem to stern). In addition, there is evidence that temples to the gods of the mariners were sited at significant locations, usually on the flanks or summits of great promontories, and thus easily visible far at sea. Atop the peak or headland, priests lit great beacons of burning pyres each night. By their light, master mariners might fix their positions or be forewarned of rocks or breakers. Millennia before Columbus, these adventurers also sailed beyond sight of land, dependent only upon dead reckoning and Polaris, the polar star. And now, in the age of Solomon, dusky men with their ancestral roots in the desert prayed to Yahweh for safe passage upon the face of the deep.

We are told that King Solomon and his Phoenician partners built their joint fleet at a port called Ezion-geber. In a biblical

Trading dhows loaded with merchandise photographed on the Nile

View of the Bay of
Eilat today. Legend
still has it that Ezion-geber
was near the modern city
of Eilat, but scholars are
becoming increasingly
convinced that it was
sited further south at
Jezirat Far'un

reference, the port is placed near Eilat on the shore of the Red Sea,
in the land of Edom. Modern Eilat lies at the southern edge of the
roasting Valley of the Arabah between the mountains of Transjordan and the badlands of the Negev. Here in our era, scientists,
scholars and laymen, lured by curiosity or by legends of Solomon's
incomparable wealth, by biblical tales of 'silver and gold, garments,
myrrh, spices, horses and mules, of riches beyond belief', have
centred their search for the lost Ezion-geber. Among the artefacts
turned up have been the remains of long nails and caulking pitch,
telltale signs of ancient shipbuilding activity.

For a time, archaeologists believed Ezion-geber to be an ancient
site 500 yards inland from the shoreline where the Arabah slopes
beneath the turquoise waters of the Gulf of Aqaba. The Arabs call
the site Tell el-Kheleifeh. Excavations at the tell – an Arabic word
meaning 'mound' – revealed the remains of a building which was
identified as a copper smelting plant and dated to Solomon's time.
The savants equated this place with the Solomonic port of Ezion-
geber, for reasons which accorded more with romantic fancy than
with fact. Later, the 'smelter' was found to be the ruins of a storehouse or granary. Nor, as cooler heads pointed out, was the installation to be considered a remnant of Ezion-geber. Among the points
of evidence cited was the fact that the tell lies some 1,500 feet from

the actual shoreline, and there is no evidence of a dramatic change in the waterline since 1000 BC.

Where, then, is the home port of Solomon's fleet? The riddle is still unsolved, but some have suggested a fascinating theory. About 10 miles south of Eilat lies one of the most dramatic and evocative sights in the Holy Land. Barely 350 metres off the rugged eastern coast of Sinai, a small island rises abruptly from the Gulf of Aqaba, rather in the fashion of a humpback whale. The Bedouin call the island Jezirat Far'un, the Island of the Pharaohs. To its undulating spine clings the ghostly ruins of a Saracen castle dating to the twelfth century AD, when the great Saladin struggled to protect Moslem shipping from the depredation of Crusader barons in search of booty.

An exploration of the island's perimeter reveals to trained observers the remains of casemate walls and fortified towers and a well-protected man-made harbour whose silted entrance once welcomed the waters of the channel. The ruins of ancient store buildings crown the encircling hillocks. Ask a knowledgeable mariner about Jezirat Far'un, and he will tell you it once constituted one of the only natural landings amid the reefs and rocky shore on either side of the tortuous coastline, one of the few anchorages offering protection from the angry southern winds.

This ostracon inscribed with the words 'Gold of Ophir belonging to Beth-horon, 30 shekels' appears to be an invoice

Pottery fragments found in the ruins of the island show it to have been in use long before the Crusaders – from the fourteenth to the eighth century BC, a span that encompasses the age of Solomon. The island's artificial harbour inspires scholarly comparisons with similar hand-carved Phoenician anchorages at Tyre, at Motia in Sicily and at Leptis Magna on the North African coast. Can it be here at Jezirat Far'un that the mariners of King Hiram helped establish the merchant navy of King Solomon? Future excavations may one day provide the answer.

We are told of the wealth which flowed through Ezion-geber northwards to Jerusalem. The Bible speaks with understated awe of long voyages by the Solomonic fleet to an exotic port or country called Ophir. Like Ezion-geber, Ophir is one of those legendary place-names drawn from the atlas to the land of the lost. We are told that such voyages lasted as long as three years. Scholars explain the biblical fact as meaning that perhaps the entire journey outward bound and home again spanned one whole year and portions of two others. Thus, the fleet could have set out into the Gulf of Aqaba for Ophir in November or December of one year and returned in the spring of the third year, to avoid the searing heat of the Arabah summer.

We learn that the fleet brought from Ophir vast quantities of gold and silver, that 'the king made silver as common in Jerusalem as stone, and he made cedar as plentiful as the sycamore of the Shephelah'. The fleet also carried back ivory, apes and peacocks (some translators prefer 'baboons' to 'peacocks'), precious stones and large amounts of a timber called almug, which was used in the construction of harps and lyres, as well as in the king's palace. Scholars variously suggest almug wood is North African thyina or Indian sandalwood. The solution depends upon where one wishes to site mysterious Ophir. Suggestions range from the African coast, perhaps Somaliland, Ethiopia or farther south, to the eastern Red Sea coast in South Arabia. Still others favour the Arabian shore of the Persian Gulf, an area believed to have produced gold in ancient times. And some insist Ophir was in India.

We are told that Solomon's vast wealth was used in part to provide lavish fixtures, fittings and decorations for the palace complex in Jerusalem, of which the Temple was a part. The latter required seven years to build, but the remainder of the royal establishment took nearly twice as long – thirteen years – to complete. It included the palace proper, most superficially described to us; the 'House of the Forest of Lebanon', the name doubtless inspired by its most distinctive feature, a foundation floor of four rows of cedar pillars; the long Hall of Pillars; and the Hall of the Throne, where Solomon pronounced judgement. Some suggest that the House of the Forest of Lebanon was used as an armoury, treasury, or storehouse for many of the precious objects, such as the following, belonging to the king:

Now the weight of gold that came to Solomon in one year was six hundred and sixty-six talents of gold, besides that which came from the traders and from the traffic of the merchants, and from all the kings of Arabia and from the governors of the land. King Solomon made two hundred large shields of beaten gold; six hundred shekels of gold went into each shield. And he made three hundred shields of beaten gold; three minas of gold went into each shield; and the king put them in the House of the Forest of Lebanon. The king also made a great ivory throne, and overlaid [perhaps 'inlaid'] it with the finest gold. The throne had six steps, and at the back of the throne was a calf's head, and on each side of the seat were arm rests and two lions standing beside the arm rests, while twelve lions stood there, one on each end of a step on the six steps. The like of it was never made in any kingdom. All King Solomon's drinking vessels were gold, and all the vessels of the House of the Forest of Lebanon were of pure gold; none were of silver, it was not considered as anything in the days of Solomon . . . Thus King Solomon excelled all the kings of the earth in riches and wisdom. And the whole earth sought the presence of Solomon to hear his wisdom, which God had put into his mind. Every one of them brought his present . . . so much year by year (1 Kings 10:14–21, 23–5).

It is considered likely that, in order to administer Solomon's commercial interests, colonies of Israelite officials and traders were established throughout the ancient world. We find a hint of this in a reference by the later Deuteronomist to the standards which should govern the conduct and actions of an Israelite king. In a possible reference to Solomon, the Deuteronomist writes that a king 'must not multiply horses for himself, or cause the people to return to Egypt in order to multiply horses . . .' There is every reason to suspect that certain singular offshoots of mainstream Judaism found in Abyssinia, Yemen and India in our own epoch are the remnants of commercial and diplomatic colonies founded in Solomon's golden age.

To sustain both his ambitious schemes and lavish life style, it was necessary that the king overhaul and further centralize the administration of Israel. Only in this way could Solomon assure himself of the revenue needed to maintain the massive royal establishment, the military establishment and the necessary man-power to carry out the monumental building projects he launched throughout the land.

As to the size of Solomon's court, we are told in the Bible:

A gothic carving of
Solomon's Throne of
Lions from the Cathedral
of Strasbourg

'Now King Solomon loved many foreign women: the daughter
of Pharaoh, and Moabite, Ammonite, Edomite, Sidonian, and
Hittite women . . . He had seven hundred wives, princesses, and
three hundred concubines . . .' Solomon's harem simultaneously

served the needs of both the flesh and of international relations.

There are also details on the court's rate of consumption: 'Solomon's provision for one day was thirty *kors* of fine flour, and sixty *kors* of meal, ten fat oxen, and twenty pasture-fed cattle, a hundred sheep, besides harts, gazelles, roebuck, and fatted fowl.'

In order to gain perspective on the daily food requirements of the court, one need only be told that one measure, or *kor*, is roughly equivalent to six bushels. Thus the court consumed some 540 bushels of flour and meal per day. Scholars' estimates place the population of the court at anywhere between five thousand and thirty thousand persons, obviously including dependants. In comparison with other royal budgets handed down to us, Solomon's requirements were not necessarily extravagant in and of themselves. But against the background of austere Israelite tradition and ingrained respect for individual rights, one can discern in the steps taken by Solomon the roots of popular grievances which would eventually re-open old political scars, fatally turn the kingdom in upon itself and precipitately ring down the curtain on the golden age.

Preserved in the First Book of Kings is a fascinating document from the records of Solomon's reign. In specifying the names and duties of his chief officials, the record advises us that 'Solomon had twelve officers over all Israel, who provided food for the king and his household; each man had to make provision for one month in the year.' In other words, the king divided greater Israel into twelve administrative districts. And upon the shoulders of their governing officials fell the burden of requisitioning from the people of each area the provisions necessary to feed the court, and perhaps the household guard as well, for a designated month in twelve. In this rudimentary system of taxation, each district officer undoubtedly reported to an official named Azariah, who is described as being 'over the officers'. Success for the twelve governors was evidently keyed to two simple but demanding requirements – the ability to meet the royal quota for meat, produce, wine, grain, oil and animal feed for the designated month; and the ability to collect it from the district population with a minimum of civil unrest. One dramatic indicator of the importance of these prefects is the fact that at least two of them became husbands to daughters of the king.

The number 'twelve', which is a key to the system, has political significance which goes far beyond the obvious requirements of the calendar. It coincides with the number of the original tribes of Israel. Yet in the case of at least six of the newly created administrative districts, the boundaries diverged from the far older

Among Solomon's wives was the daughter of the Egyptian pharaoh. The so-called Tomb of Pharoah's Daughter in the Valley of Kidron, Jerusalem

A 10th-century Latin manuscript illumination of Solomon dictating to his scribe (above) and passing judgement (below)

tribal boundaries. If revenue was the prime objective of Solomon's administrative reorganization, politics was surely a vital secondary consideration.

There was the need to incorporate into the political entity of mainstream Israel the extensive holdings won through conquest or annexation – portions of the Mediterranean coast, of large Canaanite tracts in the Valley of Jezreel and the occupied lands east of the Jordan. But some scholars point out that implicit in the administrative divisions there seems to be a deliberate effort to break up many of the tribal units in northern Israel, which were shortly to serve as the focus for the eventual collapse of the united monarchy. It is therefore not unreasonable to suggest that the reorganization also represented a calculated extension by Solomon of David's policy aimed at weakening and assimilating into a centralized political structure the older tribal order.

The demands and priorities of Solomonic grandeur manifest themselves in yet another way. We are told in the archival list of Solomon's officials of a man named Adoniram, the son of Abda, who was in charge of forced labour. An official with similar duties in the reign of David is named Adoram. This is either a copying error in the biblical transmission, and references to the same royal retainer through two reigns, or a coincidental case of two men with similar names. In any event it is clear that the policy of slavery and the forcible draft of manpower to fill the king's labour requirements was vastly expanded in Solomon's reign.

The Bible tells us that David had mobilized slave labour brigades composed of a number of vanquished peoples – such as the Ammonites, who were put to work making bricks. Impressing a defeated enemy in such a manner was an established practice in that time, and, indeed, long afterwards.

But the biblical record makes it clear that the need for labourers swelled after David. We were given some idea of the numbers involved in the Temple project – in which a total of 3,300 chief officers presided over a levy of forced labour 'out of all Israel' comprising 180,000 men. At another point in the biblical chronicle, we are advised that some 550 subordinates supervised the standing forced-labour pool under Adoniram. In one section of the First Book of Kings, the slave-labour pool of Solomon is described as being constituted solely from the remnants of the defeated peoples. The pertinent passage reads:

> All the people who were left of the Amorites, the Hittites, the Perizzites, the Hivites, and the Jebusites, who were not of the people of Israel – their descendants who were left after them in the land, whom the people of Israel were unable to destroy utterly – these Solomon made a forced levy

of slaves, and so they are to this day. But of the people of Israel Solomon made no slaves; they were the soldiers, they were his officials, his commanders, his captains, his chariot commanders, and his horsemen (1 Kings 9:20–2).

Many scholars insist that this passage represents a later addition to the biblical text and is propagandistic in nature. The aim, they believe, is to suggest that while slavery was openly accepted in Israel, Solomon in his wisdom never imposed slavery upon his own people, and that they, in their passionate embrace of freedom from the time of their early roots in Egyptian bondage, would never have submitted to any form of servitude in their own land. As an example of evidence to the contrary, these scholars cite the biblical statement that men were drafted 'out of all Israel' to work upon the Temple.

It can be argued that Solomon did impose some form of draft-labour system, or corvée, upon certain segments of the Israelite population and that resort to corvée may have been one of the royal excesses which decisively produced the division of the nation after Solomon and the eventual liquidation of the ancient Jewish state. Israelites who failed to pay their taxes, broke the law or agitated against the king may well have had to endure forced labour as their punishment.

In support of this contention, we are told of a certain royal official named Jeroboam, of the tribe of Ephraim, who apparently was in charge of certain labour detachments set to work on public improvements in Jerusalem. Solomon is portrayed as so highly pleased with the work of the young Jeroboam that he places him in charge of forced labour 'of the House of Joseph'. The reference would seem to suggest that Jeroboam served as a master over draft-labour battalions of Israelites.

Was it from their ranks, as well as those who sympathized with them, that Jeroboam – able, industrious, ambitious – recruited the force of dissidents that attempted to rise against Solomon? For we do know that Jeroboam did indeed mobilize a group of men with grievances against the king, that he may have organized an impressive chariot fleet in support and that his attempt to overthrow the king failed. Jeroboam fled to Egypt, where he found asylum, most likely under Pharaoh Sheshonk, the biblical Shishak. And there, apparently with Sheshonk's blessings, he continued to plot against Solomon, evidently drawing to him other political exiles from Israel.

Solomon continued to build, and Israel continued to prosper. But certain signs pointed to great danger. And Jeroboam bided his time.

# 12 Decline and Division

Solomon, as we have seen, was virtually without peer as a successful commercial *entrepreneur*. Nor did any Old Testament king ever equal his reputation as a builder. In addition to erecting the Temple and his lavish palace complex, Solomon, like David before him, repaired the Millo – the building terraces of Jerusalem. And he ordered the extensive reconstruction of the walls of the capital (according to present archaeological evidence, David appears to have been content merely to repair the old Jebusite walls). The Bible relates that Solomon also rebuilt or restored the great and ancient cities which Israel acquired from the Canaanites and launched other extensive construction projects throughout the land. The Bible tells us of 'all the store cities that Solomon had, and the cities for his chariots, and the cities for his horsemen, and whatever Solomon desired to build in Jerusalem, in Lebanon, and in all the land of his dominion'.

Tyrian architects, masons, carpenters and foremen, together with trained Canaanite artisans who had been absorbed into the national life of Israel, grafted their incomparable skills onto the face of Israel, and Israelite craftsmen voraciously absorbed everything they could. They learned to quarry stone, to hew, draft and dress the great building blocks so expertly that even without the use of bonding mortar it was impossible to insert the blade of the sharpest knife between them. They learned to incise decorative motifs into stone, to carve ivory, to inlay the wood of Ophir and Lebanon with gold and silver.

It would be incorrect to suggest that the prime objective of Solomonic architects was aesthetic reformation. Temple and palace aside, the aims were largely military and administrative. Solomon built feverishly as a means of defending his holdings. He built to hold the occupied territories and to seal off the invasion

The anointing and rule of King Solomon depicted in a fresco in the Basilica of St Paul, Rome

routes over which the great armies of pharaohs and kings had traditionally marched. And he built to maintain dominion over the commercial arteries which helped underwrite the lavish Solomonic budget.

For example, Solomon is believed to have contributed significantly to the construction of a series of Israelite forts along the desert trails of the Negev. These fortifications guarded Israel's southern frontier against incursions by Amalekite raiders from the south and east. Some scholars believe that Solomon also established small royal temples within the precincts of key fortress towns along the frontier, such as Arad, proclaiming the spiritual hegemony of Yahweh over his land.

But Solomon focussed his resources and efforts beyond Jerusalem upon the reconstruction and fortification of cities of great strategic importance throughout the kingdom. The Book First of Kings preserves a roster of these cities. It proclaims that Solomon was responsible for great public works at 'Hazor and Megiddo and Gezer and Lower Beth-horon and Baalath and Tamar in the wilderness, in the land of Judah. . .'

Though its precise location is forgotten, Tamar is placed conjecturally by some scholars at the site of an ancient spring the Arabs call Ain el-'Arus in the wilderness of the Arabah just a few miles below the southern rim of the Dead Sea. In the Book of Ezekiel, we are told that Tamar is located on the southern border of Israel, which is described as running 'from Tamar to the waters of Meribath-kadesh, thence along the Brook of Egypt to the Great Sea'. Thus we can be fairly certain that Tamar in Solomonic times was a vital anchor of Israel's southern border.

Baalath has been identified by some with a modern site called Qatra in the Plain of Philistia, where it would have dominated the southern flank of Judah, the Way of the Sea and a key mountain pass leading to Jerusalem. Lower Beth-horon was another important defence point on the western flank of Jerusalem. It was one of a number of strongholds overlooking the broad and fertile Valley of Ajalon, where Joshua is supposed to have stopped the sun in its orbit. The valley is one of the main approaches to Jerusalem from the coast, and Beth-horon is treated frequently in biblical references as a strategically important site.

Sadly, so little is left to us of the great public works of Solomon – not a single material trace of the original Temple (though we know its location today is marked by the Islamic religious shrine the Dome of the Rock). Nor does anything remain of the Jerusalem palace but perhaps a single proto-Ionic capital found in the rubble of the Holy City by an excavating team. Still standing are low

The sarcophagus of
King Hiram of Tyre

stone stumps of citadels where sentries of Solomon's army once gazed across the desert. For the most part, material remains of ancient Israel have been ground to dust, toppled into ruin or carted away by a seemingly endless array of conquerors.

Yet we are not totally bereft of material links to the Solomonic era. Those remnants of which we know have been dredged by archaeologists from the detritus of the many-layered necropolis over which modern Israel has been built. It was the Bible itself which led scholars with spades to the sites where the most monumental remains lay buried, the three walled cities, both great and old, of Solomonic Israel – Hazor, Megiddo, and Gezer. Today, they are tiers of frozen history, huge mounds composed of stratified ruins dating back many centuries before Israel as a nation, Israel as a people, came to exist.

Now these great tells, looming as high as 120 feet above the surrounding plains, are populated only by uncanny silence, thickets of weeds and thorns, darting lizards that burrow amid the rubble. But in 1900 BC, roughly about the time the patriarchal figure Abraham migrated to Canaan from Haran in northern Mesopotamia, Gezer was a bustling city enclosed by towering ramparts and peopled by Canaanites who owed their ultimate allegiance to the pharaoh of Egypt. Hazor had been a populated site some 1,400 years before Joshua's conquest. Roughly at the time Joshua prepared to capture it, Hazor, with a built-up area of more than 175 acres, was the largest city in Canaan and one of the most important cultural and commercial centres in the Fertile Crescent. In the twelfth century BC, during the period of the Judges, when Israelite peasants erected their crude stone dwellings and struggled to eke a subsistence living from the stony soil of the Canaanite uplands, the king of Megiddo dwelled in unsurpassed luxury and filled his treasure room in the basement of the extensive palace with magnificent carvings in ivory and fine objects of gold, faience and alabaster.

Long before Solomon, these three sites had been destined by geography to become magnets for mankind and to evolve into cities of unrivalled importance. The three cities were founded at or near the intersection of broad plains and valleys which had long served as invasion routes for conquering armies. All three were major provincial military, administrative and communications centres. All three guarded major trade arteries, and were thus important markets.

Gezer, the northernmost city of the fertile Shephelah, lay close to the Way of the Sea and the Valley of Ajalon, the route to Jerusalem from the coastal plain. The pharaoh who wished to control the littoral of the eastern Mediterranean had to control Gezer, for

The remains of stables from the Solomonic era at Megiddo

Ruins of the 'Solomonic corridor' at Megiddo looking out onto one of the trade routes that connected Syria with the coast

A proto-Ionic capital, one of the characteristic features of Solomonic architecture

it dominated a section of the Way of the Sea from Egypt.

Hazor, 10 miles to the north of the Sea of Galilee, was a vital stronghold which dominated the northern defences and commanded the roads from the coastal plain, Syria, and Mesopotamia.

The military and commercial importance of Megiddo is attested by its reputation as Armageddon of the New Testament, the legendary setting where the decisive battle was to be waged between the forces of Light and Darkness. The mound-city commanded the vital pass through the Carmel Range from the coast of Sharon to the Galilee, and, as such, earned its martial reputation from having been levelled and looted so often by marauding armies. The annals of Pharaoh Tuthmosis III, the vaunted conqueror of the fifteenth century BC, speak with pride of the successful campaign against Megiddo.

It is evident that he who controlled Gezer, Megiddo and Hazor was master of Israel.

As we have noted, it was military considerations which were paramount in the minds of those who allocated resources and manpower for public works. It is not surprising, therefore, that the monumental remains of the three biblical cities are military in character – namely, their walls and their gates – and that the design of both these elements followed a single master plan. The standardization of walls and gates points to the existence under Solomon of a strong centralized administrative structure. We seem to be dealing with the conceptions of a master architect who must have

worked in close collaboration with Benaiah, the commander of the army, and who enjoyed the confidence of the king. It seems equally certain that the plans which emerged must have been personally reviewed, perhaps altered and finally approved by but a single authority – King Solomon himself.

All three Solomonic cities were encircled by massive ramparts of the same singular construction – fortification walls of the casemate type. Casemate defences consist of a double wall, a stout outer bulwark and a thinner inner one. The space between the two walls was divided laterally by a series of crosswalls or partitions into a large number of cells or compartments. In times of peace, the cells were used to store military apparatus, to stable cavalry horses or to house soldiers within the actual outer defence perimeter without disturbing the tranquillity of the city within. Against the threatened assaults of enemy battering rams in time of siege, the cells were filled with rubble or earth, which absorbed and cushioned the impact of the blows. Even when the rams succeeded in breaching the outer wall, the enemy was forced to clear away the fill under the withering fire of the defenders from the broad parapet above, and additional reinforcements could be summoned to defend the breach while the second wall still remained to be assaulted. Casemate walls were quite clearly a technological response to the development of the battering ram. The Phoenicians and Israelites most probably borrowed the concept from its originators, the Hittites.

Not only are the design and detail of the fortification walls

This 9th-century BC Canaanite ivory carving uncovered at Megiddo shows a royal ceremonial identical at the three Solomonic cities, but their dimensions are comparable as well. The phenomenon of standardized construction is even more dramatically displayed in the Solomonic gates of Megiddo, Gezer and Hazor. As a rule, the main gate of a walled city was its most vulnerable element under siege. It had to be sufficiently narrow to constrict the passage of attackers in the event of a breach, yet wide enough to permit reasonable access and manoeuvring room for the defenders' horses and chariots. In times of peace, the gate complex also served as the administrative centre for the governor, and a sentry detail was always on duty monitoring the normal comings and goings of the population, collecting levies and accepting petitions to the governor from the populace. The sentries were also charged with the observation and interrogation of strangers.

A visitor to one of the three Solomonic cities ascended broad steps or a ramp sufficiently wide to be negotiated by chariots. He entered a guarded foregate whose roof was supported by two small flanking towers. Having satisfied the sentries at this checkpoint, he approached a broad cobbled plaza or square large enough to accomodate a chariot's turning radius. In this plaza much of the commercial life of the city revolved. After crossing it, our traveller turned sharply left and found himself before the imposing main gate, a large roofed structure some 25 feet deep, fronted by twin two-storey towers. The entranceway between them spanned over 14 feet in width. He entered an imposing gate chamber in which a pair of great wooden doors (probably covered with bronze plating) could be swung back on stone sockets and housed in great recesses. Then he passed the final security hurdle – the main entrance passage, flanked by three pairs of pilasters, which formed three cells of identical size on each side. Within each of the six recesses, or guard-rooms, soldiers were apparently stationed in time of siege, ready to spring from behind the stone piers with swords drawn to obstruct any of the enemy who had breached the main portal.

The gates of Solomon are unique. In all three cases, their measurements are nearly identical. Their magnificent masonry work is characteristic of techniques associated with Phoenician construction, recalling the biblical information that Solomon called upon King Hiram of Tyre for skilled craftsmen to assist in his great building enterprises. Technically, the gates represent the mark of Tyre; historically, they are the mark of King Solomon.

There is tentative evidence that their plan was the work of a man or men who also had a hand in the design of the First Temple. In the fortieth chapter of the Book of Ezekiel, the prophet of the Babylonian exile has 'visions of God' in which he is exalted by a dream of mystical longing and revisits the Temple in distant Jerusalem. Ezekiel describes the structure in minute detail. He approaches the eastern gate of the Temple enclosure: 'And there were three side rooms on either side of the east gate; the three were of the same size . . .'

Ezekiel also leaves us the measurements of the eastern gate in cubits, the ancient oriental unit. While the exact equivalent of the Israelite cubit is not known, scholars presume it equals or approximates the known value of the common cubit of the ancient Egyptians, 17.7 inches. If this value is applied to the dimensions bequeathed us in the Old Testament, the eastern gate of the Temple is roughly the same size as the Solomonic portals of Hazor, Megiddo and Gezer. It is far from inconceivable that the chief architect of the Temple and the three fortified cities were one and the same.

The excavators who dug into the southern quadrant of Megiddo have uncovered the remains of what was once an impressive fortified palace, its masonry drafted and dressed in the Phoenician manner. The palace is dated to the reign of Solomon. In the rubble were found two proto-Ionic capitals. Once they had crowned pilasters attached to the walls of a large room or corridor within the palace complex. The proto-Ionic design is derived from the stylized representation of a palm tree. Solomon's builders introduced it to royal Israelite construction, and it became a trademark of monumental buildings ascribed to later Israelite kings. Later borrowed from the Phoenicians by the Greeks, it evolved into the Ionic capital so familiar in classical Western architecture.

But the so-called southern palace is not the only Solomonic building of its kind at Megiddo. Excavators have also uncovered the remains of another palace in the northern sector of the mound. It was even more impressive than its counterpart. It was rectangular in plan and covered an area of some 6,500 square feet. Entering from the south, a visitor in Solomonic times found himself in a broad central courtyard bounded on three sides by spacious corridors and rooms. At one corner of the complex rose a single guard tower. The layout is typical of those found at Phoenician sites, where such buildings are believed to have served as formal or ceremonial palaces – residences in which a visiting king might dwell, conduct official business, hold audiences, as well as preside over great feasts for the notables and citizens.

Within the ruins of the Megiddo structure, archaeologists found a large amount of pottery, including hundreds of storage jars, dishes, jugs and juglets and cooking pots, all of composition and style which date them to the period of Solomon. These artefacts mark the area in which they were found as the palace kitchen.

Is it possible that Solomon himself, while on royal progress through Israel, visited this palace, walked through these hallways, tendered great banquets at which these dishes and vessels were used? The walls, gates and building remains resurrected from the tenth-century BC strata of Megiddo, Gezer and Hazor bring one closer to a sense of the times of Solomon than any other place, outside the pages of the Old Testament itself.

The Bible tells us that Solomon 'had dominion over all the region west of the Euphrates from Tiphsah to Gaza, over all the kings west of the Euphrates; and he had peace on all sides round about him. And Judah and Israel dwelt in safety, from Dan even unto Beersheba . . .'

The reign of Solomon is renowned for works of peace, not war. But a careful reading of the Bible leaves us in little doubt as to how the peace was maintained and the empire secured. We are told of 'all the store-cities that Solomon had, and the cities for his chariots, and the cities for his horsemen'. We are also informed that 'Solomon had forty thousand stalls of horses for his chariots, and twelve thousand horsemen', of the governors of the twelve administrative districts who brought 'barley also and straw for the horses and

This relief of charioteers from the Temple of Amon at Karnak, Egypt, depicts both the Egyptian chariots and the Cilician horses that made up Solomon's elaborate cavalry and chariot forces

swift steeds . . . to the place where it was required, each according to his charge [quota]'.

It is impossible to document the size of Solomon's military establishment. But it is not unreasonable to posit the existence of a sizable army, given the range of its missions within the empire – to maintain order within Israel proper and the occupied lands, to patrol the borders and to garrison the forts in the remote regions. There is evidence that the army was organized on the basis of a dual structure. There was first the professional standing army under the central command directly controlled by the king. But the standing army was supplemented by a national reserve force or militia composed of units recruited and based in the twelve districts.

It is believed that the twelve governors were required to maintain assigned force levels of militiamen and that each district militia was placed on active status, or at least on alert, on a rotating basis during an assigned month each year. The parallel structures afforded the king maximal flexibility in terms of his ability to respond to various levels of crisis. Each militia unit was available to maintain order in its immediate locality and could also be incorporated in whole or in part into the national command, the level of the call-up being determined by the scale of the emergency. In the meantime, at least one militia unit was always on stand-by alert, readily available to assist regular units in coping with sudden crisis until additional reserve units were mobilized.

For the first time in Israelite history, in the reign of Solomon elaborate chariot and cavalry forces were established, going far beyond the largely ceremonial squadron of chariotry which preceded the monarch in David's day. Inasmuch as Solomon was the supplier of the famed horses of Cilicia and the chariots of Egypt to surrounding nations, it seems reasonable that Israel itself acquired them in numbers sufficient to maintain at least parity with her neighbours. It is clear that the credibility of an army in the Solomonic era and long afterward depended in large part on the manoeuvrability afforded by the cavalry and the ability of the mobile chariot squadrons to deliver 'firepower' swiftly to that sector of a wide-ranging battle where and when it was most urgently needed.

Scholars of ancient warfare derive details of Solomon's cavalry and chariotry from contemporary records and artistic representations of neighbouring oriental civilizations. It is believed that an Israelite cavalryman controlled his horse with a bridle but rode bareback and without spurs. He was equipped with a helmet and round shield and was armed with a sword, bow, spear or javelin.

It has been calculated that Solomon possessed perhaps up to

1,400 chariots, each drawn by two horses and carrying a crew of two warriors – the driver and a companion armed with bow or spear, or sword for combat at closer range. Chariots served as the frontal cutting edge for a charge or mobile firing platforms on the flanks. Given the obvious advantages of rapidly wheeling charioteers and thundering cavalry against foot-soldiers, one can appreciate their intimidating psychological impact in the field of battle.

A fascinating duality permeates the biblical saga of Solomon, a duality which is perhaps not exceptional when we remind ourselves of the contradictions inherent in our own relationship with political leaders. It is a relationship which is highly egocentric in that it is coloured largely by self-interest. We hold our leaders in high regard when they play to our national vanity, when they enhance our self-respect, when they achieve great victories in our name and, through beneficial policies or simply good luck, when they preside over prosperous times. But political popularity is fickle. When misfortunes arise, we are as apt to curse and reject with scorn today the man we all but deified yesterday.

The fortunes of politics are ruled, also, by another operative set of seeming contradictions, one perhaps less easy for us to accept, given the conditioning of our own success-oriented epoch. It is in struggle and failure that we find the necessary preconditions for success; and, conversely, it is within the context of success that we find the seeds of decline.

Within the same pages that ennoble Solomonic grandeur and wisdom, that speak with pride of the *pax Solomonica*, of the material attainments of the reign, of the esteem in which the monarch is held through the land and the known world, we read also that 'the Lord was angry with Solomon'. We find bitter passages that recount the excesses of the Solomonic age. We are most surprised to note the tragically foreshortened life of the united monarchy, and we realize that the successes for which Solomon is acclaimed also produced strains and discontents so great that the Solomonic empire could not survive them.

The tragedy is more readily understood when we recall the inherent suspicion of kingship that was latent within the body politic of Israel, a memory of earlier times when, under the old tribal order, 'there was no king in Israel' and 'every man did what was right in his own eyes'. Some men were never prepared to accept a monarch. Others, exemplified by old Samuel, were reluctantly prepared to put up with a king, but only as a temporary expedient. Still others failed to reconcile the monarchy with Israel's Covenant, which seemed to them to exclude all but a divine ruler.

Added to these internal contradictions were the chauvinistic strains and stresses dividing north from south. We are forced to wonder, by the extent of the political trauma which seizes and shakes the kingdom to its foundations, whether the people of the north ever truly proferred their allegiance to the House of David on any but the most superficial level. As one source of continuing antagonism, one can easily imagine how the Judean establishment came to monopolize the organs of power and the positions of influence throughout the kingdom.

Perhaps this congeries of destabilizing and schismatic factors would have remained dormant but for Solomon's tendency to overextend himself and his nation. It is a malaise with which we are not entirely unfamiliar. A careful reader of the Old Testament appreciates in the emendations of post-Solomonic editors that Solomon's economic miracle was founded in part on a series of excesses, coupled with oppressive policies, which in time placed unsupportable burdens upon the material resources of a nation that had never been blessed with overabundance.

Solomon's ambitious building schemes were carried out by the enslavement of large numbers of non-Israelites and the imposition of a forced-labour draft upon his own people. The population of the captive territories must have stirred uneasily under the yoke, and

Solomon impressed into slavery many of the non-Israelite peoples that were under his rule. This relief of bound slaves is from the Temple of Abu Simbel, Egypt

Israelite resentment, too, can be easily envisioned. Jeroboam, in fact, had once tried to capitalize upon it. The concept of the corvée flew in the face of Israelite tradition and evoked grim memories of the unhappy experience of bondage which the early Israelites had borne from Egypt.

We have seen how Solomon's treaty with Hiram called for sizable shipments of grain and olive oil to Tyre. Given also the excessively high levies required to maintain the royal establishment, amounting in part to over 380,000 bushels of grain each year, the peasantry of Israel must have been forced to bear an all but impossible burden. Excessive taxation, coupled with the corvée, exacerbated popular unrest.

It is likely that, late in Solomon's reign, Israel's economy was gravely afflicted by an unending drain of resources and capital. The Bible tells us that the king tried to extricate himself from a chronic financial predicament by seeking from Hiram of Tyre 120 talents of gold. In exchange, Solomon ceded to Hiram 'twenty cities in the land of Galilee'. We are told that when the Phoenician king came to view his new possessions, he was greatly displeased and grumbled to Solomon: 'What kind of cities are these which you have given me, my brother?' As a result, the territory came to be known as Cabul, which, scholars suggest, may have meant either 'borderland' or 'good-for-nothing'. In the circumstances, both meanings seem apt. The abandonment of the Galilee holdings by Solomon could not have been a popular act. Whether the deal involved a straight capital transaction or represented an attempt to redress a deficit in the balance of trade with Tyre is not certain.

Solomon's harem was another source of irritation which zealots must surely have exploited and fanned. As has been noted, the king had taken a large number of foreign women as wives – most of them, we may assume, the close kin of dynasts and high officials from neighbouring kingdoms. Such marriages were a potent tool of diplomacy in Solomon's day. They affirmed the sealing of political and commercial covenants, ratified alliances, affirmed the termination of states of war.

As a diplomatic courtesy, temples were built on the Mount of Olives just beyond the walls of Jerusalem, in which the foreign ladies of the royal court and their personal attendants could continue to worship their native deities and observe the rituals of their cults. We are told: 'Solomon built a high place for Chemosh, the abomination of Moab, and for Molech, the abomination of the Ammonites, on the mountain east of Jerusalem. And so he did for all his foreign wives, who burned incense and sacrificed to their gods.'

As Solomon grew old, he began to adopt the religious practices of his foreign wives. 'Solomon's Idolatry' by the Dutch painter Gerbrand van den Eeckhout (1621–1674)

Devout Israelites perhaps grudgingly tolerated the foreign marriages. But the presence of a growing number of pagan temples must have served as a constant source of discontent. Irritation must surely have turned to rage when sophisticated Israelites themselves came voguishly to adopt various of these idolatries. It is alleged by later sources that not the least of these was Solomon himself. We are told in a later biblical passage: 'When Solomon was old, his wives turned away his heart after other gods; and his heart was not wholly true to the Lord his God, as was the heart of David his father. For Solomon went after Ashtoreth the goddess of the Sidonians, and after Milcom the abomination of the Ammonites . . .'

Towards the end of Solomon's long reign, mounting domestic difficulties were accompanied by political unrest in other parts of the empire. Egypt, still dreaming of the prospect of reclaiming the ancient pharaonic holdings in Asia, had given asylum and support to any enemy of the Davidic dynasty who might conceivably contribute to factionalism and unrest in the Israelite kingdom. We noted that Jeroboam had fled to Egypt after his abortive rising. He was following in the footsteps of Hadad the king of Edom, who had been given an annual stipend and lands by the pharaoh after his defeat at the hands of David. Hadad apparently never ceased hoping for a chance to reclaim Edom from the Israelite empire. In time, most likely with Egyptian assistance and support, Hadad returned to his land and wrested large portions of it from Solomon.

A second political exile in Egypt was Rezon son of Eliada. He returned to his land to lead the great city of Damascus in revolt against the Israelite masters. Damascus was the most important city of Syria, and David had selected it as the provincial capital of his northern holdings. Rezon thus founded the Aramaean state which in time would come to dominate Syria and mortally threaten later Israel.

The loss of both Damascus and Edom profoundly affected Solomon's trading monopolies and ended his effective domination of large portions of the King's Highway, as well as the caravan trails north of Palmyra. These reverses, coupled with a marked reduction in the payment of tribute, must have had a disastrous impact upon the country's economic life. The king's ability to maintain effective occupation forces in other territories must have been weakened, further accelerating the shrinking of the Solomonic empire. Perhaps Solomon tried to compensate for these losses to his treasury by imposing onerous new tax burdens on his people, further inflaming the public temper.

It must have been at this time of declining fortune that Solomon died. We know nothing of the circumstances, for we lack the intimate biographical details about him which abound in the biblical account of his father's life. The Bible states quite simply, and without emotion: 'Now the rest of the acts of Solomon, and all that he did, and his wisdom, are they not written in the book of the acts of Solomon? And the time that Solomon reigned in Jerusalem over all Israel was forty years. And Solomon slept with his fathers and was buried in the city of David his father; and Rehoboam his son reigned in his stead.'

Scholars believe that Solomon died about the year 928 BC. We know that Rehoboam's mother was a princess of Ammon named Naamah. We know little else of the origins of Solomon's successor, least of all of his knowledge of diplomacy and statecraft, the esteem in which he was held at large, his worthiness or ability to rule.

What history demanded of the House of David at this critical moment was another David. A new hero was required to prolong Israel's heroic age. Events tend to indicate that Rehoboam was not the man. Solomonic lavishness had drained an indigenously impoverished oriental state of goodwill and national purpose.

Detail of a fresco by Hans Holbein the Elder showing King Rehoboam (1530)

In their absence, the polarizing tendencies of the Israelite people again reasserted themselves, and Rehoboam was not the leader to overcome them. Under him the political structure so painstakingly constructed by his forebears fell apart. The great Kingdom of the Israelites split in twain, creating two second-rate powers fit only for the role of political pawns. The golden age had spanned but a brief eighty years.

While Rehoboam seems to have been accepted quite readily by Judah, as might be expected, it was necessary for him actively to seek the allegiance of the north. He journeyed to meet with representatives of the northern peoples at the traditional cultic centre of Shechem. Jeroboam, who had apparently found it possible to end his exile with Solomon's passing, evidently waited in the wings, offering the northerners a tempting political alternative, should Rehoboam be found unworthy.

He in fact proved both arrogant and stupid. The northern leaders presented a series of demands as the price of their acceptance of the Davidic succession, demands largely concerned with relief from the Solomonic excesses. Paramount among them was a call for the liberalization of the forced-labour system.

Rehoboam's counsellors urged him to yield, but he insisted on defending to a showdown what he considered the legitimate prerogatives of the Davidic house. The northerners rebelled; stoned to death Adoram, the royal overseer; forced Rehoboam to flee back to Jerusalem; and acclaimed Jeroboam their king. The House of David ruled Jerusalem and Judah only.

Civil war flared between Israel in the north and Judah in the

The remains of ancient Shechem, where Rehoboam was rejected by the northern tribes and Jeroboam was chosen as their king

south. In Egypt, a vigorous Libyan nobleman named Sheshonk, founder of the Twenty-second Dynasty, saw in the Israelite schism an opportunity to re-establish Egyptian authority in Asia. He launched a massive attack that amounted in the long run less to an invasion than a widespread raid in force. It is Sheshonk who is believed to have destroyed the northern palace at Megiddo. The pharaoh has conveniently left us a list incised on the Temple of Amon at Karnak of more than 150 places in Judah and Israel which he seized or devastated. The Bible tells us that Rehoboam was forced to ransom the safety of Jerusalem by turning over to the marauding pharaoh the treasures of both the palace and the Temple. In time, internal problems forced Sheshonk to abandon his campaign. But before withdrawing, he erected a triumphal stele at the fortress city of Megiddo, a fragment of which has been recovered. That stele was in fact the tombstone of Solomonic Israel.

In less than a century, the energies and ambitions of two men had converted a collection of disparate tribes, united only by a common religious covenant, into a great nation. But it required perhaps no more than five years for their political and material achievements to have been all but destroyed. The empire of Solomon and David was no more.

Yet David's Jerusalem and Solomon's Temple, together with the nucleus of biblical writings which was created in their era, have survived political disasters, statelessness, persecution and war. The Davidic tradition has come to represent an enduring triumph over the never-ending follies and misfortunes of man.

The Temple of Amon at Karnak, Egypt, where King Sheshonk left a list of the places he raided in Judah and Israel

# Epilogue

After David had brought the Holy Ark to Jerusalem, the prophet Nathan had a vision and related to the king Yahweh's promise: 'Your house and your kingdom shall be made sure for ever before me; your throne shall be established forever.' Now the kingdom of David was broken, but it was not shattered. The House of David retained the throne of Judah and would continue to rule for close to three and a half centuries. Eighteen generations of David's progeny would follow, through civil strife and the rise of great and land-hungry empires on all sides, until the dynasty, its capital and the Temple – Israel's crowning shrine to Yahweh – were destroyed and Judah scattered into exile. The perpetuity of that thread of rule is the coda to the story of the House of David.

The creation of a political boundary between north and south did not automatically divide the People of Israel into two separate nations. The lure of Jerusalem as a centre for worship and the celebration of national festivals was too deeply embedded in the popular consciousness to be wiped out by political proclamation alone. Jeroboam was not insensitive to this subtle threat from the south. To distract the attention of his subjects from Jerusalem, he created new cultic centres in Dan and Bethel, at the northern and southern ends of his kingdom, and provided golden calves as the physical setting over which the spirit of Yahweh would hover.

The House of David was enraged by such presumption, as if any high place – regardless of the trappings invented to enhance its status – could compete with the Temple. Yet more than religious fervour drove Rehoboam and his descendants. The right to rule in Judah alone did not satisfy their sense of vision. They were not prepared to accept the rebellion of the northern tribes as a *fait accompli* for all time. And they would not renounce the claim consolidated by two generations of glorious rule.

The might of Assyria, one of the empires that rose to power after the split of David and Solomon's kingdom, is shown in this relief of the siege of a city and the taking of captives, from the palace of Ashurbanipal, Nineveh

257

After Sheshonk's invasion of Judah and Israel, Rehoboam, smarting from this lesson in his own vulnerability, embarked on a programme of fortifying the cities of Judah. Curiously enough, however, he did not fortify the northern frontier with Israel, as if such an act would signify his *de facto* recognition that his hegemony ended at the border with Ephraim.

The weakness of the northern kingdom in the wake of Sheshonk's invasion prompted Abijah, Rehoboam's son, to go one step further towards unifying the kingdom again. When he attacked Israel, his battle-cry was a clear assertion of his dynastic claim to Jeroboam's territory:

Hear me, O Jeroboam and all Israel! Ought you to know that the Lord God of Israel gave the kingship over Israel for ever to David and his sons by a covenant of salt? Yet Jeroboam the son of Nebat, a servant of Solomon the son of David, rose up and rebelled against his lord; and certain worthless scoundrels gathered about him and defied Rehoboam the son of Solomon, when Rehoboam was young and irresolute and could not withstand them. And now you think to withstand the kingdom of the Lord on the hand of the sons of David, because you are a great multitude and have with you the golden calves which Jeroboam made you for gods. Behold, God is with us at our head, and his priests with their battle trumpets to sound the call to battle against you. O sons of Israel, do not fight against the Lord, the God of your fathers; for you cannot succeed (II Chronicles, 13: 4–8, 12).

And indeed, Abijah's forces dealt a crushing blow to the defenders of Israel and captured the cultic centre of Bethel. But the victory was short-lived.

A generation later, during the reign of Abijah's son Asa, Judah found itself threatened from two directions. First came an attack from the south by Zerah the Cushite, yet another warning of Egypt's strength and ill-will. Asa's defeat of the Egyptian invaders was an inspiring one; but it could not make up for his humiliation when, in the thirty-sixth year of his reign, the forces of Baasha of Israel revenged Abijah's attack and conquest of Bethel and penetrated the southern kingdom almost as far as the walls of Jerusalem.

Baasha's might was backed by the strength of his ally to the north, King Ben-hadad of Aram. When Asa saw his own forces falling back in the face of the army of Israel, he entered the arena of power politics – a game of survival that would be played for loss and gain throughout the life of the divided kingdom. Using the Temple treasure as his source of funding, he bought off Ben-hadad, and the Aramaean monarch did an about-face and astounded his former ally by invading the cities of northern Israel. At the time of the surprise attack, Baasha was off near the border with Judah, fortifying the city of Ramah in order to block traffic going from Israel to the Temple. Now the project had lost all priority, and he rushed northwards to defend his exposed northern territory. With his path to Israel open, Asa pushed north into Ephraim, destroyed the fortifications of Ramah and used the very same stones to build his own line of defence on the border with the northern kingdom. The erstwhile pretender to the throne of a united kingdom under the rule of the Davidic line sealed the border and thereby renounced his claim on the north.

That done, the years of war between the two kingdoms came to an end. And while the dream of reunification would never be realized by a king of Judah, alliances would replace bloodshed; a new form of unity would develop. Surrounded as they were by more powerful and increasingly belligerent states, Judah and Israel would, for a while, function as a unit in the power struggles of the area, despite their continued political division.

The modern site of Ramah, where Asa sealed the border between Judah and Israel

Under the rule of King Ahab, the northern kingdom gained considerable strength, and Judah benefitted from the stability which strength often provides. Jehoshaphat, who succeeded Asa in 870 BC, exploited the relative quiet to embark upon a wide-ranging programme of internal reorganization. In addition to continuing the fortification of Judah against potential danger from without, he turned his attention to restructuring his administration, building up an educational network, reorganizing judicial institutions and placing both the standing army and the reserves on a firmer footing. Judah's strength became sufficient, in and of itself, to avert an attack by any of the major powers, and Jehoshaphat was even able to extract tribute from his lesser neighbours – the Philistines on the coast and the Arab tribes to the south. He also revived trade through the Red Sea port of Ezion-geber – although his own fleet sank before it could get very far – thereby increasing the kingdom's wealth.

In the new spirit of mended relations between the two kingdoms, Jehoshaphat joined forces with King Ahab to push Aram out of Ramoth-gilead, which had formerly been the territory of the northern kingdom. He also entered into a blood alliance with Ahab by marrying his son Jehoram to Ahab's daughter Athaliah. Whether his covert intention was to gain by inheritance what warfare had failed to achieve we cannot know. But if such was his notion, it backfired in a cruel and blood-thirsty fashion and led to the only break in the continuity of the Davidic line ever to afflict the kingdom.

When Jehoshaphat died in 848 BC and Jehoram assumed the

An ivory carving from Hazor, made during the time of King Jehoram's reign, shows a pagan in the posture of worship

throne, the era of tranquillity and progress was already in the process of deterioration. The vassal state of Edom rebelled and broke away from Judah, thus closing off access to the port of Ezion-geber and causing a decline in the kingdom's prosperity. But this was only one reason for the internal dissent that plagued Jehoram's rule. More powerful still was opposition to the pagan practices introduced by his wife Athaliah, the princess of the northern kingdom. Above all, however, the extraordinary up-heavals and tragedies within the royal house itself were sufficient reason for general consternation. When Jehoram ascended to the throne, his first act was to murder all his brothers, thus securing his position against any possible rival within the dynasty. Later in his reign, while the king was absent from Judah – probably on a campaign in support of the kingdom of Israel – an alliance of

Philistines and nomadic Arabs from the Egyptian desert attacked Jerusalem and wiped out the entire royal household – with the exception of Queen Athaliah and their youngest son, Ahaziah.

When Jehoram died, evidently to no one's regret, Ahaziah continued to act under his mother's influence in religious affairs. But he hardly had time to do much damage. In the first and only year of his reign, he joined his uncle King Jehoram of Israel in yet another ill-fated attack on the Aramaeans at Ramoth-gilead. When Jehoram was wounded and retired to his palace at Jezreel to convalesce, Ahaziah followed to pay a sick-call. But his timing was fatal, for he was caught at Jehoram's side when a rebellion broke out against the king. And Ahaziah, himself a descendant of the House of Ahab, was included in the massacre against the progeny of the Israelite throne.

Now it was Athaliah's turn to act, and she was quick to do so. As soon as news of Ahaziah's death reached Jerusalem, she compounded the bloody deeds played out in the northern kingdom by murdering all of Ahaziah's sons – or so she thought – and assuming the throne herself. The shock in Judah was paralysing, but there were two people who knew that in her haste Athaliah was not quite thorough enough. She had missed Ahaziah's youngest son, Joash, who was spirited away and hidden by his aunt.

The secret of Joash's survival was firmly kept by his uncle Jehoiada, the High Priest, while he waited for the opportunity to restore the House of David to the throne. Although the ruler of Judah was not only an interloper but a confirmed heathen, Jehoiada waited seven years for the propitious moment and secured the loyalty of the palace guard. After carefully briefing the soldiers and the priesthood on the exact procedures of the anointing ceremony, Jehoiada crowned Joash in the Temple. Athaliah was drawn out of her palace by the din of trumpets and celebration, but by the time she realized what had happened, her cries of 'Treason!' were to no avail. She was trapped by the king's captains, dragged from the Temple premises and slain at the Horses' Gate to the royal palace. The House of David prevailed.

The seven-year-old Joash was groomed by the priesthood until he reached majority, and the kingdom was cleansed of pagan influences – all that remained of Athaliah. A new covenant with Yahweh was proclaimed, and Joash decreed that monies should be collected for the repair of the Temple. Twenty-three years into his reign, however, the king discovered that his implicit trust in the priesthood had been betrayed: the funds collected for repair of the holy shrine were not being used for that purpose at all. It is not surprising, therefore, that with the death of the High Priest and

The area of Beth-shemesh, the site of Amaziah's defeat by Joash

royal relative Jehoiada, the influence of the priesthood declined rapidly, and the king transferred his favour to his civil servants. Later, when Jerusalem was threatened by Aramaean forces, the king depleted the Temple treasury to ransom the city, thus crushing the power of the priesthood completely. But even the civil hierarchy was astounded by his action, taking it as a sign of Joash's impotence. In the fortieth year of his reign, this sole survivor of a brutal massacre was cut down by a conspiracy of his servants and the priesthood.

Internal strife and instability pursued his son and successor, Amaziah. But the new king himself was his own worst enemy. Amaziah campaigned successfully in Edom, but then his overconfidence led him to a strange turnabout. Despite three generations of alliance between Judah and Israel, Amaziah suddenly challenged Joash, the king of Israel, to a contest of military prowess. Joash was careful to warn Amaziah of the consequences of his bravado, but the king of Judah would not hear of withdrawing. The armies of the two kingdoms met at Beth-shemesh, and Judah was sorely defeated. With Amaziah captive, Joash marched into Jerusalem, pillaged the Temple treasure, took hostages and deposited his foolish foe back in his capital. Amaziah held out as a vassal of Israel for fifteen years before a revolt broke out against him. He fled to the fortified city of Lachish, but the rebels pursued him and killed him there. His sixteen-year-old son Uzziah assumed the throne.

During this period, the centre of power in the Fertile Crescent was shifting from Aram, directly north-east of Israel, to Assyria, east of the Euphrates; and with Aram's decline, the kingdoms in Palestine were freed from external pressure and allowed to concentrate on internal development. Uzziah's reign was characterized by a renewed strengthening and expansion of Judah. The sister kingdoms pushed the territory under their rule back to the borders of David's empire. Uzziah made peace with the Israelite kingdom and proceeded to expand in every other direction: he re-established his rule over Edom, reconstructed Ezion-geber on the Red Sea, broadened out into Philistia and thoroughly fortified his entire kingdom. But then the king was stricken with leprosy in the middle of his reign, and it became necessary to proclaim his son Jotham co-regent. When Uzziah died, Jotham continued the policy of expansion, conquering Ammon and extracting tribute from it.

But the days of renewed glory were numbered, for during the reign of Jotham's son, Ahaz, both Aram and Israel were to fall to Assyria, and Judah would become a vassal state to the Assyrian king, Tiglath-pileser III.

All too quickly, the achievements of Uzziah and Jotham began to dissolve. Edom revolted successfully, and the Philistines not only recouped their coastal territories but achieved a foothold in the Shephelah as well. The social fabric of the kingdom was shredding equally rapidly, for idolatry reached the height of child sacrifice, and even the king burned his sons. When Ahaz refused an appeal from Israel and Aram to join their forces against Tiglath-pileser, the two northern kingdoms invaded Judah in an effort to depose the uncooperative monarch and place their own puppet on the throne.

Judah was helplessly exposed to attack from all sides. And when the Edomites and Philistines took a stab at the defenceless kingdom, Ahaz – against pleas from the prophet Isaiah – turned in despair to Tiglath-pileser himself for aid. The mighty king of Assyria knew that he had nothing to gain by defending this little monarchy, so he, too, turned against Ahaz and extracted tribute from Judah. In 722 BC Israel fell to Tiglath-pileser's successor, Shalmaneser V, and Judah remained intact only by virtue of the heavy ransom it paid to the new overlord of the Fertile Crescent.

When Hezekiah ascended to the throne of Judah in 716 BC, the flow of tribute to Assyria had won peace for the small kingdom. Israel had become a province of the Assyrian Empire, and Judah – assumed to be pacific, considering the odds against surviving in any other posture – was allowed to develop. Hezekiah took the administration of the kingdom firmly in hand. He purged the

Isaiah's prophecies of salvation gave King Hezekiah the courage to hold out against Sennacherib and refuse to surrender Jerusalem. A 12th-century relief of Isaiah from Souillac, France

country of the idolatrous practices that had become widespread in his father's reign, cleansed the Temple and invited his brethren in the former Kingdom of Israel to worship in Jerusalem. These religious reforms undoubtedly had a nationalistic motive behind them. Hezekiah was attempting to re-unite his people around the standard of the House of David as the only means of survival as long as Assyria was just one step away from robbing Judah of self-rule.

The death of King Sargon II of Assyria prompted a new spirit of revolt among the conquered peoples of the Assyrian Empire, and Hezekiah was caught up in the mood of rebellion that extended from Babylon to Egypt. Thinking first of his own kingdom, he refortified Jerusalem and built a unique system to transfer the city's water from its source outside the walls into Jerusalem in the event of siege. This marvel of engineering, known as Hezekiah's tunnel, is one of the few archaeological remnants of the First Temple period to have survived the centuries, and one can follow its course to this very day.

Such preparations were not in vain. When the anti-Assyrian rebellion came to a head, Sennacherib, the new ruler of Assyria, proved his mettle against all his opponents by defeating first

*left* Hezekiah's tunnel, the system built to transfer Jerusalem's water supply from its source at the Gihon Spring, outside the city walls, into the city in the event of siege
*right* King Ashurbanipal, the last of the great Assyrian monarchs, shown hunting lions in this relief from his palace at Nineveh

Babylon, then Philistia and finally routing the Egyptian forces that had come up the coast to Hezekiah's aid. Then, in 701 BC, Sennacherib turned on Judah, occupying forty-six towns, taking captives and reaping the spoils of conquest. Still set on bringing his message of might to the very heart of Hezekiah's kingdom, he advanced upon Jerusalem, and Hezekiah – fearing the worst – repented his lapse from submission and offered tribute. The Assyrian accepted gladly, but he did not renounce his designs on Jerusalem and nonetheless sent envoys to demand its surrender. Encouraged by the prophet Isaiah's visions of salvation, Hezekiah stood firm and refused to open the gates of the city to the Assyrians. But Sennacherib probably realized that taking Jerusalem was an unnecessary expense of energy: Judah was already in his power. So he withdrew his armies, leaving the holy city intact and Hezekiah on the throne.

With Judah reduced to submission, Hezekiah's religious zeal was abandoned by his son Manasseh, who introduced idol worship into the very Temple itself. Then Manasseh was captured, evidently while off on an anti-Assyrian campaign, and carried off to Babylon in chains. When he was returned to Judah and his throne, in sheer relief he repented his pagan ways, purified the Temple and strengthened the walls of Jerusalem. His son Amon, however, was the victim

Pharaoh Neco (right) before the goddess Hathor (left) in a carving bearing the inscription '[I give] you every country . . . ' Neco's plan was to wrest Palestine from the grasp of Assyria by supporting the declining empire against the rise of Babylon

of poor political judgement in placing his support behind Assyria just as the mighty and hated empire was showing signs of decline. The error earned him the fate of assassination by court officials in the second year of his reign.

The era of King Josiah, who succeeded Amon, was again the time of a great power shift in the Near East. With Babylon on the rise, Pharaoh Neco of Egypt chose to shore up the declining Assyrian Empire against the new and even greater threat from the east – and in the hope of taking Palestine out of Assyria's steadily weakening grasp. Josiah was sensitive to the political changes taking place around him, and he followed Hezekiah's example of re-uniting his people around the dynasty by embracing a programme of religious reform. In 612 BC, towards the end of Josiah's reign, Assyria was attacked by Babylon, and Pharaoh Neco rushed north to the aid of his new ally. Josiah had a different vision of the future, however, and attempted to thwart the arrival of Egyptian relief forces by blocking their advance at Megiddo. It was there that he was mortally wounded, and his death signalled the beginning of the end for Judah.

Egypt was out for vengeance. Three months after Jehoahaz was placed on the throne by the nobles of Judah, he was summoned by Neco to the pharaoh's field headquarters, where his welcome was politically fatal. Neco deposed the newly installed king and exiled him to Egypt, appointing his half-brother Jehoiakim in his stead. Jehoiakim then paid dearly for his throne by functioning as a puppet of the Egyptian court. But all his loyalty to his southern neighbour held him in no stead when Nebuchadnezzar of Babylon defeated the Egyptians at the battle of Carchemish in 609 BC and Judah came into his sphere of influence. Jehoiakim was evidently unhappy with his new master, for three years later he revolted against Babylon. Armies of Nebuchadnezzar's vassal states east of the Jordan, being the closest at hand, were sent in to quell the uprising, but Judah held out. Finally, in 597, Nebuchadnezzar himself marched on Judah, and Jehoiakim was carried off to captivity in fetters.

Jehoiachin, his eight-year-old son and successor, ruled for only three months and ten days before being exiled to Babylon and replaced by his uncle Zedekiah, a Babylonian appointee. Zedekiah remained subdued for nine years and angrily watched Judah being stripped of its territory. But in 589 BC, against the advice and dire prophecies of Jeremiah, he joined a revolt by Tyre and Ammon against the Babylonian governors of the area. This again brought Nebuchadnezzar to the gates of Jerusalem, determined to wipe out the spirit of rebelliousness once and for all. The Holy City was besieged for a year and a half until the Babylonians succeeded in breaching the northern wall. Zedekiah tried to escape, but he was caught near Jericho, forced to witness the slaughter of his sons, blinded and then taken captive to Babylon. All of Judah was reduced to ruins, and its population was scattered into exile.

The anguished prophet Jeremiah, who had warned that 'Jerusalem shall become a heap of ruins, a lair of jackals', now led the mourning rite for the ravaged city and the humiliated and chastised population of Judah:

> Our inheritance has been turned over to strangers,
>   our homes to aliens.
> We have become orphans, fatherless;
>   our mothers are like widows.
> The joy of our hearts has ceased;
>   our dancing has been turned to mourning.
> The crown has fallen from our head,
>   woe to us, for we have sinned!
> (Lamentations 5: 2–3, 15–16)

The child-king Jehoiachin thrived in exile and was even honoured by a seat at the king's table. So David's line continued, but the age of royal rule had ended. Israel would regain its land, but David's seed would never rule it again. Yet the deeds and glories of King David would live on in the imagination of his people. And David's city, the prize possession of his dynasty, would be rebuilt again and again – and is still being rebuilt – in testimony to his memory.

# Selected Sources

Aharoni, Yohanan, *The Land of the Bible: A Historical Geography*, Philadelphia, Westminster Press, 1967.

Albright, W. F., *From the Stone Age to Christianity*, Baltimore, Johns Hopkins Press, 1940.

————, *Archaeology and the Religion of Israel*, Baltimore, Johns Hopkins Press, 1953.

Bright, John, *A History of Israel*, London, SCM Press, 1972.

Cooper, Duff, *David*, New York, Harper & Row, 1943.

Gordon, Cyrus H., *The Ancient Near East*, New York, W. W. Norton & Co., 1965.

Hitti, Philip K., *History of the Arabs*, London, Macmillan and Company, 1970.

Kollek, Teddy and Moshe Pearlman, *Jerusalem*, London, Weidenfeld and Nicolson, 1968.

Maly, Eugene H., *The World of David and Solomon*, Englewood Cliffs, N.J., Prentice-Hall, 1966.

May, G. Herbert, ed., *Oxford Atlas of the Bible*, London, Oxford University Press, 1962.

Moscati, Sabatino, *The Face of the Ancient Orient*, Chicago, Quadrangle Books, 1960.

Rowley, H. H. and M. Black, eds, *Peake's Commentary on the Bible*, London, Thomas Nelson & Sons, 1962.

Thomas, David Winton, ed., *Archaeology and Old Testament Study*, Oxford, Clarendon Press, 1967.

Wright, George Ernest, *Biblical Archaeology*, Philadelphia, Westminster Press, 1962.

Yadin, Yigael, *The Art of Warfare in Biblical Lands*, London, Weidenfeld and Nicolson, 1963.

# Index